The Civil Rights Act of 1964

SUNY Series in Afro-American Studies
John Howard and Robert C. Smith, editors

The Civil Rights Act of 1964

The Passage of the Law That Ended Racial Segregation

edited by Robert D. Loevy

with contributions by Hubert H. Humphrey, Joseph L. Rauh, Jr., and John G. Stewart

State University of New York Press

Cover photo of Senators who had key roles in the Civil Rights cloture battle after the cloture vote (June 1964), Hubert H. Humphrey Photograph Collection, courtesy of the Minnesota Historical Society

Published by
State University of New York Press, Albany

© 1997 State University of New York

All rights reserved

Printed in the United States of America

No part of this book may be used or reproduced in any manner whatsoever without written permission. No part of this book may be stored in a retrieval system or transmitted in any form or by any means including electronic, electrostatic, magnetic tape, mechanical, photocopying, recording, or otherwise without the prior permission in writing of the publishers.

For information, address State University of New York Press, State University Plaza, Albany, NY 12246

Production by Dana Foote
Marketing by Theresa Abad Swierzowski

Library of Congress Cataloging-in-Publication Data

The Civil Rights Act of 1964 : the passage of the law that ended racial segregation / edited by Robert D. Loevy ; with contributions by Hubert H. Humphrey, Joseph L. Rauh, and John G. Stewart.
p. cm. — (SUNY series in Afro-American studies)
Includes bibliographical references and index.
ISBN 0–7914–3361–7 (hc : alk. paper). — ISBN 0–7914–3362–5 (pb : alk. paper)
1. Afro-Americans—Civil rights—History—20th century. 2. Segregation—Law and legislation—United States—History—20th century. 3. United States. Civil Rights Act of 1964. I. Loevy, Robert D., 1935– . II. Series.
KF4757.C59 1997
342.73'0873—dc21 *97–687*
CIP

10 9 8 7 6 5 4 3 2 1

Contents

Preface *vii*

1. Introduction: The Background and Setting of the Civil Rights Act of 1964
   Robert D. Loevy **1**

2. The Role of the Leadership Conference on Civil Rights in the Civil Rights Struggle of 1963–1964
   Joseph L. Rauh, Jr. **49**

3. Memorandum on Senate Consideration of the Civil Rights Act of 1964
   Hubert H. Humphrey **77**

4. Thoughts on the Civil Rights Bill
   John G. Stewart **93**

5. The Senate and Civil Rights
   John G. Stewart **149**

6. The Civil Rights Act of 1964: Strategy
   John G. Stewart **167**

7. The Civil Rights Act of 1964: Tactics I
   John G. Stewart **211**

8. The Civil Rights Act of 1964: Tactics II
   John G. Stewart **275**

9. Independence and Control
   John G. Stewart **321**

Contents

10. The Impact and Aftermath of the Civil Rights Act of 1964
Robert D. Loevy *333*

11. A Chronology of the Civil Rights Act of 1964
Robert D. Loevy *353*

Bibliography *365*

Index *371*

Preface

The Civil Rights Act of 1964 was described at the time of its enactment as the most significant piece of legislation to be passed by the U.S. Congress in the twentieth century. This titanic legislative struggle produced the longest continuous debate ever held in the U.S. Senate. The resulting legislation eliminated virtually overnight legal racial segregation, particularly in the American South, where public separation of black Americans from white Americans had long been codified in state laws.

A number of those who participated in congressional enactment of the Civil Rights Act of 1964 clearly understood the great historical significance of what they were doing. Joseph L. Rauh, Jr., one of the chief lobbyists supporting the bill, wrote a long magazine article (never accepted for publication) analyzing the various legislative strategies employed to try to get the bill passed. U.S. Senator Hubert H. Humphrey, the Democratic floor leader for the bill in the Senate, dictated a personal recollection of his all-important role. John G. Stewart, the chief legislative assistant to Senator Humphrey, dictated a long series of notes candidly reporting the daily triumphs and failures as the Senate slowly but surely made up its collective mind on an issue of searing national importance.

John G. Stewart also wrote a Ph.D dissertation (University of Chicago, 1968) on the general subject of Senate leadership and civil rights. The latter portion of Stewart's dissertation contained an in-depth analysis of the passage of the Civil Rights Act of 1964. Stewart completed his dissertation four years after the new civil rights law was enacted. He thus was able to bring added research and timely reflection to the subject.

Preface

This book brings together in one place these four first-person accounts of the passage of the Civil Rights Act of 1964. An opening chapter by the editor reviews the history of civil rights legislation and civil rights events from colonial times to the early 1960s, thereby setting the scene for this great legislative struggle. Following the first-person accounts, the book concludes with a chapter by the editor detailing changes in both congressional procedures and the civil rights movement from the 1960s to the 1990s. This closing chapter describes the several additional civil rights bills passed since 1964 and explains the widespread effects the Civil Rights Act of 1964 continues to exert on American life and American politics.

At the end of the book, for handy reference and clarification of events, is a chronology of the major dates and developments in the enactment of the Civil Rights Act of 1964.

These first-person accounts have been edited, but only for grammatical and typographical errors. Deletions (. . .) and bracketed inserts ([ ]) have been kept to a minimum and only used to give the reader a clearer explanation of the congressional procedures involved. Great care has been taken to preserve the original content and flavor of these historic documents.

Acknowledgments

I am grateful to the following individuals and institutions for permission to publish their materials in this book:

John G. Stewart, for permission to publish portions of his doctoral dissertation "Independence and Control: The Challenge of Senatorial Party Leadership" as chapters 5, 6, 7, 8, and 9 in this book and to publish his anonymous notes on the passage of the Civil Rights Act of 1964, which are collected in the Hubert H. Humphrey Papers, Minnesota Historical Society, Senatorial Files, 1949-1964, Legislative Files: Area Redevelopment Admin-Civil Rights 1964 (23.K.10.6F), as chapter 4 in this book.

Joseph L. Rauh, Jr., for permission to publish his manuscript on the role of the Leadership Conference on Civil Rights in the passage of the Civil Rights Act of 1964, as chapter 2 in this book.

The Minnesota Historical Society, for permission to publish the "Memorandum on Senate Consideration of the Civil Rights Act of 1964," by Hubert H. Humphrey, from the Hubert H. Humphrey Papers, Senatorial Files, 1949-1964, Legislative Files, Civil Rights, 1961-1964, C[ivil] R[ights] Diary, as chapter 3 in this book.

Chapter 1

Introduction
The Background and Setting of the Civil Rights Act of 1964

Robert D. Loevy

The first permanent English colony in North America was founded at Jamestown, Virginia, in May 1607. Twelve years later, in 1619, a Dutch ship sailed into the harbor at Jamestown and sold twenty African slaves to the Virginia colonists. Thus did "slavery" and "involuntary servitude," as they are referred to in the United States Constitution, come to the American South.

Negro slaves, brought in chains from their original homelands in central and southern Africa, proved useful and profitable in what was to become the southern United States. The flat farmlands, served by meandering tidewater rivers, were ideal for creating large plantations for growing cotton and other agricultural products. The African slaves provided a cheap and reliable source of agricultural and household labor for the emerging southern economy.

North of Virginia, where there were more hills and a harsher climate, the use of human slaves was not as successful. This part of the American colonies, the North, harnessed the labor of yeoman farmers and men and women working for wages. This created one of the great sectional differences of United States history—a group of southern states that relied heavily on slave labor and a group of northern states emphasizing the work and industry of free citizens.

By the time of the Declaration of Independence in 1776 there were almost half a million black persons in the colonies. A thriving slave trade had developed in which men, women, and children were sold, often at public auction, from one owner to another. Thomas Jefferson, a slave holder from Virginia, had included a condemnation of the human slave trade in the original draft of the Declaration of Independence, but his impassioned words were deleted to keep the support of the southern colonies during the Revolutionary War against Great Britain.

The United States next confronted the slavery problem at the time of the drawing up of the federal Constitution at Philadelphia, Pennsylvania, in the summer of 1787. The delegates provided for the abolition of the importation of slaves twenty years after the Constitution was adopted, but the institution of slavery was allowed to remain. In addition, in a famous compromise, each slave was to be counted as "three-fifths" of a person for establishing how many representatives each state could have in the lower house, the House of Representatives, of the national Congress.

Throughout the early 1800s the South and the North drifted progressively further apart over the issue of allowing the institution of human slavery to continue in the United States. As the nation expanded westward across the North American continent, particularly hard political battles were fought over the issue of "slavery in the territories." Finally, after Abraham Lincoln was elected president in 1860, the southern states seceded from the federal union rather than run the risk of having the U.S. Congress in Washington abolish slavery outright.

The Civil War

President Lincoln refused to let the southern states "go in peace," and the result was the American Civil War. The

North achieved by force of arms that which it had not been able to achieve through legislative politics. On January 1, 1863, President Lincoln issued his Emancipation Proclamation, thereby freeing the slaves in those states that had seceded from the Union.

After the Civil War was over, large Republican Party majorities in the national Congress passed and sent to the states for adoption the three great "Civil War Amendments." The 13th Amendment abolished "slavery" and "involuntary servitude." The 14th Amendment guaranteed the newly freed Negroes equal protection of the laws and the right to "life," "liberty," and "property." The 15th Amendment guaranteed all American citizens the right to vote no matter what their "race, color, or previous condition of servitude." It is important to note that all three Civil War Amendments—the 13th, 14th, and 15th—expressly gave *Congress* the power to enforce the provisions of the amendment by appropriate legislation.[1]

The Black Codes

The Civil War Amendments "worked" but only for a short while. During a twelve-year period of "Reconstruction" in the South following the Civil War, blacks were allowed to vote and a number were elected to important state and national political offices. But, after the Civil War ended, white southern politicians and government officials went to work subverting and reducing the position of blacks in the American South. As early as 1865, the year the Civil War ended, a number of southern state legislatures began passing Black Codes, laws designed to put black citizens in a state of near slavery by limiting their rights and privileges.

The Republican majority in the United States Congress responded to the Black Codes with the Civil Rights Act of 1866, which made it illegal to deprive a person of his civil rights regardless of race, color, or previous servitude. Additional civil rights laws were passed by Congress in 1870, 1871, and 1875, all of them designed to have the national government in Washington, D.C., protect black Americans from white-dominated southern state governments. Throughout this period, the Republicans in Congress sought to "nationalize" the issue of black civil rights so that southern white-state legislatures could not undo the work of the Civil War.[2]

The End of Reconstruction

This effort to have the United States Government protect black rights in the South received a major setback in 1876. In the presidential election that year (the famous Tilden-Hayes contested election), the Republicans garnered the necessary electoral votes to elect Rutherford B. Hayes by agreeing to remove all Union troops from the southern United States. As Republican fortunes continued to wane in the late 1870s and the 1880s, the Republican Party became less and less interested in protecting black civil rights in the South and more and more interested in winning white votes anywhere they could be found. This problem was further complicated by the fact that the more "civil rights oriented" Republicans of the Civil War period, those most committed to the cause of the recently freed slaves, were growing old and retiring from active politics. The younger members of the Grand Old Party simply did not share their deep devotion to protecting black civil rights in the South.

The nationalization of black civil rights came to a complete end in 1892 when the Democrats gained control of the presidency and both houses of Congress for the first time since the Civil War. By 1894 this Democratic Congress had succeeded in repealing most of the civil rights laws that had been enacted during the post-Civil War period, most importantly the provisions that had to do with voting rights.[3]

This wholesale removal of protections left the black citizen in the South almost completely at the mercy of southern state governments, and the result was a rash of state laws protecting the right of white citizens to segregate themselves from black citizens in many aspects of social and political life. Southern whites particularly used state law to deny black citizens access to places of "public accommodation," such as restaurants, hotels, and swimming pools, which could be designated by their private owners as "for whites only."

The Political Party Problem

The change in the Republican Party attitude toward black Americans that occurred in the late 1870s was an important event in the history of civil rights in the United States. It marked the beginning of a long period of time in which the interests of black Americans were made secondary to the needs of the two major political parties to win national elections. Time and again over the following ninety years, both the Republican and Democratic parties would sacrifice civil rights programs and civil rights bills on the altar of "not losing white votes" in the next election. This situation was exacerbated, of course, by the fact that, after the 1890s, southern whites were eligible to vote but most southern blacks were barred from voting by poll taxes, literacy tests, and "white-only" primary elections.

Thus black Americans were faced with what could be called the "political party problem." The political power to pass civil rights laws rested with the two major political parties—the Republicans and the Democrats—but both parties had more to gain by appealing to the votes of enfranchised segregationist southern whites rather than the non-votes of disenfranchised southern blacks.

The Civil Rights Cases of 1883

Although the United States Supreme Court played a significant role in the mid-twentieth century where protecting black civil rights was concerned, such was not the case in the late nineteenth century. In fact, the protections guaranteed by the constitutional amendments and congressional statutes enacted following the Civil War were largely taken away by the court.

In the *Civil Rights Cases of 1883*, the Supreme Court ruled that the protection of rights guaranteed by the 14th Amendment applied only to the states and not to individuals. Thus an 1875 act of Congress prohibiting discrimination against blacks in inns, public conveyances, theaters, and other public accommodations or amusements was declared unconstitutional because it was limiting *private* behavior rather than *state* behavior.

In retrospect, it is interesting to ponder how different United States history might have been if the Supreme Court had not ruled as it did in the *Civil Rights Cases of 1883*. Congress, after all, passed a public accommodations law, much the same law that members of the civil rights movement worked for so diligently in the 1950s and early 1960s. If the Supreme Court in the early 1880s had upheld the power of Congress to pass such a law and prohibit racial discrimination in public places throughout the entire nation, the course of civil rights history in the United States could have been completely different.

A careful reading of the relevant portions of the 14th Amendment, however, reveals why the Supreme Court ruled as it did. "No *state* shall make or enforce any law which shall abridge the privileges or immunities of citizens of the United States; nor shall any *state* deprive any person of life, liberty, or property, without the due process of law; nor deny to any person within its jurisdiction the equal protection of the laws." Clearly the 14th Amendment prohibitions were on the state governments and not upon the private individuals who lived within those states.

The impact of this decision on the position of blacks in the South was extensive. It meant the 14th Amendment could not be used to protect black Americans from mistreatment by southern individuals—it could only be used to protect black Americans from official actions by the states. The result was a system of oppression in which private individuals could not only discriminate against blacks but could actually terrorize them, confident in the knowledge that the power of the United States Government in Washington, D.C., would not be used to punish them. The state governments, which were limited by the 14th Amendment, thus needed only to stand aside and let private individuals do the discriminating and/or terrorizing, simply being careful not to pass any state laws or initiate any state actions that took away any of the rights protected by the 14th Amendment.

This was the legal situation that made the beating, the lynching, and the assassination such effective weapons for subjugating blacks to white majority rule in the South. Beatings, lynchings, and assassinations were carried out by individuals rather than by state governments, thus preventing the national government in Washington, D.C., from using the 14th Amendment as an excuse to intervene. Throughout the late nineteenth and early twentieth centuries, national law enforcement officials were unable to act to stop lynchings and racial murders in the South because, according to the Supreme Court, the 14th Amendment only limited the states. If white individuals who beat, lynched, or murdered blacks were to be caught and punished for their crimes, it would be up to the state governments, and not the national government, to do it.

"The Free White Jury That Will Never Convict"

Another part of the southern system of black oppression was "the free white jury that will never convict." In most southern states, white citizens who beat, lynched, and murdered blacks could do so with almost complete confidence that state and local police, being committed themselves to the doctrine of white supremacy, would be less than zealous about investigating the crimes and catching the perpetrators. In the few cases where arrests were made and trials were held, lynch mobs and race murderers could be certain that a jury of their white neighbors and friends would find them "Not Guilty" and let them go free. The end result of the *Civil Rights Cases*, therefore, was to give white individuals in the South almost complete license, including lynching and murder, to personally enforce racial segregation, all of it done without any sense that there would ever be any official punishment.

Beatings, lynchings, and racial murders were not isolated instances in the American South during the late nineteenth and early twentieth centuries. By the early 1890s a black was lynched in the South an average of every three days.[4] By the turn of the century it was well known that even "respectable" white leaders "tolerated" lynching as a way of enforcing racial segregation in the South.

Although the number of lynchings had decreased by the middle of the twentieth century, murders and assassinations remained an ever-present personal technique for frightening southern blacks into submission to white supremacy. On Christmas night in 1951, Harry T. Moore, the Florida secretary of the National Association for the Advancement of Colored People (NAACP), was killed along with his wife when a bomb was thrown into their home. Moore had been organizing Florida blacks to register and vote. No one was arrested or tried for the crime. Clarence Mitchell, Jr., the Washington, D.C., representative of the

NAACP, put the role of state government in perspective when he charged: "The state of Florida for political reasons does not try to stop that kind of thing."[5]

Separate but Equal

In 1896 racial segregation in the American South was upheld by a decision of the United States Supreme Court. This landmark decision, *Plessy v. Ferguson*, arose when a railroad company refused to provide a sleeping car berth to a black train passenger. The Supreme Court ruled the railroad could segregate white sleeping car passengers from black sleeping car passengers, but the railroad had to provide sleeping accommodations for blacks that were equal to similar accommodations for whites. This decision promulgated for the first time the famous "separate but equal" doctrine. That doctrine was used extensively by southern states to justify racially segregated public schools, from kindergarten to graduate school, throughout all of Dixie.

Plessy v. Ferguson did produce a stirring dissenting opinion. In a lone voice strongly opposed to the majority opinion, Justice John Marshall Harlan wrote: "Our Constitution is colorblind and neither knows nor tolerates classes among citizens."

Renationalizing the Civil Rights Issue

Despite Justice Harlan's inspiring words, the major characteristic of southern blacks at the beginning of the twentieth century was that they were "governmentally isolated." They lived in a world in which, by both congressional action and Supreme Court decision, the protections of the national government had been removed from them. They were subjected simultaneously to the will of segregation-oriented state governments and, more threateningly, white individuals who could beat, lynch, or murder them with no fear of substantial punishment by either the national or state governments. After 1892, when the Congress repealed national voting rights laws, black southern males were even denied the vote, guaranteed by the 15th Amendment to the Constitution, as a way of improving their position in society.

It thus was clear to many by the start of the twentieth century that, if southern blacks were ever to be freed from southern white oppression, both official and unofficial, the national government in Washington, D.C., would have to do the job. There thus arose a constant call by those interested in black civil rights for action by the national government. Simultaneously, southern segregationists, realizing that the only potential threat to their "peculiar institution" came from Washington, D.C., became strong advocates of states' rights and dedicated opponents of national power. If southern blacks were to ever be free, the national Congress in Washington, D.C., would have to "renationalize" the civil rights issue.

But any new national laws protecting black civil rights would have to pass both houses of Congress—the Senate as well as the House of Representatives. In the Senate was a rule guaranteeing unlimited debate, the famous filibuster rule. Any civil rights bill to come before the U.S. Senate would face a filibuster by a determined group of southern senators, and the filibuster could only be stopped by a "cloture vote," which required a two-thirds vote in the Senate. Thus, from the very beginning of the black civil rights movement, the Senate filibuster was regarded as the great obstacle—and a successful cloture vote to stop a civil rights filibuster was the great goal.

The Early Civil Rights Movement

Following a particularly violent race riot in Springfield, Illinois, in 1908, a group of humanitarian whites formed a new organization to help combat racial discrimination. Joining forces with a group of black intellectuals, they met in New York to organize the National Association for the Advancement of Colored People (NAACP).

It is important to note the NAACP was formed by both blacks and whites. Integration of the races was the goal and practice of the organization from the moment of its founding. Even more important was the principal technique adopted by the NAACP—the use of the Constitution and the court system of the United States to bring equality for African-Americans through law. This emphasis on having lawyers file lawsuits to guarantee blacks their legal rights as United States citizens identified the NAACP as a "conventional" and "mainstream" American interest group.[6]

Some early gains for blacks came from the Supreme Court. In 1938 in *Missouri ex rel. Gaines v. Canada,* the court took up the question of whether the "separate" black facilities were indeed "equal" to the white facilities. The facility in question was the University of Missouri's whites-only law school, and Missouri had no equivalent black law school. The court ruled that Missouri must provide its black citizens with a black law school equal to the white law school.

This decision was a step forward in the cause of black civil rights. Anywhere it could be shown that segregated black facilities were not equal in quality to the equivalent white facilities, a suit could be filed seeking improved facilities for blacks.

Throughout the early twentieth century, there was a slow but steady movement of blacks out of the South and into the North, particularly into the central cities of large northern metropolitan areas. In 1900 only 10 percent of American blacks lived outside the South, but by 1930 more than 20 percent of blacks lived outside of Dixie.[7]

In the South most blacks were prevented from voting by literacy tests, a technique by which white election judges refused to allow blacks to register to vote if the blacks could not read and analyze an obscure section of the state constitution. When blacks moved to the North, however, they came into a political arena where they could register and vote and have an impact on state and national politics.

As the percentage of blacks living outside the South swelled to 23 percent by 1940, significant numbers of U.S. senators and U.S. representatives from the North came to have sizable numbers of black constituents living and voting in their states and congressional districts. There thus came into existence a sizable group of U.S. senators and U.S. representatives from the North who were interested in actively pursuing the cause of black civil rights on Capitol Hill in Washington, D.C.

Black Voters and the Democratic Party

Prior to the stock market crash of 1929 and the Great Depression of the 1930s, the vast majority of American blacks voted for the Republicans, the party of Abraham Lincoln, the Great Emancipator. In the 1932 presidential election, in the depths of the depression, when one-third of all black males were jobless, the incumbent Republican president, Herbert Hoover, drew more than three-fourths of the black vote over the Democratic candidate, Franklin D. Roosevelt.

Roosevelt won the election, however, and went on to institute a broad program of economic reforms known as the New Deal. The economic benefits of the New Deal were distributed more or less equally to blacks and whites, and by January of 1935 more than three million blacks, one-fifth of the black labor force, were employed on relief projects instituted by the United States Government. By the time of the 1936 presidential election, millions of black voters began switching from the Republicans to the Democrats because of their strong support for Franklin D. Roosevelt and his New Deal economic programs.[8]

In the years following the New Deal, the Democratic Party found it best to win black votes with economic benefits rather than by advancing the cause of black civil rights. Franklin D. Roosevelt had been elected by an uneasy coalition of northern liberal voters, both black and white, on the one hand and white southern Democratic voters on the other hand. This so-called Roosevelt Coalition was strengthened by economic programs, which simultaneously aided southern whites and northern blacks, but it was split apart by civil rights programs, which appealed strongly to northern Democrats but stirred inflamed opposition from segregation-oriented southern Democrats.

Presidential Action for Civil Rights

Because the southern Democrats were a key part of the large Democratic majorities that controlled both the Senate and the House of Representatives during the New Deal period, Franklin D. Roosevelt had neither the inclination nor any reason to believe he would be successful at getting a civil rights bill through Congress during the 1930s. Roosevelt therefore adopted a policy that served as a working model for subsequent presidents of both political parties. He would use the *executive powers* of the presidency to further the interests of black Americans, doing those things which a president could do unilaterally without having to get legislative authorization from Congress.

Roosevelt used his executive powers of appointment to name large numbers of blacks to United States Government jobs. Not only did the number of black appointments increase, but so did the quality of the jobs blacks were given.

Most important, Roosevelt bypassed Congress and, by executive order, established the Civil Rights Section of the Justice Department. Although it started slowly at first, the Civil Rights Section began building a skilled bureaucracy of lawyers and other trained professionals to further the cause of black civil rights in the United States. For the first time since the Reconstruction period following the Civil War, there was a definite place in the United States Government where blacks could go for legal and governmental help in the fight to win their civil rights.

In its early days the Civil Rights Section devoted itself to fighting for the right of blacks to vote in national elections and to opposing police brutality to blacks. Later on the Civil Rights Section became an ally of the NAACP in filing suits to bring about school integration and in lobbying Congress to pass civil rights laws.

In 1941 Franklin D. Roosevelt's efforts on behalf of African-Americans encouraged black leaders to press for even more integration of the races. Six months before the Japanese attack on Pearl Harbor, as defense plants were gearing up for anticipated U.S. involvement in World War II, black leaders saw an opportunity to make substantial progress. A group of nationally prominent blacks, headed by A. Philip Randolph of the Brotherhood of Sleeping Car Porters, began to organize a mass march on Washington, D.C., to demand more and better jobs for blacks. As the number of anticipated marchers rose to over one hundred thousand, President Roosevelt agreed to create a Fair Employment Practices Committee (FEPC) and ban discrimination in defense plants if the so-called March on Washington was called off.

Roosevelt issued an executive order creating the Fair Employment Practices Committee, and the planned March on Washington never took place. Roosevelt's good judgment in using an executive order, rather than a law of Congress, to establish the FEPC was supported by subsequent events. In 1946 Congress abolished the Fair Employment Practices Committee, thereby wiping out some of the employment gains that had been made by blacks during the wartime period. The House of Representatives voted to create a permanent Fair Employment Practices *Commission* in

1946, but the bill was rejected in the Senate. The House passed the Fair Employment Practices Commission bill a second time in 1950, but once again the proposal died in the Senate.

Following Franklin D. Roosevelt's death in the spring of 1945, Democratic president Harry S. Truman continued the use of executive action as the principal means of furthering black civil rights. When Congress refused to pass a Selective Service Act that would eliminate all racial discrimination in the United States armed forces, Truman in 1948 issued an executive order that integrated the Army, Air Force, Navy, and Marine Corps and specifically banned "separate but equal" recruiting, training, and service.

Truman also appointed a presidential Committee on Civil Rights. The committee issued a lengthy report, *To Secure These Rights*, which presented factual data and gripping personal testimony on the denial of black civil rights in the South. The reaction of Congress to *To Secure These Rights* was not a civil rights bill but a number of speeches by southern Democrats condemning the report as factually untrue and an attempt by the U.S. Government to interfere in matters that should be left exclusively to the states.

By furthering black civil rights through executive orders, Roosevelt and Truman created a situation in which black Americans came to regard the presidency as responsive to their needs. Simultaneously the Congress, and particularly the Senate, came to be seen by blacks as the enemy of civil rights. Among segregationist southern whites, on the other hand, the Senate came to be regarded as the great protector of states' rights, and the presidency was seen from Dixie as an interfering force trying to overthrow southern institutions from afar.

The Eisenhower Administration

In 1952 Dwight D. Eisenhower, the commanding general of Allied Forces in Europe during World War II, was elected president of the United States. A Republican, Eisenhower followed Roosevelt's and Truman's example of using the powers of the presidency to further the cause of black civil rights.

One achievement of President Eisenhower in the civil rights field was the appointment of Earl Warren to be chief justice of the United States. Eisenhower had promised Warren the first vacancy on the Supreme Court but had not expected that vacancy to be the chief justiceship. Nonetheless, when Chief Justice Fred Vinson died of a heart attack, Eisenhower named Warren, the Republican governor of California, to lead the high court.

The appointment of Warren as chief justice of the United States is significant because of Warren's subsequent leadership in the Supreme Court's unanimous decision to declare racial segregation in public schools unconstitutional (*Brown v. Board of Education of Topeka, Kansas*). Although many scholars pointed out that Eisenhower later expressed regrets about appointing Warren and questioned the wisdom of integrating public education in the segregationist South, the fact remains that Eisenhower appointed the chief justice of the Supreme Court who produced the *Brown* decision.[9]

Almost as important as the appointment of Earl Warren to the Supreme Court was Eisenhower's decision to allow his attorney general, Herbert Brownell, to argue the case against racial segregation before the Supreme Court. Although Eisenhower separated himself publicly from Brownell's arguments supporting public school integration, in private he helped Brownell write his opinion.

Having the attorney general, or an assistant attorney general, be the strong administration spokesperson for civil rights was an Eisenhower trait that was continued by the Kennedy and Johnson administrations in the 1960s. As Eisenhower relied on Brownell (and his successor, William Rogers) in the civil rights area, President Kennedy relied on his attorney general—his brother Robert Kennedy—to be the "front person" on civil rights. Following President Kennedy's assassination, President Lyndon Johnson placed equally heavy and public civil rights responsibilities on Deputy Attorney General (later Attorney General) Nicholas Katzenbach.

Brown v. Board of Education of Topeka, Kansas

When handed down in May 1954, the landmark decision, *Brown v. Board of Education of Topeka, Kansas,* called for the desegregation of all public school systems in the nation "with all deliberate speed." The court unanimously ruled that separate facilities were, by definition, unequal and, therefore, unconstitutional. Most important, however, was the breadth of the decision. In outlawing segregation in *all* public education throughout the entire nation, the court thereby implied that all forms of segregation were illegal. It could now be assumed that the court would uphold new civil rights legislation banning all forms of public discrimination, provided, of course, Congress could be persuaded to pass such legislation.[10]

The *Brown* decision was a turning point for the executive branch of the United States Government as well as the judicial branch. Minority Americans had won much more than the right to seek a court order to integrate any public school at any educational level anywhere in the United States. The court order would have to be enforced, and the obvious group to do the enforcing would be the Civil Rights Section of the United States Department of Justice. Civil Rights Section lawyers, when needed, could begin moving into the American South to oversee the orderly desegregation of public schools. Desegregation orders from U.S. courts would be enforced, if enforcement became difficult, by U.S. marshals. The judicial branch of the United States democracy had given the executive branch the legal justification—if it cared to use it—to go into the South and become directly involved in the enforcement of public school integration.

The Eisenhower Administration responded—and with a great deal of foresight—to the fact that U.S. marshals were the logical instruments to enforce public school integration. As more and more efforts to integrate public schools in the South resulted in strident white opposition, the Eisenhower Justice Department began training a sizable group of U.S. marshals to be used in the South. Herbert Brownell's successor as attorney general, William Rogers, trained an elite crew of six hundred marshals whose significance reached well beyond the Eisenhower years. When President John Kennedy needed marshals to enforce school integration at the University of Mississippi and the University of Alabama in the early 1960s, he was able to draw on the elite crew of U.S. marshals trained under Eisenhower.[11]

Massive Resistance

It was originally hoped that state and local governments in the South would comply voluntarily with the *Brown* decision. In many areas, however, the decision was met with "massive resistance." White political and governmental leaders worked to put off as long as possible the racial integration of their local schools. Segregationist-dominated southern state legislatures soon joined the act, enacting state laws that cut off state educational funding to any school system that had the temerity to racially integrate. In some cases, amendments to state constitutions were adopted that required shutting down public schools rather than allowing them to desegregate.

President Eisenhower often vacationed and played golf in the South. He thus was well aware of the strength of southern attitudes on the race issue, particularly as they applied to school integration. Eisenhower often expressed the fear that, if the U.S. Government pressed too hard on the issue of public school integration, many communities in the South might abandon public education altogether. Whites would then have their own private or church-related schools while blacks, particularly poor blacks, would have no schools at all. Eisenhower frequently used the word *dilemma* to describe this problem of total southern intransigence on the subject of public school integration.[12]

The *Brown* decision thus had two simultaneous but contradictory effects. On the one hand, it inspired northern liberals and black political activists to press ever more strongly for racial integration in the American South and the Border States. On the other hand, it unified much of the official white South in its all-out opposition to race mixing in any form. Conflict between these two forces became ever more inevitable during the later years of the Eisenhower administration.

By the early 1960s, the lack of progress on school integration in the South became one of the strongest arguments for the Civil Rights Act of 1964. As the tenth anniversary of the *Brown* decision approached in the spring of 1964, civil rights supporters pointed out that a decade had gone by since the Supreme Court's landmark decision but very few southern blacks were attending integrated schools. Such a conspicuous example of lack of state action on desegregating schools dramatized the need for congressional—and thus national government—intervention.

The Nonviolent Movement

The Congress of Racial Equality (CORE) was founded in Chicago, Illinois, in 1942 and became a national organization in 1943. Based on the nonviolent principles of Mahatma Gandhi of India, CORE sought to integrate restaurants, snack bars, lunch counters, and public rest rooms throughout the North, the border states, and the upper South. (Any attempt to integrate such facilities in the "Deep South" states of South Carolina, Georgia, Alabama, Mississippi, and Louisiana was regarded as too dangerous and very unlikely to be successful.) CORE was dedicated to pushing southward the "Jim Crow" line, an indeterminate east-west line across the United States above which black customers could be served along with whites in public places and below which they could not.

CORE's preferred techniques for pressing the cause of integrated public facilities were the "freedom ride" and the "sit-in" demonstration. The first freedom ride was staged in 1947. The Supreme Court had outlawed segregation in buses and bus stations operating in interstate commerce (across state lines), so CORE sent a group of its members through the upper South by bus to see if the court decision was being obeyed.

Socio-dramas were used to train CORE members. Acting out the roles of demonstrators and arresting officers, experienced CORE members would teach newcomers how to curl their bodies and put their arms around their heads so as to reduce the effects of physical violence. CORE members were taught to be nonviolent but determined. They were trained not to leave a demonstration site unless actually arrested. If restaurant or snack bar personnel would not serve the demonstrators, they were to remain in their seats until they were either served or arrested. No matter how hard a CORE demonstrator might be struck with a fist or a club, the CORE demonstrator was never to strike back.

Similar to the NAACP, CORE had both black and white members and would send "integrated" teams on freedom rides and to sit-ins. Only half the members of a CORE team would actually participate in the demonstration. The other half would behave legally in order to be able to render medical assistance if necessary or bail arrested demonstrators out of jail.

When traveling through the upper South in the late 1940s, CORE freedom riders held their meetings and stayed overnight in local black churches. This was because the local black church was the only place where CORE members were reasonably safe from being harassed by southern opponents of racial integration.

The NAACP frowned on CORE's form of nonviolent direct action because of the NAACP's preference for using court suits as the best method of securing black civil rights. After CORE began drawing significant national press attention in its efforts to integrate public facilities throughout the South, however, the NAACP began to take over the role of defending CORE demonstrators in southern court rooms after they were arrested and came to trial.

In addition to freedom rides through the upper South, CORE in the late 1940s was busy integrating the swimming pool at Palisades Amusement Park in New Jersey. By 1949 CORE was working at integrating all downtown eating places in St. Louis, Missouri, and by 1953 they were working toward the same goal in Baltimore, Maryland.

By the mid-1950s CORE had refined the sit-in demonstration into a highly perfected and effective technique. Integrated groups of demonstrators would fill a certain number of tables and chairs in the restaurant or lunch counter in question, thus denying the owner the income that those tables and chairs would ordinarily be earning. One demonstrator would have a sign on his back stating the number of hours and minutes the demonstrators had sat there without being served. In some instances CORE would use a "trying on" technique, sitting in at the particular restaurant for only one or two hours, one day a week, in order to show the restaurant owner that having blacks in his or her eating place did not really harm business.

Throughout the 1940s and early 1950s, CORE did not generate much national or local publicity with its various freedom rides and sit-in demonstrations. In the South and the border states, newspaper editors simply did not bother to cover CORE demonstrations or report on CORE's isolated victories in integrating a snack bar here and a bus station rest room there. Until the year 1955, fighting for black civil rights was neither a popular cause nor a hot news item.

It can be argued that those CORE demonstrators who labored in relative obscurity during the 1940s and early 1950s were some of the real heroes of the civil rights movement. They did win some important victories, but their most important contribution may have been that, when the civil rights movement did become a big national news story, the nonviolent techniques of the freedom ride and the sit-in demonstration were perfected, tested, and ready to go.[13]

The Montgomery Bus Boycott

Although blacks and whites were permitted to ride the same city buses in Montgomery, Alabama, seating on the buses was racially segregated. Whites were to sit at the front of the bus and fill seats toward the rear. Blacks were to sit in the back of the bus and fill seats toward the front. If the bus was so crowded that a white person had to stand, a black bus rider was required by Montgomery city law to give up his or her seat to the white person.

Riding the bus home after a tiring day at work, Mrs. Rosa Parks, a black seamstress, refused to give up her seat on a city bus to a white man. The date was December 1, 1955, now regarded by many observers as the beginning of the modern civil rights movement. Mrs. Parks was arrested. Subsequently, she was bailed out of jail by E. D. Nixon, the Montgomery representative of the Brotherhood of Sleeping Car Porters and a local leader of the NAACP. Later that evening Nixon was struck with the idea of having Montgomery's black citizens boycott the city's segregated bus system.

Other groups, including an organization of black women known as the Women's Political Council, also decided a bus boycott was the best way to respond to the arrest of Rosa Parks. An organizational meeting was held at the Dexter Avenue Baptist Church, and subsequently the minister at that church, the Reverend Martin Luther King, Jr., was elected to lead the bus boycott. Montgomery's forty thousand blacks stayed off the city buses for more than a year, vowing not to return until the buses were totally desegregated. Many of the boycotters walked to their destinations. Others rode in car pools or received free automobile rides from volunteer drivers supporting the bus boycott.

> The major accomplishment of the Montgomery bus boycott was that it turned a nonviolent demonstration for racial integration into a national news story. Because of the large number of boycotters involved, and because boycotters carpooling and walking made good television film, the national television networks covered the bus boycott extensively. When the white community in Montgomery reacted with random acts of violence (buildings bombed, buses fired upon, physical harm to boycotters, etc.), there was even more national coverage. It was this news attention that made Martin Luther King, Jr., a national symbol of the new black resistance to segregation and enabled him to present to the American people his ideas on the nonviolent demonstration as a means of producing political and social change.[14]

The bus boycott failed to convince the white political and governmental leadership in Montgomery to desegreate the city's buses. In November of 1956, almost one year after the bus boycott had begun, the United States Supreme

Court ordered the city bus system in Montgomery to integrate racially. The court proved willing to act when the local white leadership would not. On December 21, 1956, with every word and move recorded by national and international television news, Martin Luther King and his supporters boarded a Montgomery city bus and were able to sit in any empty seat they wanted.

The most important result of the Montgomery bus boycott was that "it made nonviolent forms of protest against racial segregation big news items, both in the national and the local press. After Montgomery, no longer would demonstrators work in relative obscurity. Race relations, civil rights demonstrations, and violent white reactions to demonstrations henceforth were big news and played accordingly."[15]

The emergence of Martin Luther King, Jr., in the mid-1950s was a key event in the escalating fight for civil rights. Through the experience gained during the Montgomery bus boycott, King learned that the northern and western United States were most likely to press for civil rights reform when a dramatic instance of racial segregation was presented on the news media, particularly television. King quickly became adept at organizing racial protests in southern cities, specifically choosing as his opponents racist public officials who would react against the demonstrators with violent means such as police clubs, police dogs, high pressure fire hoses, etc.[16]

Two of these massive racial protests in the 1960s produced major civil rights bills. The impetus for Congress to enact the Civil Rights Act of 1964 (which banned racial discrimination in public places) occurred following brutal white suppression of racial demonstrations led by Dr. King in Birmingham, Alabama, in the spring of 1963. An equally brutal reaction to a voting rights march led by King in Selma, Alabama, in 1965 produced the Voting Rights Act of 1965 (which gave the U.S. Government the power to register blacks to vote in southern states).[17]

THE EISENHOWER CIVIL RIGHTS PROGRAM

During Dwight D. Eisenhower's first three years in office—1953 to 1955—he presented no civil rights bills to Congress. The president and his cabinet members were well aware that Eisenhower's predecessor in office, Democrat Harry S. Truman, had not only failed to get a civil rights bill from Congress but had ruined his relationships with the southern Democrats by his efforts to get a bill passed. Eisenhower also believed that strongly held political opinions—such as a firm belief in racial segregation—could not easily be changed, even by U.S. Government legislation. Eisenhower told a new conference in 1954: "I believe there are certain things that are not best handled by punitive or compulsory Federal law."[18]

Although he declined to ask Congress for a civil rights bill in his first years in office, President Eisenhower was quietly determined to eliminate racial discrimination in those areas where the president had clear-cut authority and there was no question of overriding states' rights. Eisenhower therefore issued executive orders ending any segregationist practices that remained in the District of Columbia, in the military, and in the U.S. Government bureaucracy. He was the first president to appoint a black, Frederic Morrow, to an executive position on the White House staff. Eisenhower's record of achievement in the civil rights field was sufficiently impressive that he gained considerable support among black voters when he successfully ran for reelection to the presidency in 1956.[19]

Eisenhower's policy of minimizing legislative requests and maximizing executive action was followed by his successor as president, John F. Kennedy. It can even be argued that President Kennedy, by delaying signing an executive order to racially integrate public housing in the United States for more than two years, was less willing to use executive action on behalf of civil rights than Eisenhower was. To

Kennedy's credit, following the violent and well-publicized racial demonstrations in Birmingham in 1963, he sent a major civil rights bill to Congress and worked diligently for its passage.

The Civil Rights Act of 1957

On March 9, 1956, Attorney General Herbert Brownell circulated to Eisenhower and his cabinet a four-part civil rights bill to be presented to Congress.[20] Part I provided for creation of a bipartisan United States Commission on Civil Rights for the purpose of studying racial discrimination in the United States and recommending remedial legislation to Congress. It was hoped the Civil Rights Commission's investigations and written reports would provide factual data and reasoned arguments for civil rights supporters in subsequent legislative fights.

Part II provided for transforming the small Civil Rights *Section* of the Justice Department into a Civil Rights *Division* headed by an assistant attorney general. The proposed Civil Rights Division would enjoy the enhanced status of being created by congressional legislation rather than executive order. It also would have more lawyers and more money with which to pursue civil rights objectives.

Part III of Herbert Brownell's proposed civil rights bill provided that the attorney general of the United States be granted the power to secure court injunctions in civil rights cases and that such cases be removed from state courts to United States courts. Civil rights supporters had long argued that only intervention by the United States Government would end civil rights violations against blacks in the South.

> This provision soon became known on Capitol Hill as "Part III" because it was the third title of

> the proposed Eisenhower administration civil rights bill. Part III was an extremely important proposal to civil rights supporters. It would permit the U.S. attorney general to file civil rights suits, thus relieving the black individual in a hostile southern community of the responsibility of filing such a suit. Many black individuals would not think of filing a civil rights suit, mainly because the threat of white retaliation, possibly in the form of a bombing or a lynching, was so great. The attorney general and the Civil Rights Division of the Justice Department would have no such fears, however, and could pursue civil rights cases in a vigorous and public way that would never occur if such cases were left to the individual initiative of isolated southern black citizens.[21]

The Eisenhower Part III was not adopted until 1964, but almost all civil rights bills brought to Congress in the 1957-1964 period contained a provision similar to Part III. This provision invested the attorney general with the power to seek court injunctions to protect the civil rights of African-Americans throughout the South. The concept retained the identifying label "Part III" even when it was not the third part of the particular bill in question.

Part IV would increase the power of the Justice Department to seek injunctions against actual or threatened interference with the right to vote. It also extended U.S. election laws to cover primary elections and special elections as well as general elections.

At first President Eisenhower endorsed only the first two points of Brownell's proposed legislation. By October of 1956, however, late in his successful campaign for reelection, Eisenhower declared his support for all four provisions. In his 1957 State of the Union message he urged Congress to enact all four points into law.[22]

CONGRESSIONAL ACTION

Because there is no filibuster rule in the United States House of Representatives, the southerners opposed to civil rights had no way of stopping the Eisenhower civil rights bill in the House. All four of Herbert Brownell's recommended provisions were, with only minor amendments, passed by the House on June 18, 1957.

Easy passage in the House of Representatives became, from this point on, one of the established principles of legislative strategy making for enacting civil rights bills. By the early 1960s civil rights supporters assumed passage in the House was a foregone conclusion. They would schedule a civil rights bill for passage in the House when it suited their strategy for getting the bill through the Senate, which was much more difficult. When the bill that became the Civil Rights Act of 1964 was before the House of Representatives in February 1964, civil rights strategists added and deleted provisions according to how it would effect passage in the Senate rather than the House of Representatives.[23]

The first major problem confronting the Eisenhower civil rights bill was the Senate Judiciary Committee and its strongly segregationist chairman, James O. Eastland of Mississippi. Eastland had used his powers as committee chairman to kill every civil rights bill that came to the committee during the 1950s. Eastland and his Judiciary Committee thus were famous as the "burial ground" in the Senate for civil rights bills.

The strategy devised in 1957 for bypassing the Senate Judiciary Committee was used repeatedly with civil rights bills during the 1960s. The House-passed civil rights bill was intercepted at the moment a clerk carried it over to the Senate from the House of Representatives. Before the bill could be routed to the Senate Judiciary Committee, the Senate leadership took the bill and put it directly on the Senate calendar for debate at a future time.

The vote to bypass the Senate Judiciary Committee in 1957 received only lukewarm support from Democratic senators. Only ten of them voted to bring the bill directly to the Senate floor for debate. The Republicans in the Senate were virtually unanimous in their support for the 1957 bypass motion, however, and that support is what enabled it to be narrowly adopted. Senate Republicans probably supported the bypass motion so strongly because it was a Republican president's civil rights bill.

This technique for bypassing the Senate Judiciary Committee, pioneered in the Eisenhower years, was quite well established by 1964. When the bill that became the Civil Rights Act of 1964 reached the Senate from the House, the southerners decided to filibuster the motion to bypass the Judiciary Committee. Incredibly to civil rights supporters, this southern filibuster of the motion to bypass the committee lasted for almost three weeks. Then the filibuster of the civil rights bill itself began.[24]

The southern attack on President Eisenhower's 1957 civil rights bill centered on Part III, the provision permitting the attorney general to file suits in civil rights cases. Georgia Senator Richard Russell, the post-World War II leader of the pro-segregation southern Democrats in the Senate, condemned Part III as an all-out invasion of states' rights. Russell told the Senate:

> The bill is cunningly designed to vest in the attorney general unprecedented power to bring to bear the whole might of the federal government, including the armed forces if necessary, to force a commingling of white and Negro children in the state supported schools of the South.[25]

Russell concluded his speech by noting that many Americans living outside the South "would not approve of another Reconstruction at bayonet point of a peaceful and patriotic South."

In this speech, Senator Russell established the expansion of U.S. Government power as the principal issue on which civil rights bills would be opposed during the late 1950s and 1960s. This issue had particular appeal to prosegregationists because it rested on constitutional grounds —the U.S. Government should not be given too much power at the expense of the states—rather than on racial segregation as such. By the early 1960s Russell was referring to the tendency of all civil rights bills to expand the powers of the national government over the state governments as the "Federal blackjack."[26]

Russell's attack on Part III in the 1957 bill was successful. Even President Eisenhower, after analyzing Russell's interpretation and seeing its effect on public opinion, told a news conference he could not support giving the attorney general such vast powers. With Part III eliminated, the southerners no longer considered the bill a threat and let the other three provisions pass into law without a filibuster. Russell called the removal of Part III "the sweetest victory in my twenty-five years as a senator."[27]

The most important lesson learned from the 1957 Civil Rights Act by civil rights supporters was that any deal with the southern senators on a civil rights bill would result in "cutting the heart out" of the bill. By the early 1960s, this had produced a "no compromises" attitude on the part of civil rights supporters where the southerners were concerned. The lesson of 1957 was that any bill that the southerners approved of would not be worth having. A favorite expression at the time was that the bill would have been "gutted." In both 1964 and 1965, pro-civil rights forces adopted the strategy that a meaningful civil rights bill would have to undergo a determined southern filibuster in the Senate and that filibuster would have to be ended by a successful cloture vote (two-thirds of senators present and voting).

President Eisenhower's 1957 Civil Rights Act should not be regarded as a failure, however. The new law established a Civil Rights Commission to study racial problems in the United States and, based on the results of the study, make recommendations to Congress. In 1961 the Commission issued a major report to Congress thoroughly documenting the effects of racial segregation and oppression in the South. The Commission's findings served as the basis for the Kennedy administration civil rights bill that eventually became the Civil Rights Act of 1964.[28]

Equally important in the 1957 Civil Rights Act was the creation of the Civil Rights Division in the Department of Justice. Under both President Kennedy and President Johnson, the Civil Rights Division worked to further the civil rights of blacks in the American South and sought to reduce the conflict and violence produced by civil rights demonstrations. Under the leadership of Assistant Attorney General Burke Marshall, a Kennedy appointee, the Civil Rights Division of the Justice Department accomplished many important civil rights tasks in the early 1960s.

Little Rock

In an effort to voluntarily comply with the Supreme Court's *Brown* decision, the school board in Little Rock, Arkansas, began the process of desegregating that city's Central High School.[29] As school opened in September of 1957, nine black students were scheduled to attend classes at the previously all-white high school. Before the African-American students could even enter the building, however, the governor of Arkansas, Orval Faubus, sent in the Arkansas National Guard to "maintain law and order" by keeping the black students out of school. By sending in the National Guard to prevent racial integration, Governor Faubus was directly challenging the authority of the U.S. Supreme Court. Indirectly, he was challenging the ability of the U.S. Government to enforce the orders of its highest court.

President Dwight D. Eisenhower responded immediately to this challenge to court-ordered school integration. Acting under his authority as Commander in Chief of all U.S. armed forces, he "federalized" the Arkansas National Guard, thus putting it under his control rather than Governor Faubus's control. The Arkansas National Guard was ordered out of Little Rock, and regular U.S. Army troops were sent in to occupy the area around Central High School and see that school integration proceeded in an orderly and peaceful manner.

These decisive actions at Little Rock by a U.S. president made a significant impact on public opinion throughout the nation. For the first time since the Civil War period, United States military forces had entered a southern city and state to enforce a national policy (racial integration) strongly opposed by a state government official (Governor Faubus).

For southern blacks, this national intervention was a critical development. Up until the time President Eisenhower acted so swiftly and decisively at Little Rock, there had been no guarantee that national government power would be used to uphold the Supreme Court's order on school integration. After Eisenhower's actions at Little Rock, however, "the precedent was set." From that point forward, blacks could always hope for United States Government intervention on behalf of their efforts to integrate public schools. Little Rock motivated black civil rights leaders in the South and their white supporters to work even harder to end racial segregation.[30]

Little Rock's Central High School was integrated by military force for the 1957-1958 school year. The following year, however, Governor Faubus closed the schools rather than allow them to be desegregated. For a brief period, therefore, President Eisenhower's powerful intervention in the school integration crisis in Little Rock resulted in Little Rock public schools being closed. President Eisenhower's fear that going too rapidly with integration might result in closed public schools in the South had proven to be realistic, at least in the short run.

The Civil Rights Act of 1960

In 1959 the Eisenhower administration presented a civil rights bill to Congress which, among other things, extended the life of the Civil Rights Commission and gave the U.S. attorney general the power to inspect state and local voting records in elections for U.S. Government offices.[31] The bill received immediate consideration in the House of Representatives, where House Judiciary Committee Chairman Emanuel Celler referred it to a special subcommittee headed by himself. Celler had very carefully appointed a number of pro-civil rights supporters to this subcommittee—Subcommittee No. 5. Southern members of the House frequently charged that the subcommittee had been "stacked" in favor of civil rights.

As would be expected, the subcommittee took the Eisenhower proposals and added to them. A Part III was included in the subcommittee bill, even though President Eisenhower had refused to include Part III in the administration proposals.

The creation and use of Subcommittee No. 5 was one of the important civil rights developments during the Eisenhower years. In the years following 1960, House Judiciary Chairman Celler continued to groom the subcommittee as a strong pro-civil rights group. When the bill that eventually became the Civil Rights Act of 1964 came before Subcommittee No. 5 in the fall of 1963, the subcommittee reported out one of the strongest civil rights bills that had ever been presented to the U.S. Congress. The subcommittee bill was so pro-civil rights that President Kennedy called Chairman Celler to a series of meetings at the White House at which the bill was toned down so that it would have a better chance of eventual passage in the Senate.[32]

Following consideration by the House Judiciary Committee, President Eisenhower's 1959 civil rights proposal ran into a stone wall of opposition in the House Rules Committee. The chairman of the House Rules Committee, Representative Howard Smith of Virginia, would disappear from Washington for long periods of time when a bill he disliked was supposed to be under consideration by his committee. With the Rules Committee chairman absent, no action could be taken on the bill in question. When the 1957 civil rights bill came before his committee, Chairman Smith left town for his Virginia farm because, he said, his dairy barn had caught fire and burned down. He went back to the farm again in 1959, arguing that his dairy cattle were sick and needed him close by.

House Judiciary Chairman Celler sought to solve the problem of Smith's stalwart opposition by circulating a discharge petition. If one-half of the members of the House signed the discharge petition, the 1959 Eisenhower civil rights bill would move automatically from the Rules Committee to the House floor for debate and passage. The petition came within 10 names of the 218 required signatures when Chairman Smith relented and allowed the Rules Committee to vote out the bill. Apparently only the "threat" of a successful discharge petition was enough to shake the bill free.[33]

This technique for overcoming the obstacle of Chairman Smith and the House Rules Committee was used over and over again during the 1960s. For instance, when the Civil Rights Act of 1964 was mired in the House Rules Committee in January 1964, circulation of a discharge petition helped to inspire Chairman Smith to let the committee majority release the bill.[34]

By February 1960 the Eisenhower civil rights bill was, as expected, mired in the Senate Judiciary Committee. At this time Eisenhower's attorney general, William P. Rogers, proposed that court-appointed referees be sent into the

South to register black citizens to vote. The Rogers proposal, which had the support of President Eisenhower, called for U.S. judges to send in referees wherever they found a "pattern or practice" of discrimination in the voter registration process.

Democratic members of the Senate criticized the Eisenhower voting rights plan. They pointed out that blacks would have to go through lengthy and legally treacherous court proceedings in order to get court-appointed referees sent into the South to register black voters. The Democrats argued the president of the United States, and not the courts, should dispatch U.S. registrars down into Dixie to put blacks on the voting rolls.

This controversy over how to register blacks to vote in the South, first aired publicly in early 1960, would continue until the enactment of the Voting Rights Act of 1965. In the end, it was the president-appointed registrars rather than the court-appointed referees who were sent into the South to put large numbers of blacks on the voter registration rolls.

Perhaps more important was the development of the concept of "pattern or practice" for determining when the U.S. Government should override states' rights and enforce national civil rights laws. In the final stages of the Senate debate on the Civil Rights Act of 1964, an aide to Republican Senator Everett M. Dirksen of Illinois proposed that U.S. Government laws banning racial segregation in public accommodations and employment only apply in those states where there was a "pattern or practice" of discrimination. This compromise language, first proposed in 1960 by Attorney General Rogers, broke a stalemate and helped gain needed votes to cloture a southern filibuster and enact the 1964 civil rights bill into law.[35]

A legislative maneuver was used to get Eisenhower's 1960 civil rights bill past Chairman James Eastland (Dem., MS) and the Senate Judiciary Committee. On February 15, 1960, the civil rights bill came up for debate on the Senate floor as an amendment to a minor bill concerning the leasing of a surplus U.S. Army building to a school district in Missouri. The southern Democrats in the Senate immediately began a filibuster, primarily against the prospect that Part III would be adopted and would give the U.S. attorney general the power to intervene directly in racial relations in the South.

Late in February, in an effort to break the filibuster, the Senate went into round-the-clock sessions. The eighteen filibustering southerners, divided into six teams of three senators each, had no trouble keeping one three-person team on the Senate floor while the other five teams rested. Those opposing the filibuster, however, had to keep fifty-one senators (a quorum) at the Capitol ready to meet a quorum call at any time. The result of round-the-clock sessions was to exhaust the pro-civil rights senators, not the southerners.

The failure of round-the-clock sessions to break the filibuster of the 1960 civil rights bill was a lesson to civil rights supporters that dominated their thinking during the early 1960s. The southerners could not be exhausted by twenty-four-hour-a-day sessions, but the pro-civil rights senators could be. It meant that there was only one way to end a filibuster—get two-thirds of the Senate to vote cloture. Thus, when the Civil Rights Act of 1964 and the Voting Rights Act of 1965 were undergoing southern filibusters in the Senate, round-the-clock sessions were not attempted to break the filibuster. In both cases civil rights supporters, from the very beginning, saw a successful cloture vote as the only way to end the filibuster and get meaningful civil rights legislation passed in the Senate.

Once it became clear that round-the-clock sessions would not stop the southern filibuster of the 1960 civil rights bill, pro-civil rights senators attempted a cloture vote even though they did not know if they had enough votes for cloture. The results were disastrous. The cloture motion did not even receive a majority vote, let alone come close to the required two-thirds vote. The Senate quickly defeated Part

III, the southerners ended their filibuster, and the Civil Rights Act of 1960, which now dealt weakly with voting rights, was enacted into law.[36]

The failed cloture vote on the 1960 Civil Rights Act strongly influenced civil rights legislative strategy making in both 1964 and 1965. The lesson was clear: Never attempt a cloture vote until absolutely positive that two-thirds of the senators are going to vote for cloture. Neither the Civil Rights Act of 1964 nor the Voting Rights Act of 1965 were brought to a cloture vote until civil rights supporters were certain they had the necessary votes. Attempts to hold cloture votes before the votes were in hand were assiduously avoided.[37]

Student Sit-In Demonstrations

One of the most visible forms of racial discrimination in the late 1950s and early 1960s was the refusal of snack bars, lunch counters, and restaurants to serve African-Americans. On February 1, 1960, four black college students staged a "sit-in" at a lunch counter in Greensboro, North Carolina. Although the Congress of Racial Equality (CORE) had been using sit-ins to publicly oppose racial segregation since the early 1940s, this particular sit-in, perhaps because it involved college students, received extensive coverage in the national news media, particularly on network television news.

All at once students at other black colleges throughout the South began staging sit-ins in an effort to end racial segregation in nearby eating places. Students at white colleges often joined these sit-in demonstrations, as did sympathetic high school students and adults of both races. Frequently these demonstrations resulted in white segregationists taunting and beating up the persons sitting-in, thereby producing even more coverage by the news media. By January 1961, as Eisenhower was leaving office, over seventy thousand black and white youngsters had participated in the sit-ins. A new civil rights organization, the Student Nonviolent Coordinating Committee (SNCC), was formed to organize sit-in demonstrations throughout the South.[38]

It can be argued there is something of a connection between President Eisenhower's swift intervention in the Little Rock school crisis in 1957 and the rise of the sit-in movement early in 1960. Eisenhower had made it clear that, in the end, the U.S. Government would support, militarily if necessary, those who were working for civil rights in the southern United States. Although the sit-in demonstrators were protesting local and state laws, Little Rock had given them much reason to believe that the U.S. Government would eventually come into the dispute on their side.

President Eisenhower's support for civil rights might have been considerably more positive and dramatic if the sit-in demonstrations had occurred early in his administration rather than at the very end. The civil rights issue so completely divided the American body politic that no president took action on meaningful civil rights legislation until a dramatic national event forced him to take action. Thus President Kennedy did not persuasively support what was to become the Civil Rights Act of 1964 until civil rights demonstrations and riots erupted in Birmingham, Alabama. President Johnson did not press for the Voting Rights Act of 1965 until the violent suppression of the voting rights march to Selma, Alabama. If the sit-in demonstrations had begun taking place earlier in the Eisenhower years, and Eisenhower had been presented with a serious situation involving equal access to public accommodations, there well could have been considerably more action by Eisenhower in the civil rights field.

The Kennedy Administration

John F. Kennedy succeeded Dwight D. Eisenhower to the presidency on January 20, 1961. The racial unrest that had characterized the Eisenhower years continued and increased.[39]

In the fall of 1962 James Meredith, a black, sought to be admitted to the all-white University of Mississippi. Furious legal manipulations by Mississippi Governor Ross Barnett and the Mississippi state legislature to keep Meredith out of "Ole Miss" resulted in Meredith's legal case being taken up by both the NAACP and the Civil Rights Division of the Department of Justice. As a result, when Meredith came onto the Ole Miss campus the day before he was to register for classes, the case had been extremely well publicized and Meredith was under the personal protection of United States marshals.

A large mob of white demonstrators gathered on the Ole Miss campus to protest Meredith's entrance. Time and again the mob assaulted the U.S. marshals as they stood guard in front of the building in which Meredith was to register the next day, pelting both the marshals and the building with eggs, rocks, and bottles. One marshal was severely wounded in the neck. A bystander was killed by a stray bullet, and a news correspondent was mysteriously shot to death at close range. Although snipers fired bullets repeatedly at the university building in which Meredith was to register, miraculously none of the U.S. marshals or Justice Department lawyers there were killed.

As the evening riot increased in intensity, President John F. Kennedy went on national television to explain why the court order admitting Meredith to the University of Mississippi had to be carried out: "Americans are free, in short, to disagree with the law," the president told the nation, "but not to disobey it." President Kennedy subsequently realized that Governor Barnett was not going to send adequate police or National Guard troops to relieve the beleaguered U.S. marshals at Ole Miss, so he "federalized" the Mississippi National Guard and dispatched twenty-five thousand U.S. Army troops to the campus. After they arrived, Meredith was registered at the University of Mississippi without incident.[40]

Eight months later the U.S. marshals and the Justice Department lawyers would play much the same scene at the University of Alabama, only this time the confrontation would be with Alabama Governor George Wallace rather than a mob of segregationist rioters. In a well-publicized political speech, Wallace had pledged to the people of Alabama that he would "bar the school house door" rather than permit school integration in their state. Wallace stood in a doorway at the University as two black students, Vivian Malone and James Hood, sought to register for classes. The students were closely guarded by Justice Department officials and U.S. marshals. After reading a short speech condemning "the trend toward military dictatorship" in the United States, Wallace "stood aside" and permitted the students to register. Wallace did so, however, only after being ordered out of the doorway by the general in command of the Alabama National Guard. The Alabama Guard had been "federalized," and the orders to the general had come directly from President Kennedy.[41]

A Unique Legislative Environment

It can be said of the Civil Rights Act of 1964 that, short of a declaration of war, no other act of Congress had a more violent background—a background of confrontation, official violence, injury, and murder that has few parallels in American history. By late 1962 and early 1963 the South was the site of many confrontations between black demonstrators on the one hand and segregationist whites on the other. Justice Department personnel were traveling through Dixie enforcing school integration orders, looking for civil rights violations in the arrests and trials of sit-in demonstrators, and working to mediate peaceful settlements between the warring forces.

Several factors contributed to the confrontational background of this legislation. Franklin D. Roosevelt's executive order creating the Civil Rights Section of the Justice Department (later the Civil Rights Division) provided a government agency to aid southern blacks in their efforts to gain integration. The 1954 Supreme Court school integration decision had given black leaders a legal basis for arguing for equal treatment, not only in the school room but in the community generally. The Montgomery bus boycott had legitimated the nonviolent demonstration as an acceptable, and effective, means of gaining black rights.

Also important was the use of television to dramatize racial repression in the South. Network television news in the 1950s and 1960s originated and was edited almost totally in the North. Most networks news chiefs sent liberal, northern reporters down South to cover the civil rights movement rather than recruiting local reporters in the South who might have been more sympathetic to the segregationist cause. When white segregationist rioters realized they were being presented in an unfavorable light on the television screen, they made the mistake of beginning to rough up reporters and television crews and to destroy cameras and film. Such physical attacks on the press simply made northern editors more determined than ever to carry the civil rights story to the American people in terms as favorable as possible to the integrationists.

The impact of television on the civil rights movement was not limited to television viewers in the North and the West. Newspapers and local television and radio stations in the South, being local businesses and edited locally, tended to play down civil rights stories or edit them out altogether. There was no such local editing of network television news reports. People in southern cities who heard little about racial problems through their local news media were exposed to a constant barrage of civil rights stories on the national news on TV. The "Cotton Curtain" which used to prevent unpleasant racial items from getting into local southern news media was completely torn asunder by national network television news.

It has been argued that Martin Luther King, Jr., and his associates had an unspoken strategy of using nonviolent demonstrations to deliberately provoke attacks from violence-prone white southern officials and white segregationist mobs. It was well known to King and his associates, so the argument goes, that it was the opposition white violence that would attract widespread and sympathetic media coverage of their activities.

Whether or not King and his associates had such an unspoken strategy, their efforts resulted in the media coverage they needed. The civil rights movement thus became one of the most publicized events in United States history. It set the stage for the Civil Rights Act of 1964 to be one of the most extensively publicized legislative battles in United States history.

In June of 1963, following particularly violent demonstrations and counter-demonstrations in Birmingham, Alabama, President Kennedy sent a very strong civil rights bill to Congress designed to end all racial segregation in places of public accommodation (hotels, motels, restaurants, etc.).[42] Due to the awesome power of the southern Democrats, particularly in the Senate, a major civil rights bill had not been enacted in Congress since the aftermath of the Civil War. A great legislative showdown was about to begin.[43]

Notes

1. For discussion of the 13th, 14th, and 15th Amendments, with selections from congressional debates on these amendments, see Bernard Schwartz, *Statutory History of the United States: Civil Rights* (New York: Chelsea House, 1970), Part I, pp. 3-439.

2. For discussion with selections from congressional debates on the various civil rights acts of the 1870s, see Schwartz, *Statutory History of the United States: Civil Rights*, Part I, pp. 443-799.

3. See "The 1894 Repeal of Voting Rights Legislation" in Schwartz, *Statutory History of the United States: Civil Rights*, Part I, pp. 803-834.

4. Samuel Lubell, *White and Black: Test of a Nation*, 2d ed. (New York: Harper and Row, 1966), p. 19.

5. James L. Sundquist, *Politics and Policy: The Eisenhower, Kennedy, and Johnson Years* (Washington, D.C.: Brookings, 1968), p. 221. See also *Commission on Civil Rights*, Hearings before the Subcommittee on Constitutional Rights of the House Judiciary Committee, 83 Cong. I sess. (January 26, 1954), pp. 45-47.

6. Sean Dennis Cashman, *African-Americans and the Quest for Civil Rights, 1900-1990* (New York: New York University Press, 1991), pp. 20-23. See also Robert Weisbrot, *Freedom Bound: A History of America's Civil Rights Movement* (New York: Norton, 1990), p. 8. Both Cashman and Weisbrot give comprehensive book-length histories of civil rights in the United States. For an account of NAACP activities during the civil rights movement of the 1950s and 1960s, see Roy Wilkins with Tom Mathews, *Standing Fast: The Autobiography of Roy Wilkins* (New York: Viking Press, 1982).

7. Statistics on blacks moving north are from Lubell, *White and Black*, pp. 35-36.

8. Lubell, *White and Black*, pp. 57-58.

9. For discussion of Eisenhower's statements—and Warren's—about the *Brown* decision, see Stephen E. Ambrose, *Eisenhower: Volume Two: The President* (New York: Simon and Schuster, 1984), p. 308.

10. Peter Evans Kane, "The Senate Debate on the 1964 Civil Rights Act" (Ph.D. diss., Purdue University, Lafayette, In., 1967), p. 13.

11. Lubell, *White and Black*, p. 109.

12. Stephen E. Ambrose, *Eisenhower: Volume Two: The President*, p. 308.

13. For discussion of the Congress of Racial Equality (CORE), see James Peck, *Freedom Ride* (New York: Simon

and Schuster, 1962) and August Meier and Elliott Rudwick, *CORE: A Study in the Civil Rights Movement, 1942-1968* (New York: Oxford University Press, 1973). For a first-person account by a national leader of CORE, see James Farmer, *Lay Bare the Heart: An Autobiography of the Civil Rights Movement* (New York: Arbor House, 1985).

14. Robert D. Loevy, *To End All Segregation: The Politics of the Passage of the Civil Rights Act of 1964* (Lanham, Md.: University Press of America, 1990), p. 22.

15. Loevy, *To End All Segregation*, pp. 22-23. There are many accounts of the Montgomery bus boycott. Martin Luther King, Jr., wrote his own account, *Stride Toward Freedom: The Montgomery Story* (New York: Harper and Row, 1958). For additional first-person accounts see David J. Garrow, ed., *The Montgomery Bus Boycott and the Women Who Started It: The Memoir of Jo Ann Gibson Robinson* (Knoxville: University of Tennessee Press, 1987), and Rosa Parks with Jim Haskins, *Rosa Parks: My Story* (New York: Dial Books, 1992). For a brief account see Sean Dennis Cashman, *African-Americans and the Quest for Civil Rights, 1900-1990*, pp. 124-130. For a documentary history see Peter B. Levy, ed., *Let Freedom Ring: A Documentary History of the Modern Civil Rights Movement* (New York: Praeger Publishers, 1992), pp. 51-64.

16. For a detailed biography of Martin Luther King, Jr., which also serves as an account of the civil rights movement from 1954 to 1968, see David J. Garrow, *Bearing the Cross: Martin Luther King, Jr., and the Southern Christian Leadership Conference* (New York: William Morrow, 1986). See also David L. Lewis, *King: A Biography* (Urbana: University of Illinois Press, 1978); Stephen B. Oates, *Let the Trumpet Sound: The Life of Martin Luther King, Jr.* (New York: Harper and Row, 1982); and Taylor Branch, *Parting the Waters: America in the King Years, 1954-1963* (New York: Simon and Schuster, 1988).

17. For a discussion of the effect of the Birmingham demonstrations on the Civil Rights Act of 1964, see Loevy,

To End All Segregation, pp. 10-16. For the relationship between the Selma march and the Voing Rights Act of 1965, see David J. Garrow, *Protest at Selma: Martin Luther King, Jr., and the Voting Rights Act of 1965* (New Haven, Conn.: Yale University Press, 1978).

18. News conference, March 3, 1954, *Public Papers of the Presidents*, 1954, p. 48.

19. Lubell, *White and Black*, pp. 75-76.

20. For a summary of the Civil Rights Act of 1957 going through Congress, see Sundquist, *Politics and Policy*, pp. 222-238. See also John G. Stewart, *Independence and Control: The Challenge of Senatorial Party Leadership* (Ph.D. dissertation, University of Chicago, Chicago, Ill., 1968), pp. 141-150. For analysis and selections from the congressional debate, see Schwartz, *Statutory History of the United States: Civil Rights*, Part II, pp. 837-932. See also J. W. Anderson, *Eisenhower, Brownell, and the Congress* (published for Inter-University Case Program by University of Alabama Press, 1964). See also *Revolution in Civil Rights* (Washington, D.C.: Congressional Quarterly, 1965), pp. 27-30.

21. Loevy, *To End All Segregation*, p. 29.

22. For President Eisenhower's own account of his early civil rights record and his role in the enactment of the Civil Rights Act of 1957, see Dwight D. Eisenhower, *The White House Years: Waging Peace: 1956-1961* (Garden City, N.Y.: Doubleday, 1965), pp. 148-162

23. Loevy, *To End All Segregation*, pp. 317-318.

24. Loevy, *To End All Segregation*, ch. 9, "Filibuster #1: The Motion to Consider," pp. 167-185.

25. *Congressional Record*, 103 (July 2, 1957), p. 10771.

26. For a complete history of Senator Russell's opposition to civil rights, see David Daniel Potenziani, *Look to the Past: Richard B. Russell and the Defense of Southern White Supremacy* (Ph.D. dissertation, University of Georgia, Athens, Ga., 1981).

27. *Congressional Record* 103 (August 30, 1957), p. 16661.

28. For a summary of the five-volume Civil Rights Commission Report of 1961, see *Congressional Quarterly Almanac—1961*, pp. 394-398.

29. For a summary of the Little Rock crisis, see Cashman, *African-Americans and the Quest for Civil Rights, 1900-1990*, pp. 137-141. For a first-person account by one of the African-American students and President Eisenhower's address to the nation, see Levy, *Let Freedom Ring*, pp. 44-48. For President Eisenhower's own account, see Eisenhower, *The White House Years: Waging Peace: 1956-1961*, pp. 162-176. See also Ambrose, *Eisenhower: Volume Two: The President*, pp. 413-423.

30. This analysis of the effect of President Eisenhower's actions at Little Rock on the civil rights movement is based on Lubell, *White and Black*, pp. 101-102.

31. For a book-length analysis of the Civil Rights Act of 1960, see Daniel M. Berman, *A Bill Becomes a Law: Congress Enacts Civil Rights Legislation* (New York: Macmillan, 2d ed., 1966). See also *Revolution in Civil Rights*, pp. 31-36; Sundquist, *Politics and Policy*, pp. 238-250; and Stewart, *Independence and Control*, pp. 150-158. For analysis and highlights of the congressional debate, see Schwartz, *Statutory History of the United States: Civil Rights*, Part II, pp. 935-1013.

32. Loevy, *To End All Segregation*, ch. 4, "Subcommittee No. 5: 'Out of Control' for Civil Rights," pp. 35-81.

33. Berman, *A Bill Becomes a Law*, pp. 26-33, 88-95.

34. Berman, *A Bill Becomes a Law*, pp. 32-33, 95-97. See also Loevy, *To End All Segregation*, pp. 90-95.

35. The Dirksen assistant who made the proposal was Clyde Flynn, Republican Counsel, Subcommittee on Constitutional Amendments, Senate Committee on the Judiciary. See Loevy, *To End All Segregation*, pp. 258-259.

36. Berman, *A Bill Becomes a Law*, p. 77.

37. Berman, *A Bill Becomes a Law*, pp. 77-81; Loevy, *To End All Segregation*, pp. 276-286; Garrow, *Protest at Selma*, pp. 123-126.

38. For descriptions of the sit-in movement see ch. 2, "The Sit-ins," in Robert Weisbrot, *Freedom Bound: A History of America's Civil Rights Movement*, pp. 19-44, and ch. 9, "1960: Origins of a Decade of Disruption," in Aldon D. Morris, *The Origins of the Civil Rights Movement: Black Communities Organizing for Change* (New York: Free Press, 1984), pp. 195-228. For book-length treatments see Miles Wolff, *Lunch at the Five and Ten: The Greensboro Sit-ins: A Contemporary History* (New York: Stein and Day, 1970), and William H. Chafe, *Civilities and Civil Rights: Greensboro, North Carolina, and the Black Struggle for Freedom* (New York: Oxford University Press, 1980). For the history of SNCC, see Howard Zinn, *SNCC: The New Abolitionists* (Boston, Mass.: Beacon Press, 2d ed., 1965); Clayborne Carson, *In Struggle: SNCC and the Black Awakening of the 1960s* (Cambridge, Mass.: Harvard University Press, 1981); Cleveland Sellers with Robert Terrell, *The River of No Return: The Autobiography of a Black Militant and the Life and Death of SNCC* (New York: William Morrow, 1973); and James Forman, *The Making of Black Revolutionaries* (Washington, D.C.: Open Hand, 1985).

39. For book-length treatments of John F. Kennedy and civil rights, see Carl M. Brauer, *John F. Kennedy and the Second Reconstruction* (New York: Columbia University Press, 1977) and Harris Wofford, *Of Kennedys and Kings: Making Sense of the Sixties* (New York: Farrar, Straus, and Giroux, 1980). For an analysis of Robert F. Kennedy's civil rights record as attorney general, see Victor S. Navasky, *Kennedy Justice* (New York: Atheneum, 1971). See also ch. 18, "The Fight for Equal Rights," in Theodore C. Sorensen, *Kennedy* (New York: Harper & Row, 1965), pp. 470-506, and ch. 3, "The Travail of Equal Rights," and ch. 36, "The Negro Revolution," in Arthur M. Schlesinger, Jr., *A Thousand Days: John F. Kennedy in the White House* (Boston, Mass.: Houghton Mifflin, 1965), pp. 924-977.

40. For a detailed description of the riot at the time of James Meredith's admission to the University of Mississippi,

see Michael Dorman, *We Shall Overcome* (New York: Delacorte Press, 1964), ch. I, "Riot at Ole Miss," pp. 1-120.

41. For a detailed description of U.S. efforts to integrate the University of Alabama, see Dorman, *We Shall Overcome*, ch. IX, "Tuscaloosa," pp. 270-334.

42. For a detailed description of the civil rights demonstrations and resulting violence in Birmingham, Alabama, see ch. IV, "Birmingham," in Dorman, *We Shall Overcome*, pp. 143-187. See also David J. Garrow, ed., *Birmingham, Alabama, 1956-1963: The Black Struggle for Civil Rights* (Brooklyn, N.Y.: Carlson, 1989).

43. For book-length treatments of the enactment of the Civil Rights Act of 1964, see Loevy, *To End All Segregation*, and Charles and Barbara Whalen, *The Longest Debate: A Legislative History of the 1964 Civil Rights Act* (Cabin John, Md.: Seven Locks Press, 1985). See also Kane, *The Senate Debate on the 1964 Civil Rights Act*, and Norbert Mills, *The Speaking of Hubert Humphrey in Favor of the 1964 Civil Rights Act* (Ph.D. dissertation, Bowling Green State University, Bowling Green, Ohio, 1974).

Chapter 2

The Role of the Leadership Conference on Civil Rights in the Civil Rights Struggle of 1963–1964

Joseph L. Rauh, Jr.

Joseph L. Rauh, Jr. (1911-1992) was a familiar figure in liberal Democratic circles in Washington, D.C., in the 1960s. An attorney, he was the vice-chairman of Americans for Democratic Action (ADA), a national lobbying organization that traditionally supported liberal causes.

In his younger years, Rauh had worked in the presidential administration of Franklin D. Roosevelt. He wrote FDR's 1941 executive order that set up a Fair Employment Practices Committee to work against racial discrimination in World War II defense plants.

Joe Rauh was the major lobbyist for the Leadership Conference on Civil Rights, a group of about fifty labor and religious organizations that had banded together to lobby Congress on the general issue of civil rights. Rauh thus organized and led the major lobbying effort on behalf of the civil rights bill that eventually became the Civil Rights Act of 1964. Rauh, who was white, was joined in this effort by a black lobbyist, Clarence Mitchell, Jr., director of the Washington Office of the National Association for the Advancement of Colored People (NAACP).

Shortly after President Lyndon B. Johnson signed the Civil Rights Act of 1964 into law on July 2, 1964, Joe Rauh wrote this article about his experiences as one of the two main lobbyists for the bill and submitted it for magazine publication. The article was rejected for publication and remained for years in Rauh's personal files in his office in Washington, D.C. To the best of the editor's knowledge, it has not been previously published.

Joseph Rauh, Jr., wrote an account that is both chronological and thorough. He described the passage of the Civil Rights Act of 1964 from the pro-civil rights point of view, but he also was careful to describe the various actions of the opponents of the bill.

The Rauh manuscript is most significant for its coverage and description of many of the private meetings and private conversations held by those who were working hard to enact the civil rights bill. It also is the only detailed first-person account available covering House of Representatives consideration of the Civil Rights Act of 1964. There are a number of first-person accounts of the Senate action, but only this one on the House as well as the Senate.

Joseph Rauh, Jr., begins his account in January 1963, when President John F. Kennedy sent a civil rights message to Congress that civil rights supporters considered comparatively weak. Rauh follows the civil rights bill for its entire journey through Congress, concluding when the bill is finally signed into law.

On February 28, 1963, President Kennedy sent Congress his long-awaited message on civil rights legislation. The need for legislative action was forthrightly stated: "The [black] baby born in America today . . . has about one-half as much chance of completing high school as a white baby born in the same place on the same day—one-third as much chance of completing college—one-third as much chance of becoming a professional man—twice as much chance of becoming unemployed— . . . a life expectancy which is seven years less—and the prospects of earning only half as much."

But President Kennedy was never one to demand congressional action on need alone. His sense of timing told him he could not overcome the legislative roadblocks in the way of civil rights legislation, and defeat, no matter how gallant, had no appeal for him. So, instead of moving to implement the Democratic platform promises of a Fair Employment Practices Commission [FEPC] law, authority for the attorney general to file civil injunctive suits in civil rights cases (the old Part III deleted from the 1957 bill), and immediate first-step school desegregation, the president limited himself to recommending patchwork improvements in existing voting legislation, technical assistance for school districts voluntarily seeking to desegregate, and extension of the Civil Rights Commission. He would run in 1964 on his unprecedented record of [black] appointments and aggressive executive action.

Civil rights leaders were dismayed. The Leadership Conference on Civil Rights, consisting of 50 civil rights organizations including the NAACP, ADA [Americans for Democratic Action], labor, Jewish groups and others, met promptly to survey the wreckage. The consensus was clear: President Kennedy had yielded on civil rights legislation before the fight had even begun. The proposed bill was hardly worth fighting for. Clarence Mitchell [Jr.], the legislative representative of the NAACP, whose dogged optimism and courage were to make him the leading figure in the enactment of the 1964 legislation, walked into the meeting with a sheaf of civil rights bills just then being introduced by liberal Republican senators and covering much of what the Democrats had promised—and a public accommodations bill to boot. But there was not much solace in bills introduced by a handful of the Senate Republican minority, and the meeting broke up in disarray. Such comfort as there was came from the hope that the second Kennedy administration would be different.

[Birmingham]

Two men changed the picture. In May of 1963, Martin Luther King, shrugging off advice that he withhold his protest demonstrations in Birmingham until the newly elected moderates took over the city government, started massive protests in the streets of Birmingham. [Police Commissioner] "Bull" Connor, never one to use a scalpel with an axe at hand, brought out the dogs, the fire hoses, the electric cattle prods. Front page pictures of Birmingham atrocities began to arouse the slumbering conscience of the nation. King lost the battle of Birmingham for his immediate demands, but the noble suffering of his protesters did not go unheard.

The Kennedy legislative proposals of February appeared shabby indeed in May and June. New proposals were inevitable. But what additional legislation would the president now ask of Congress? The civil rights groups sent message after message to the White House and the Justice Department urging that, in this time of crisis, the president demand of Congress what was really needed: a law providing access to all public accommodations, an FEPC to deal with the drastic [black] unemployment, immediate first-step school desegregation everywhere, [black] registration and voting before federal registrars, and, of course, a Part III giving the attorney general power to enjoin state interference with peaceful protests, as in Birmingham.

Disquieting reports emanated from [Kennedy] administration sources that no such all-out proposal would be forthcoming. In addition to the February package, the major proposals were to be a public accommodations bill limited in scope, power in the attorney general to sue for school desegregation (but without any requirement for immediate desegregation), and withholding of federal funds supporting segregated or discriminatory state or local activities.

[Labor Concerns]

The labor movement was especially alarmed over the rumored failure to include a [Fair Employment Practices Commission (FEPC)] in the upcoming bill. A labor-civil rights group led by Andy Biemiller, director of the AFL-CIO's Department of Legislation, met with Senate Assistant Majority Leader [Hubert H.] Humphrey [Dem., MN] on June 5th, to demand an administration bill worthy of the times. The delegation argued that the administration's proposed bill would be "a patent compromise in a no-compromise situation. All-out fights are made on all-out measures." Senator Humphrey was wholly in agreement that the strongest possible bill should be sent to Congress, and he urged his views upon President Kennedy both orally and by memorandum.

To no avail. On June 19th, the president sent his civil rights bill to Congress without change. It contained the administration's best estimates of what could be enacted, rather than what was needed. A single concession was made to the pressure from the left. The president's message carried "support of pending Federal Fair Employment Practices legislation," though the omnibus bill which he recommended did not include it. But, even without FEPC and Part III, President Kennedy's bill was the most comprehensive civil rights proposal ever made to Congress.

Two days later, the president called the civil rights leaders to the White House. He was obviously worried, but equally determined. He referred to the now famous, although never subsequently revealed, poll showing his popularity down below 50 percent for the first time [in his presidency]. He said he realized that this fight might even endanger his reelection, but here was a moral issue and he was determined to wage the battle come what may. He stressed the need for an all-out effort by everybody in the room to mobilize the public behind his bill. The only light note crept in when one of those present referred in some hostile way to "Bull" Connor [the Birmingham police commissioner]. The president dryly responded that "'Bull' Connor has done more for civil rights than anyone in this room."

[A Go-Sign from the Vice President]

The latter part of the meeting was chaired by then Vice President Johnson. When my turn to speak came, I asked what attitude the [Kennedy] administration would take if the civil rights groups sought to strengthen the bill by amendments, including an FEPC and Part III, and whether this would cause friction. Mr. Johnson responded that there had to be "flexibility" in a campaign of this kind, and he saw no difficulty in the civil rights groups going beyond the administration in their demands. This was the go-sign for the Leadership Conference strategy from then on.

After the meeting at the White House broke up, Walter Reuther got together ten or twelve of the participants to discuss ways and means of implementing President Kennedy's request for a mobilization of public support behind the bill. Dr. King spoke of a gigantic March on Washington as the best means of ensuring legislation. Roy Wilkins spoke of enlarging the Leadership Conference to include all organizations favoring the legislation and galvanizing them into grass roots pressure for the bill. Speedy action on both fronts followed.

Roy Wilkins, who was Chairman of the Leadership Conference as well as head of the NAACP, promptly called a meeting for July 2nd at the Roosevelt Hotel in New York. Not only were the 50 long-time civil rights organizations then in the Leadership Conference invited, but another 50 or so religious and other potentially helpful groups were also asked to come. The mood was one of excitement that, at long last, there was a bill in the hopper worthy of a real struggle. The consensus was easily arrived at. The civil rights movement gave its wholehearted support to the administration bill. But it demanded more—an FEPC, Part III, [and] all public accommodations covered. Not only were these additional provisions urgently needed, but a good offense was obviously the best defense against weakening amendments.

["Mrs. Murphy's Boarding House"]

Already there was grave concern over the wide-spread newspaper talk that the public accommodations section would be gutted, possibly by an exemption for "small" public accommodations. "Mrs. Murphy's boarding house" with a few rooms was one thing, for her right of privacy cut across the [black person's] right to a room. But a general exception for all small public accommodations was something else again. A [black] laborer entering a small diner could be quite as hungry as a [black] banker seeking service at the Waldorf [Hotel in New York].

The congressional roadblocks were outlined to the meeting. The conservative character of the House Judiciary Committee; the Dixicrat-Republican control of the House Rules Committee; the Senate filibuster—these and other obstacles were carefully weighed. Dr. King whispered at one stage: "Mighty complicated, isn't it?" But, complicated or not, there was unanimous determination to overrun these roadblocks by mobilizing the nation behind the bill.

There was need for speed, not only to utilize the momentum created by the president's message, and by the continuing protest movement in both North and South, but equally to calm the stormy racial tensions shaking the country. Walter Reuther offered the Leadership Conference office space in Washington, and he and others raised the necessary funds. Arnold Aronson, whose brilliance and dedication to civil rights was never more in evidence, took over the management of the Washington office. Marvin Caplan, a reporter with wide experience in neighborhood racial work, and Violet Gunther, former ADA executive director, joined the staff. The drive to mobilize support was on in force.

[Subcommittee No. 5]

The first target was House Judiciary Subcommittee No. 5, to which the civil rights bill had been referred. While the hearings before the subcommittee were in progress, Clarence Mitchell, Andy Biemiller, Jim Hamilton of the National Council of Churches, Walter Fauntroy of [the Southern Christian Leadership Conference (SCLC)], and I, opened negotiations for strengthening amendments with the Justice Department and the White House. Our position was simple. Since a majority of the subcommittee was for civil rights, let them add Part III, FEPC, and all public accommodations to the pending bill. The Justice Department representatives opposed Part III on the merits. If the attorney general enjoined local police interference with peaceful demonstrations, they argued, the police would abdicate and total federal intervention would become necessary.

Justice was not opposed to the other two amendments, but argued that the full Judiciary Committee would not include them and, even if it did, the House and Senate would not pass them. In a word, the Leadership Conference wanted to get the best possible bill out of the subcommittee and then fight for it every inch of the way. Justice wanted only what they thought they could hold in full committee, the House, and the Senate.

Stalemated in the discussions with the [Kennedy] administration, Leadership Conference representatives went directly to [Emanuel Celler (Dem., NY), chairman of the House Judiciary Committee and Subcommittee No. 5.] Chairman Celler promptly agreed to the inclusion of FEPC, and said he would keep an open mind on other strengthening amendments offered in subcommittee. [Representative Peter W.] Rodino [Dem., NJ] agreed to offer the FEPC; [Representative Byron G.] Rogers [Dem., CO] agreed to offer Part III; [Representative Robert W.] Kastenmeier [Dem., WI] agreed to offer the broad public accommodations section.

The hearings before the subcommittee droned on through July and into August. The public accommodations section received the bulk of the attention. Democrats, in line with the position taken by the [Kennedy] administration, argued that the commerce clause gave the correct constitutional base for the bill. The Republicans, who had always resisted the broad application of the commerce clause to social and economic legislation, and who looked back with pride to the adoption of the Fourteenth Amendment by a Republican Congress, appeared to feel more comfortable with the Fourteenth Amendment as the predicate of the legislation. The Leadership Conference repeatedly urged that the public accommodations title be bottomed upon both the commerce clause and the Fourteenth Amendment, and that all public accommodations be covered by the statute. Some of the Republican enthusiasm for the Fourteenth Amendment approach began to evaporate when it became clear that the Fourteenth Amendment approach would broaden the bill.

[The "Calendar Wednesday" Flap]

While the subcommittee hearings were proceeding, there was a short flap with Representative Adam Clayton Powell [Dem., NY]. On July 24th, at the regular Wednesday afternoon meeting of the Washington representatives of the Leadership Conference organizations, staff members of Powell's committee urged the conference to help bring his committee's FEPC bill to the House floor at once through the "Calendar Wednesday" procedure. This is a procedure whereby a committee chairman (in this case, Powell) can bring a bill to the floor on a particular Wednesday without going through the House Rules Committee. But the bill must pass the House *before* adjournment that same day. The Calendar Wednesday strategy would have been a big show for Mr. Powell, but there was no chance of passing FEPC that way, and a defeat would have been a serious blow to the pending Kennedy civil rights bill. The Leadership Conference turned thumbs down, and Powell promptly announced that, since there were many more white representatives than [blacks] in the Leadership Conference, he was not bound by their decision. He did not, however, try the Calendar Wednesday procedure.

[The March on Washington]

As the subcommittee was deliberating, the historic August 28th [1963] March on Washington gave the legislative drive new inspiration. The fears of many that the march would result in incidents on Capitol Hill proved groundless. Instead, [representatives] and senators came to the Lincoln Memorial in buses and, sitting on the steps, heard the crowd chant "pass the bill, pass the bill." And House Speaker [John W.] McCormack [Dem., MA], after meeting with the leaders of the march, announced that he thought an FEPC could pass the House.

Nevertheless, the administration clung to its position against strengthening the initial Kennedy bill. The hearings had ended, August was gone, and most of September, too. Finally, Chairman Celler, caught between the administration and the Leadership Conference, decided to go ahead without administration okay. He called a press conference on September 25th and announced that the subcommittee had approved a "very strong bill." Included in it were FEPC, Part III, all public accommodations, and even some secondary items requested by the Leadership Conference.

[Chairman] Celler's press conference was a happy hour, but two clouds hovered over the gathering. The first was the obvious displeasure of Representative William McCulloch [Rep., OH], the ranking Republican on the House Judiciary Committee, who saw his previous agreement with the Justice Department for a much milder bill wiped out by the liberal Democratic majority on the House subcommittee. The other was a tragic, if understandable, mistake by the over-worked and conscientious committee counsel, William Foley. When [Representative Byron] Rogers [Dem., CO] offered his Part III in subcommittee, it was carefully limited to the rights of minorities under the Fourteenth Amendment. Foley rewrote the amendment to cross-reference to other statutes, and in doing so made it far broader than the situation warranted and vulnerable to later attack.

The Leadership Conference immediately called upon the full House Judiciary Committee to approve the subcommittee bill "without dilution or delay." But this was not to be. Hardly had the ink dried on the stories of [Chairman] Celler's news conference when the pundits moved to the attack with the label "extreme." Despite entreaties that he stick with the subcommittee bill, Attorney General [Robert Kennedy] went before the full Judiciary Committee on [October] 15th and argued for the more moderate initial administration version.[1] Particularly did he strike at Part III, pointing out that it would bring the attorney general into disputes involving censorship, church-state relations, confiscatory rate-making, searches and seizures, and other matters totally unrelated to minority rights. That this was easily remediable by returning to the original Rogers draft of Part III was never mentioned.

But the full Judiciary Committee, conservative or not, now had the bit in its teeth. On October 22nd, a motion to adopt the subcommittee bill was made by Republican Representative [Arch] Moore of West Virginia. Recognizing that the votes were there to pass the motion opposed by the administration, Chairman Celler adjourned the meeting and then cancelled one scheduled for the next day.

[The White House Intervenes]

Now President Kennedy took over. He called the congressional leaders together [at the White House] on the night of October 23rd and, after five days of negotiating, forced a compromise. FEPC was retained with enforcement in the courts; Part III was retained but limited to attorney general intervention; public accommodations were limited in scope. On October 29th the House Judiciary Committee finally met, voted down the motion to approve the subcommittee bill, and voted out the [Kennedy] compromise version.

The Leadership Conference was well satisfied. Its efforts had strengthened the bill, and the Republican leadership, including McCulloch and Minority Leader [Charles A.] Halleck [Rep., IN] were now tied to the bill. As the *New York Post* said editorially on October 31st: "The civil rights bill voted by the Judiciary Committee is an improvement over the administration's original proposal. It vindicates the fight waged by the Democratic and Republican liberals for a stronger measure. . . . The lesson of this episode so far is that faint heart rarely prevails on Capitol Hill."

The southerners on the [Judiciary] Committee stalled the report until November 21st [when the committee bill was forwarded to the House Rules Committee]. That afternoon, Chairman Celler asked the Rules Committee to send the bill to the House floor for action. [The Rules Committee chairman], Howard Smith [Dem., VA], made clear his intention to bottle up the bill, and there the matter rested when, 24 hours later, President Kennedy was assassinated.

[Lyndon Johnson Takes Over]

As if to quell any doubts that a Texan would carry on the struggle commenced by his northern predecessor, President Johnson wasted little time in making his own position crystal clear. On November 27th, in his address to the Joint Session of the House and Senate, he said: "We have talked long enough in this country about equal rights. . . . It is time now to write the next chapter—and to write it in the books of law." He called in civil rights leaders one by one and discussed ways and means of getting the bill through Congress unscathed. He never wavered from this course.

Now it was southerner against southerner—President Johnson against [Rules Committee Chairman] Howard Smith. Hardly had President Kennedy's funeral ended when [Representative] Richard Bolling [Dem., MO] filed a resolution to bring the civil rights bill before the House. Then, on December 9th, [Representative] Celler filed the inevitable petition to discharge the Rules Committee. The target was the required 218 signatures (a majority of the House) by December 13th, so that the civil rights bill could be called up in the House on December 23rd [1963] and passed before year's end. But only about 150 signatures had been obtained by the 13th (including, significantly enough, 8 or 9 Texans), and Congress went home for Christmas with the bill still in Smith's firm grasp.

Things changed immediately after the recess. [Representatives] had found real support for the bill in their districts at Christmas time. Additional signatures on the discharge petition were virtually certain. Furthermore, a majority of the Rules Committee can act without the chairman, and there were stirrings on that front, too. Of the 10 Democrats on the 15-man Rules Committee, 6 were already committed to action. Only two Republicans were needed, and Clarence Brown [of Ohio], the ranking Republican, began to pressure Smith.

Speaker [of the House] McCormack and Majority Leader [Carl] Albert [Dem., OK] supported the efforts of Bolling and Brown, and Chairman Smith opened public hearings on the bill on January 9th [1964]. After a couple of weeks of desultory hearings before the Rules Committee, Chairman Smith gave in, saying: "I know the facts of life around here." Majority Leader Albert announced that the bill would be reported out by the Rules Committee on January 30th and move to the floor the following day. This timetable fitted in quite nicely with the desire of Republican [representatives] to get away for Lincoln's Birthday speeches at home.

[To Amend or Not?]

The Leadership Conference [on Civil Rights] had a tactical problem as the bill faced the House floor. [Should they] seek strengthening amendments? The [Leadership] Conference was on record asking that the House Judiciary Committee bill be strengthened by making the public accommodations section all-inclusive; by including a Part III to permit the attorney general to initiate, not just intervene, in civil rights suits; and by strengthening the FEPC provision to permit administrative rather than judicial enforcement. Sticking to its principle that a good offense is the best defense, the Leadership Conference had continued to support these amendments even in the face of increasing reports and newspaper speculation that the bill would be weakened on the House floor, even that FEPC might be wiped out entirely.

In a meeting with President Johnson on January 21st, the president informed Clarence Mitchell and myself, representing the Leadership Conference, that he opposed any change in the bill. Recognizing the unlikelihood of strengthening amendments and the danger in adopting a different strategy on the House floor from that of the [Johnson] administration, the Leadership Conference modified its position to one of opposition to all weakening amendments and reserving decision on strengthening amendments. No such decision was ever required.

[Gallery Watchers]

Mobilizing for a battle on the floor of the House requires unusually detailed preparation. When the House takes up a bill, it goes into "the Committee of the Whole" for the purpose of considering amendments. In Committee of the Whole there are no record votes, only teller votes in which the members parade down the aisles to be counted. Writing in the galleries is not permitted. To keep a list of how [representatives] voted requires enough watchers to cover each [representative] and to remember whether and how each voted. Over 220 [representatives] had committed themselves to the bill without dilution, but these commitments were of little value unless the [representatives] were on the floor.

Leadership Conference organizations sent delegations, some large and some small, to help with the effort on the House floor. These delegations, plus the regular Washington representatives of the Leadership Conference organizations, met at the Congressional Hotel each day an hour before the House went into session to go over the schedule for the day. One or more persons would contact each [representative] to make sure he [or she] would be on the floor for teller votes and would oppose all weakening amendments. Full galleries let the [representatives] know that, though there was no record in the House, there would be one in the minds of the watchers.

[Representative] Frank Thompson [Dem., NJ] was in charge of the "whip" system to keep pro-civil-rights [representatives] on the floor. Leadership Conference [members] met with Thompson a half hour before the opening of the House each day to exchange information on present and absent [representatives]. The [Leadership] Conference office in the Congressional Hotel helped Thompson and his colleagues run down straying [representatives]—one as far as Europe. Chuck Daly, the president's [lobbyist], joined in the effort. When the Tuesday-to-Thursday eastern [representatives], even including [Republican Representative] Buckley of New York, answered present to a quorum call on a Saturday, old-timers began talking about miracles.

[House Debate]

The debate on the House floor was noteworthy for its moderation. Only Howard Smith [the Rules Committee chairman] went beyond the pale. Referring to the fact that a chiropodist [foot doctor] in a hotel would be covered by the public accommodations section, he shouted: "If I were cutting corns I would want to know whose feet I would have to be monkeying around with. I would want to know whether they smelled good or bad." But Smith was a leader without [enough] troops. Southern representatives knew they were beaten after the first few teller votes.

For ten days the debate continued as the House went through the bill title by title. First the voting rights section, then public accommodations, then public facilities, then school desegregation. Amendment after amendment was offered. If it was a weakening one, [Representative] Celler and [Representative] McCulloch would speak against it, assisted by such able lieutenants as Rodino, Rogers, Corman, Kastenmeier, Edwards, Lindsay, MacGregor, and Mathias. Amendment after amendment was defeated. Only negligible amendments were adopted. Then came the FEPC, the provision that the pundits had been so sure would never pass the House. But here again little damage was done. The House did adopt an ugly amendment denying atheists the right to protection under FEPC (later removed in the Senate), but that was all. The FEPC was safely in the bill.

As the House completed action on FEPC on February 6th and went on to the remaining more or less uncontested sections, there was a general feeling of relief in the galleries and even a hope for a moment of rest. Fifteen minutes later a message came for me to call the Leadership Conference office at the Congressional [Hotel], where I found that the president was calling. His first words were simple and direct: "What are you fellows doing about the Senate?" Then he banged out suggestions a mile a minute. The Commander- in-Chief was very much at his post.

The House passed the bill Monday night, February 10th, by a vote of 290 to 130. A bipartisan coalition had succeeded in enacting a far better bill than the one that President Kennedy had sent to Congress 8 months earlier. [Representative James A.] Haley [Dem., FL] called the bill "monstrous" and said it could not have been done without the "vultures in the galleries." Quite possibly, he was half right.

[Bypassing the Senate Judiciary Committee]

The bill reached the Senate right after the Lincoln Day recess. Democratic Majority Leader Mike Mansfield of Montana blocked the bill at the desk, announcing that in the near future he would propose that it be placed on the Senate Calendar without referral to Senator [James O.] Eastland's [Dem., MS] Judiciary Committee, the graveyard of civil rights legislation. True to his word, Mansfield moved, on February 26th, to place the civil rights bill directly on the Senate Calendar. Senator [Richard] Russell [Dem., GA], leader of the southern opposition, raised a point of order which the Senate overruled 54 to 37. On March 9th, Senator Mansfield moved to take the civil rights bill from the calendar, and the 3-month talkathon was under way.

[Organizing to Beat the Filibuster]

The question now was whether the Senate filibuster could defeat the House-passed bill or gut it as had been done in 1957. The southerners had always been well organized for their filibusters. Divided up into teams of three or four, one senator spoke, [one] or [two] others sat at his side, and the remainder rested.

This time, however, the civil rights forces were equally well organized. Senator Humphrey was named floor leader for the Democrats and Senator Kuchel for the Republicans.

Individual senators on both sides were designated to handle specific titles of the bill. A bipartisan newsletter was published early each morning reporting on the previous day's activities and giving the schedule for the day. Regular meetings between the senators leading the civil rights effort, their staffs, Ken Teasdale and Charles Ferris of the [Democratic] Policy Committee, Deputy Attorney General Katzenbach, and Leadership Conference [lobbyists] were held each Monday and Thursday a half hour before the Senate convened. Hour-to-hour contact was maintained with the Leadership Conference through Clarence Mitchell, who seldom left the Capitol during the entire three-month struggle. This time the outcome would not be determined by superior southern organization.

The civil rights side had much going for it. President Johnson had made it clear to Clarence Mitchell and me at the January 21st meeting that he would not care if the Senate did not do another thing for three months until the civil rights bill was enacted. He [also] made this crystal clear to the Senate leadership. This removed the filibusterers' greatest weapon—that they could hold out until other needed legislation required the Senate to put aside the civil rights bill. Furthermore, a substantial majority of the Senate favored the bill without dilution. [Republican] Leader [Everett] Dirksen's opposition to public accommodations and FEPC was truly a minority viewpoint.

As the Leadership Conference assessed the situation with the opening of the Senate debate early in March, the greatest danger was the possibility of an early and unsuccessful cloture vote. [This] would force a compromise to obtain the missing votes for cloture. The Conference strategy was predicated on avoiding such an early cloture vote at all costs. At one of the first Monday and Thursday meetings [with the Leadership Conference], both Senator Humphrey and Senator Kuchel committed themselves not to call for cloture until they had the required two-thirds vote in hand. This proved to be the crucial decision.

[The Motion to "Take Up"]

The southerners had indicated to the Senate leadership that they would not filibuster very long on the Mansfield motion to take up the civil rights bill, probably not more than 4 or 5 days. But these feelers had been put out to keep Senator Mansfield from ordering longer sessions. Actually, [the southerners] held up a vote on this preliminary motion for three weeks. Finally, on the eve of the Easter recess, the southerners finally yielded, and the Mansfield motion to take up the bill was adopted 67 to 17. [The 17 "No" voters were] all southern Democrats.

Hours later Senator [Wayne] Morse's [Dem., OR] motion to send the bill to the Judiciary Committee for a limited time [and no amendments] was tabled 50 to 34. The crusade of the religious groups in behalf of the bill was beginning to pay off. Two of the most conservative members of the Senate—Republican senators [Karl E.] Mundt of South Dakota and [Roman L.] Hruska of Nebraska—voted with the civil rights forces against the Morse motion amid mutterings about pressure from the ministers back home. The Pope may not have many divisions in the midwest Republican heartland, but the National Council of Churches certainly did.

The Easter recess was limited to a weekend, and on March 30th senators Humphrey and Kuchel presented the case for the bill, to be followed in the ensuing days by the senators responsible for each of the titles. Although these detailed presentations took time and gave the southern senators a respite, a record had to be made for the bill. [Also] the civil rights senators were unwilling to abandon [all the] press and television to southern propaganda. The affirmative speeches were soon finished, and now the floor belonged almost exclusively to the opposition. Even here, however, civil rights senators, by questions and interjections, were able to make the case for the bill without unduly prolonging debate.

[The Saturday Debacle]

The major problem facing the Senate leadership was keeping a quorum on tap at all times. The favorite southern harassing tactic was "suggesting the absence of a quorum" and then sitting peacefully by while the northerners struggled to muster the necessary 51 bodies. On Saturday, April 4th, only 39 [of the 51 needed] senators responded to the quorum call, and the Senate had to recess for the day. Senator Humphrey bluntly asserted: "The only way we can lose the civil rights fight is not to have a quorum when we need it."

The civil rights forces reacted sharply to this Saturday debacle. A study of the quorum calls for the first month of debate revealed a high rate of absenteeism by civil rights senators, and they began to hear from home in no uncertain terms. The following Saturday, after some frantic Friday night telephoning, a quorum was quickly present, and there was not too much difficulty after that. Indeed, on April 13th, when Senator Holland of Florida pulled the unclublike gambit of calling for a quorum while much of the Senate was attending the opening-[day] baseball game with President Johnson, fast moving limousines raced the [civil rights] senators back from the ball park. A quorum was obtained in just 23 minutes.

As the debate rolled on through April and into May, the activities of the civil rights forces began to bear fruit. Senators reported that their mail was changing from opposition to support. In no small part [this was] due to the widespread distribution of several hundred thousand Leadership Conference question-and-answer pamphlets refuting misstatements of the Mississippi-financed Coordinating Committee for Fundamental Freedoms. [There was] a smaller, but also effective, post-card campaign by the Americans for Democratic Action (ADA). [Visiting] delegations from the various states reported their senators for the bill without dilution. Religious groups visiting Senator Dirksen reported his opposition subsiding. The Harris poll for early May reported 70 percent [of Americans] for the bill (up 7 percent since the previous November) and even a wider margin against the filibuster.

[Preventing an Early Cloture Vote]

But now a new cloud appeared on the horizon. Some senators were becoming weary of endless Saturday and dinner-time quorum calls. Others were anxious [to begin passing] legislation for constituents back home. The words, "Let's try cloture and see what happens," were beginning to be heard.

The matter came up at one of the Monday and Thursday meetings. Clarence Mitchell repeated the strong opposition of the Leadership Conference to any cloture vote that might be lost and thus force a compromise. He said that if southern senators were going to use the rules to wear out the civil rights forces with quorum calls, the time had come to use the rules by having the Sergeant-at-Arms arrest the southern senators and bring them to the floor to help make the quorums. I suggested that another Senate rule be used—the one under which no senator can make more than two speeches on any given matter. In this way it might be possible to cut off debate without gambling the whole effort on a risky cloture vote. Neither suggestion was ever adopted—but the talk of cloture died down.

[Dealing with Senator Dirksen]

Then came the break. Senator Dirksen [Rep., IL] had, on April 16th, offered ten amendments which would have gutted the FEPC provision. Bad amendments or not, the senator was moving and obviously ready to negotiate. Senator Humphrey was unwilling to enter into negotiations until he had in hand the full complement of Dirksen demands, not only on the FEPC, but on the public accommodations title and the rest of the bill.

Finally, in early May, all was in readiness, and negotiations commenced between Senator Humphrey and Senator Dirksen, their staffs, and the Justice Department. Other Democratic and Republican senators joined the negotiations from time to time. The fate of the bill hung on the outcome.

At the regular Monday and Thursday meeting the Leadership Conference [lobbyists], who had been able to obtain relatively accurate reports on what was going on in the negotiating sessions, strongly urged Senator Humphrey to hold fast. One of the other senators present suggested that some concessions might be required. Clarence Mitchell, eyes flashing, exploded that the [black people] of America would never understand weakening the civil rights bill. He eloquently portrayed the depth of feeling and the violence that would inevitably flow from any weakening of the bill. Senator Humphrey smilingly broke the tension [by saying]: "Clarence, you are three feet off your chair." But the no-compromise message had been heard.

About this same time, on May 6th, Walter Reuther wired senators Humphrey and Kuchel that the UAW rejects "both as unwise and unnecessary current suggestions that concessions must be made to Senator Dirksen in order to purchase his vote for cloture. We firmly believe that the compelling urgency of this great moral issue of civil rights will persuade Senator Dirksen to vote for cloture in June whether his proposed amendments are adopted or not."

Negotiations continued with messages, phone calls and personal visits pouring in to both Humphrey and Dirksen urging a strong bill. Finally, on May 13th, a tentative agreement was reached. The next morning the Leadership

Conference [lobbyists] received the still unpublished text of the tentative agreement. Reading the changes with trepidation, it soon became evident that Humphrey's patience, good humor and courage had won the day.

True, under the Humphrey-Dirksen package those discriminated against in public accommodations and employment must first seek their remedy before the appropriate state agency, but there are no such state agencies in the South. Senator Russell [the southern leader] was not far from right when he suggested that Senator Dirksen had thus aimed the bill more directly at the South. True, under the Humphrey-Dirksen package the attorney general cannot bring suit on behalf of aggrieved individuals, but he can intervene in such a suit by an individual and, even more important, he can sue wherever there is a "pattern or practice" of discrimination against any person or group of persons. True, concessions had been made to Senator Dirksen in language, and on occasion in substance, but the basic structure of the House-passed bill remained intact.

The Leadership Conference representatives met at the AFL-CIO to chart its course in the light of the Humphrey-Dirksen package. Everyone quickly recognized that at long last here was an agreed-upon strong bill. The quandary on what to do was this. If civil rights advocates claimed victory, this would undoubtedly lead Senator Dirksen to ask for new concessions and might also weaken the cloture efforts. If, on the other hand, civil rights advocates charged that the bill had been weakened, [and demanded more] concessions, such a charge would dismay civil rights forces throughout the country and intensify racial tensions. The resulting statement issued by the Leadership Conference that afternoon was a masterpiece of saying both and neither at the same time.

Two weeks of efforts by both sides to modify the Humphrey-Dirksen package resulted in little change. On May 26th the Humphrey-Dirksen package was formally introduced in the Senate by Mansfield, Humphrey, Dirksen, and Kuchel as a substitute for the pending bill. Now the drive for cloture was on in earnest. Senator Dirksen had promised 25 votes [for cloture] for the new package. With the forty-odd Democratic votes [for cloture], the required two-thirds seemed assured.

[The Hickenlooper Revolt]

On Monday, June 1st, Senator Mansfield announced that he would file a cloture petition during the week and there would be a vote on it the following Tuesday, June 9th. This looked like the homestretch at last. But a new obstacle suddenly appeared. For some time, Republican Senator [Bourke B.] Hickenlooper of Iowa, always jealous of Senator Dirksen's leadership in his party, had been sniping at the Humphrey-Dirksen package. He had walked out of the negotiating meetings and was not bound by the results. The marginal votes that Dirksen was counting on to make up his 25 promised cloture votes were those from western areas most subject to the Hickenlooper influence. Then on Tuesday, June 2nd, the day after Mansfield had announced the upcoming cloture vote, Dirksen took sick. In the two or three days he was away from the Senate, some of the western Republicans started to backslide on cloture.

On Friday, June 5th, Hickenlooper made his move. Senator Mansfield had announced that morning that on Saturday [the next day] he would present the cloture petition to the Senate, which would bring it to a vote on the following Tuesday. Later in the day Hickenlooper took the floor to ask unanimous consent that three amendments be acted upon before [the] cloture vote: Senator [Thruston B.] Morton's [Rep., KY] amendment for jury trial in cases of criminal contempt; Senator [Norris] Cotton's [Rep., NH] amendment to restrict FEPC to employers of 100 or more; and his own amendment to delete all provisions of the bill relating to assistance for desegregating public schools.

This move posed a dilemma for the Humphrey-Dirksen forces. If they refused the unanimous consent agreement, Hickenlooper would undoubtedly have the votes to prevent cloture. If they agreed to it, the amendments might well pass, because many senators might feel this was the price of cloture. Senator Dirksen bluntly told his colleagues at 4:30 that afternoon that they had better accept [Hickenlooper's request to vote on the amendments], because [Dirksen] simply did not have the votes for cloture as it then stood. Still, decision was withheld, and the matter went over to Saturday.

Everybody was on hand Saturday morning. . . . Senator Mansfield filed his cloture petition and said he would withdraw it for a day if the Hickenlooper unanimous consent agreement [request to vote on amendments] went through. The Humphrey-Dirksen forces had made their decision. They would accept [Hickenlooper's] unanimous consent agreement. This time it was Senator Russell [the southern leader] who had the dilemma. If he permitted the agreement to go through, cloture was assured. If he objected to it, Hickenlooper's wrath might come down upon him and insure cloture anyway. Russell took the course of least resistance and withheld his objection.

As the [Johnson] administration and the Leadership Conference worked feverishly over the weekend to line up votes against the three amendments, it soon became clear that only the jury trial provision had a chance of passage. It was nip and tuck. With Senator [Henry R. (Scoop)] Jackson's [Dem., WA] office stating he would vote against the amendment, chances of defeating it appeared brighter. But when the roll call came on Tuesday, Senator Jackson cast his vote for jury trial and it carried 51 to 48.

A pair could have been arranged for the absent Senator [Clair] Engle [a civil rights supporter who was seriously ill with cancer. That would have made the vote 50 to 48.] If Senator Jackson had voted with the liberals, the amendment would have lost 49 to 49, there being no vice president [due to John F. Kennedy's assassination] to break the tie. The other two amendments went down to overwhelming defeat later in the day.

[The Cloture Vote]

The next day came the cloture vote. Every senator was on hand, Senator Engle having been wheeled in [in a wheel chair] moments before the vote. Senator [Howard W.] Cannon [Dem., NV] cast his first vote for cloture, and Senator [Carl] Hayden [Dem., AZ] did not answer to his name. It was clear the civil rights forces had won. Senator [John J.] Williams [Rep., DE] was the 67th vote for cloture, and the final tally was 71 to 29, four more than the requisite two-thirds.

Senator Hayden [did not want to vote for cloture unless it was absolutely necessary. The reason was a filibuster had gained statehood for his home state of Arizona.] But Carl Hayden, who had apparently promised the White House he would [support cloture] if this were required, now walked onto the floor and voted "No", as though to underscore the magnitude of the civil rights victory.

Operating under cloture the southerners never had a chance. No significant amendment was adopted. An amendment would be read, a southerner would use one minute of his hour's allotment, and the roll would be called. Dirksen's forces stood loyally by the package to which he had agreed, helping vote down each [southern] amendment as it came up. Four senators—[Paul] Douglas [Dem., IL], [Edmund] Muskie [Dem., ME], [Kenneth] Keating [Rep., NY], and [Clifford] Case [Rep., NJ]—had perfect voting records. The roll was called 114 times, and they were never absent nor did they ever vote against the civil rights forces.

After ten days of amendments and roll calls, on June 19th [1964], one year after President Kennedy had sent the initial bill to Congress, the Senate passed the Humphrey-

Dirksen bill 73 to 27. (Senator Goldwater and five fellow Republicans voted no.) For the second time in ten days all 100 senators, including ailing Senator Engle who could [no longer] speak, answered the roll call.

The House followed suit on July 2nd [1964] after only token resistance by Howard Smith [Dem., VA] [chairman of the House Rules Committee]. Among those who voted for the bill on final passage was [Representative] Charles L. Weltner, a young first-termer from Atlanta, Georgia. Speaking to applauding colleagues, he said: "I shall add my voice to those who seek reasoned and conciliatory adjustment to a new reality." A few hours later President [Johnson] signed the bill saying: "We have come now to a time of testing." The end of the legislative road was also a beginning.

Notes

1. In his manuscript Joseph L. Rauh, Jr., used the date "August 15th," but he clearly means Attorney General Robert F. Kennedy's testimony before the House of Representatives Judiciary Committee in mid-October of 1963. See *Congressional Quarterly Weekly Report*, 18 October 1963, 1814.

Chapter 3

Memorandum on Senate Consideration of the Civil Rights Act of 1964

Hubert H. Humphrey

Hubert H. Humphrey (1911-1978) was born and raised in South Dakota. He was educated at the University of Minnesota, and he had a long and illustrious career in Democratic Party politics in that state. In 1948, when he was the mayor of Minneapolis, he went to the Democratic National Convention and led the fight to put a strong civil rights plank in the 1948 Democratic Party Platform. "The time has come," Mayor Humphrey told the convention, "for the Democratic Party to get out of the shadow of states' rights and walk forthrightly into the bright sunshine of human rights."

The 1948 Democratic National Convention took Humphrey's advice and adopted a pro-civil rights platform. Humphrey subsequently was elected to the U.S. Senate from Minnesota, and in 1960 he ran for the Democratic nomination for president. Humphrey lost the nominating race to John F. Kennedy, of Massachusetts, who defeated Humphrey in both the Wisconsin and the West Virginia presidential primaries and then went on to win the presidency for the Democrats the following November.

In 1961 Humphrey was elected the assistant Democratic leader, more often called the Democratic whip, in the United States Senate. This meant he was the No. 2 person in the Senate, second in power only to Democratic leader Mike Mansfield of Montana. When the civil rights bill that later became the Civil Rights Act of 1964 passed the House and arrived for consideration in the Senate, Democratic Leader Mike Mansfield named Democratic Whip Hubert Humphrey the Democratic floor leader for the bill.

That meant it was Humphrey's job to plot the strategy and mobilize the forces that would defeat the expected southern Democratic filibuster and get the civil rights bill enacted in the Senate.

Immediately following the successful cloture vote in the Senate on the Civil Rights Act of 1964, Hubert Humphrey did something few U.S. senators have ever done. He sat down at his dictaphone and dictated a lengthy memorandum describing the techniques he had used to defeat the southern filibuster and thereby get the civil rights bill through the Senate. Humphrey's memorandum is one of the few first-person accounts ever written by a major congressional leader on his or her immediate role in getting major legislation enacted. Humphrey did not put his name on the memorandum, but every scholar who has worked with it has concluded that it is definitely Humphrey's.

Humphrey begins his account of the enactment of the Civil Rights Act of 1964 in the early summer of 1963, immediately after the civil rights demonstrations in Birmingham have inspired President Kennedy to send a strengthened civil rights bill to Congress. Humphrey's account is shorter and less detailed than that of Joseph Rauh, Jr., but Humphrey gives insights that only a member of the Senate leadership could provide.

This is a memorandum concerning the civil rights bill, its background and the procedures, tactics, and strategy used to accomplish its passage.

This memo starts in the early summer of 1963. I recall that, after the troubles in Birmingham, President [John F.] Kennedy had Attorney General Robert Kennedy discuss with Senator [Mike] Mansfield and myself, along with a few others in the Senate, the possibility of some legislation in the civil rights field.

It should be recalled that the Kennedy administration had not presented a civil rights program other than a leprosy bill. As I recall it, it was sometime in April that we started discussing in a serious vein civil rights programs and messages. There were innumerable meetings. Some [were] at the majority leaders's office, some at the White House, some at the Department of Justice. Generally present at these meetings were the attorney general, Senator Mansfield, myself, occasionally Senator [Clinton] Anderson [Dem., NM], Senator [Joseph] Clark [Dem., PA], and on occasion, some of the Republicans including [Everett] Dirksen [Rep., IL], [Thomas] Kuchel [Rep., CA], [Kenneth] Keating [Rep., NY], [Jacob] Javits [Rep., NY], and [Hugh] Scott [Rep., PA].

There was no real program until somewhere in May when President [Kennedy] decided, after a number of discussions, that we would prepare a rather comprehensive program. We discussed this at many of the breakfast meetings on Tuesday mornings. The main argument for some period of time was whether or not the president's message, and the bill which the [Kennedy] administration was to send to Congress, would have FEPC [Fair Employment Practices Commission] and would have statutory authority for the president's Committee on Equal Employment Opportunities. [There was also an argument over] whether a type of over-all Powell Amendment, namely cutting off federal funds where such funds were used in a discriminatory manner—whether such an amendment would be included.

[Humphrey Presses for a Strong Bill]

I urged upon President [Kennedy] a broad, comprehensive program. I recall saying to the president one time that the leadership for civil rights had to either take place in the White House or it was going to take place on the streets. I fought hard in the breakfast meetings of the congressional leaders for a broad program of civil rights and for a strong message on the part of the president. I urged the president to take command, to be the moral leader, and recall time after time urging that his message go all the way. [The message should include] voting rights, school desegregation, public accommodations, F.E.P.C., the cutoff of federal funds where discrimination exists, and the right of the attorney general to move into court and protect the rights of American citizens. This [last] is what we call the old Part III of the 1957 act.

There was considerable discussion of the civil rights message itself, and I recall President [Kennedy] having me look it over in the early part of June. In fact, I talked with the president just a short time before he sent the message to the Congress, and also spoke several times with Ted Sorensen [President Kennedy's speech writer], who was doing a great deal of the writing of the message. I urged that if the president was not going to include FEPC in his bill, that he surely should include it in his message. This is what he did. In fact, it was only a few hours before the message came to the Congress that this matter was settled, along with the matter of what is now Title VI in the bill, the cutoff of federal funds.

[House Action]

So much for the background. The summer of 1963 was spent in hearings, primarily in the House. Little or nothing [was] done in the Senate, except the attorney general testifying [at committee hearings] and being cross-examined at length by Senator [Sam] Ervin [Dem., NC].

And then in the fall of 1963, when things were sort of bogged down in the House, Attorney General [Robert Kennedy], [Deputy Attorney General] Nick Katzenbach, [Assistant Attorney General] Burke Marshall, and President [Kennedy] met with the Republican and Democratic leaders of the House, including [Charles] Halleck [Rep., IN], Bill McCulloch [Rep., OH], Carl Albert [Dem., OK], Manny Celler [Dem., NY], and House Speaker [John McCormick (Dem., MA)]. They put together the package that was finally passed by the House.

The bill was reported out of subcommittee and out of full committee and therefore was ready for action in the

House right after the first of the year, 1964. The House did proceed. It got a rule and, as we know, there were over 100 amendments, some 30 or more being adopted, and a good bill came from the House.

[The Farm Bill]

Then it came to the Senate. It rested on our Senate calendar for some time until we were able to take up the Farm Bill [containing subsidies] for wheat and cotton. I insisted on this because I felt there would be serious economic consequences [in the farm states] if we failed to take such action. President [Johnson], however, was very adamant about taking up civil rights, and so was Mansfield. However, I pleaded the case for the cotton and wheat bill over at the White House and finally was joined by Mansfield, providing that the bill wouldn't take too long. The Republicans tried to stall [the Farm Bill] a bit, but we were able to put it over without too much trouble, and then on March 9 we took up the civil rights bill.

[Preparing for the Filibuster]

Prior to this, I had been named as the floor manager for the bill. This assignment was one that I appreciated, and yet one that I realized would test me in every way. I had to make up my mind as to my mental attitude and how I would conduct myself. I can recall literally talking to myself, conditioning myself for the long ordeal. I truly did think through what I wanted to do and how I wanted to act. I proceeded to cancel a number of engagements that were on my calendar. I insisted on being on the floor of the Senate, in particular in the early days when the bill was just being brought up, lest it be derailed.

We then had meetings to set up our team captains and to spread the work and responsibility. Because Senator [Joseph] Clark [Dem., PA] had handled FEPC in committee, and Senator [Warren] Magnuson [Dem., WA] had handled public accommodations in committee, they were made team captains. Also, Senator [Philip] Hart [Dem., MI], who was on the Judiciary Committee and had handled much of Title I [voting rights] there, was made a team captain. And others were brought in to handle each title. I determined that it would be best to divide up the work on the bill title by title, asking certain senators to be responsible for the titles and sharing that responsibility with the Republicans.

The material on this is in our records, in the newsletters, which, by the way, was another innovation. We decided to put out a civil rights newsletter each day, and have done so. It was sort of a review of the day's proceedings. Each evening the debate was analyzed and capsuled in our newsletter. This was an innovation which commanded attention, and I think demonstrated that we knew what we were doing and were capable of mobilizing our resources.

We also decided to work out what we call a quorum duty list, recognizing that some senators had to be away part of the time, particularly those who were running for [reelection]. Each day we had a quorum duty list of 36 Democrats and, as I recall, there were to be 16 or 18 Republicans. These did not include the southerners, so each day we were to have 4 captains who would monitor the floor. All of [this was] worked out. We also set up a command center for quorums with Pauline Moore in charge. We also set up a research center where we could have staff members, including members of the Department of Justice, working with us closely on all amendments and other items relating to the bill. Senator Magnuson provided us with [a] room. Our group then was called into meeting several times so that we knew what we were doing.

We also met regularly with the Leadership Conference on Civil Rights [lobbyists], particularly Clarence Mitchell [Jr.] and Joe Rauh [Jr.]. We were in close liaison with them all of the time. Andy Biemiller, from the AFL-CIO, also. We realized at the beginning that we needed the active cooperation, support, and understanding of the so-called Leadership Conference on Civil Rights. We also needed more active participation from business and church groups. We had the full participation of the civil rights groups and the labor movement and the Jewish community, but even there we needed to accelerate or improve our contacts.

We met early in March with the representatives of the three faiths—Catholic, Protestant, and Jewish—in my office. We selected the date of April 28 [1964] at that time for the interfaith civil rights convocation to be held at Georgetown University. This was a plan that was worked out almost two months in advance. Plans were also designed to have civil rights meetings in the states, such as we were doing in Washington, with the clergy taking the lead. Close contact was maintained at all times with the clergy. Often this contact was due to the Leadership Conference on Civil Rights or through our staff. The staff work was excellent. Ray Wolfinger, John Stewart, Charlie Ferris, Ken Teasdale, Jerry Greenfeld—all of these were hard at work every minute keeping a watchful eye on the legislation, as well as on quorum problems.

[Ready to Debate the Southerners]

We determined early not to let the southerners occupy the press, so in the very opening days, starting with March 9 [1964] on the motion to take up, we proceeded to debate the southerners. We took the offensive and we were able to get good press. We followed up by taking the offensive when finally on March 30 [1964] we were able to get the bill before us and have it as the pending business. I opened the debate, followed by Kuchel. Each day a team of our people would take a title so that, for better than 12 days, we held the floor giving detailed information about the bill and being able to get the public's attention as to what was in this bill.

It is fair to say that, for about one month, the proponents of the legislation were able to demand press attention more often than the opponents. We encouraged our people, that is, the pro-civil rights senators, to be on radio and television. I wrote to each senator suggesting radio and television programs, suggesting newsletters [and] enclosing sample copies of newsletters that other senators had prepared. We encouraged reprints of key material that had been put in the *Congressional Record* so that there could be answers to the questions of the people back home. We answered the propaganda of the anti-civil rights groups.

In other words, we were active, at no time passive, and at all times challenging the opposition. Furthermore, when each senator had a chance to debate the bill, title by title, they also had an opportunity to get some press for themselves, to be known as part of the team fighting for civil rights. This was good not only for the issue itself, but also for the senators and their public relations, and they seemed to like it. It involved them also in active floor duty, in constant and in sharp debate with the opposition. They became ever more committed.

[Republican Efforts]

The Republicans set up early a team of captains headed by Senator [Thomas] Kuchel [Rep., CA], who was my copartner. We emphasized the bipartisan , nonpartisan nature of this struggle and, indeed, that is exactly what it was, is, and will continue to be. Regrettably, one or two of the Republicans were not too deeply committed. In fact, [some were] opposed to certain sections. I refer to [Roman] Hruska [Rep., NE] and [Norris] Cotton [Rep., NH]. Neither of them were willing to stay with their duties and asked to be relieved later on. However, men like [Hugh] Scott [Rep., PA], [Kenneth] Keating [Rep., NY], [Jacob] Javits [Rep., NY], [Thomas] Kuchel [Rep., CA], [Gordon] Allott [Rep., CO], and

[John Sherman] Cooper [Rep., KY] were good and helpful.

We did have a number of meetings between Republicans and Democrats, and this was particularly true when we met with the Leadership Conference on Civil Rights. These meetings were held every morning, one-half hour before the session, sometimes at 9:30, sometimes at 10:30.

We determined early that it would do little or no good to have round-the-clock sessions. It was possible for the southerners to amend and amend and thereby to keep going, but we preferred to make the sessions long enough to be disagreeable, and to continue the sessions so that senators recognized that their time was being frittered away.

[Importance of Quorum Calls]

Furthermore, we put great emphasis upon the quorum calls. And one time—and only once—were we unable to get a quorum. This focused public attention upon the situation, and senators were very much aware of the fact that they were supposed to be present for quorums. Newspapers, magazines and periodicals kept constant watch on who was present and who wasn't. To be present for a quorum became very important, and this meant that senators had to cancel engagements. This made them all the more unhappy when the filibuster was under way, because it meant they had to be away from their duties back home and be present in Washington only to answer quorums and, frankly, to get very little else done. It was a pre-determined program on our part to arouse the public, to create a sense of wrath and indignation in the public, and also in the Senate.

The heavy barrage of newsletters going out from senators pointed out that this filibuster was wasting time. The refusal of [the southern] senators to [allow] any voting, except in one or two instances on minor amendments, contributed to this situation. Frankly, I was rather surprised at the southerners' tactics. I never could quite understand why they didn't let us vote more often, because they had so many amendments in. If they had done so, they could have insisted that the legislative process was working, that amendments were being voted upon. Instead of that, they just kept talking and talking. It seemed to me that they lost their sense of direction and really had little or no plan other than what they used to have when filibusters succeeded.

[Patient and Friendly]

Now a few more observations. I made up my mind early that I would keep my patience. I would not lose my temper and, if I could do nothing else, I would try to preserve a reasonable degree of good nature and fair play in the Senate. I had good working relationships at all times with the southerners, even on some of the more difficult days. Only once or twice did I appear to be quick tempered, and on one occasion it was by design and not by accident.

I knew that, if the southerners could get the pro-civil rights people divided and fighting among themselves, the opponents would win. I also knew that it would hurt me politically and reflect adversely upon the Senate if we got into an acrimonious, bitter name-calling debate. And therefore at all times I tried to keep the Senate on an equilibrium with a degree of respect and friendliness. I believe that we succeeded.

[Winning Senator Dirksen's Support]

I also recognized that we must have the closest bipartisan cooperation, and this included the help of Senator [Everett] Dirksen [the Republican leader in the Senate]. On my very first TV appearance—Meet the Press—I praised Senator Dirksen, telling the nation that he would help, that he would support a good civil rights bill, that he would put his country above party, that he would look upon this issue as a moral issue and not a partisan issue. I believed it then, and my faith has been vindicated.

Several times on other occasions I praised Dirksen. I did so not only because I believed what I said, but because we also needed him. I knew that it was impossible to pass a civil rights bill, because we couldn't possibly get cloture without Dirksen and his help. Therefore every effort was made to involve him. With few exceptions, I visited with Senator Dirksen every day, encouraging him to take a more prominent role, asking him what changes he wanted to propose, urging him to call meetings and discuss his changes.

You may recall that [Dirksen] was opposed to the compulsory enforcement powers of Title II [integration of public accommodations] at the beginning. He also was opposed to anything called FEPC, such as Title VII. He had his doubts also about Title VI, the funds cutoff. This is where Dirksen was in March and April, and by working with him, talking with him day after day, appealing to his sense of patriotism and duty, which I did regularly, I was able to involve Dirksen more directly into this legislation.

I can recall, time after time, asking him: "Well, Dirk, when do you think we ought to meet and talk over some of your amendments?" And he'd say: "Well, give us a couple more days. It isn't time yet." And this went on week after week. And finally we were able to get him to call a meeting.

In the meantime he had been working with his staff and had gone over this bill very carefully. The meetings in Dirksen's office were, as we know, successful. Actually, Dirksen gave a great deal of ground. The bill which he finally supported—the substitute—in my mind is as good or better a bill than the House bill. Dirksen supported with his own amendments an effective enforcement of Title II, integration of public accommodations, but he mainly insisted on some time for conciliation and more involvement of local and state government, both of which were very good ideas, and I vigorously supported them.

In fact, I worked very closely with Dirksen at all times so there would be no split between us. I was told a number of times by Democrats that Dirksen was stealing the show, that I should be out in front. I knew that if I tried to push myself [into the spotlight] any more than I had, the bill would fail. Dirksen had to be out in front. Dirksen is a leader, he is a great dramatist, and a fine legislator. He had the right to be out in front, and I gave him every opportunity to be so.

[Involving Senator Mansfield]

I also knew that we needed [Senate Democratic Leader Mike] Mansfield more directly involved. Mansfield gave me all possible cooperation. He wanted to be at liberty to work closely with Dirksen and not be too directly involved with the day-to-day details on the floor, and that's the way we did it. He was more or less a free man, able to contact Dirksen at will, while I was in charge of the routine day-to-day duties on the floor of the Senate.

I knew that to get Mansfield involved it would require that he become a bit angry, and this worked out even better than I planned or hoped for. It came about when Senator [Richard] Russell [Dem., GA] [the southern leader] refused to let the Senate proceed to vote on some of the jury trial amendments. Mansfield thought he had an understanding with Russell on two occasions for votes. On both occasions Russell blocked the votes and didn't let us proceed. In each instance Mansfield had announced to the Senate that we would be voting, and then, of course, found out that no votes were permitted. This irritated Mansfield in particular. As time went on, he became more irritated and more involved. At all times he was a great help and constant source of encouragement and strength.

[Building National Support]

We needed the help of the clergy, and this was assiduously encouraged. I have said a number of times, and I repeat it now, that without the clergy, we couldn't have possibly passed this bill. They were very helpful.

We had close contact with key people back in the states. Particularly where we had senators who were doubtful on cloture, these [home town] people were brought into the contest again and again by telephone calls and asked to get hold of their senators [and lobby them to vote for the bill].

And as we know, there were a number of visitations to Washington by church people, and these people repeatedly called on their senators. I met with them time after time. I must have had better than a hundred meetings during this period of time, all of them, with a few exceptions, at the Capitol. I would talk privately with the civil rights groups who came to our Capitol, and labor groups and others. My staff man, John Stewart, was very busy doing the same thing. We knew that we must keep the public stirred up [and], at least, genuinely interested in passing this legislation. Too, the leaders of this public must be [made] aware of the inside details of what was going on. I tried to keep them so informed. It was quite a job.

We did not bother President [Johnson] very much. We did give him regular reports on the progress of civil rights over at the Tuesday morning breakfasts. But the president was not put on the spot. He was not enlisted in the battle particularly. I understand he did contact some of the senators, but not at our insistence. I felt we would need the president when the bill went to the House again, and I'm sure we will, and he should save himself for that situation, particularly the Rules Committee, and I'm confident he can be very helpful in this instance.

[Trouble with Senator Hickenlooper]

It became apparent after a while that there was a growing conflict between Dirksen and [Bourke] Hickenlooper [Rep., IA]. Senator Hickenlooper is the chairman of the Republican Conference Committee. He was resenting the publicity and the play that Dirksen was getting. Therefore, Hickenlooper started to balk, and not only to balk quietly, but openly and publicly. He started to hold meetings, particularly when Dirksen was ill. I had a way of knowing what was going on at those meetings. One of the members attending was reporting to me quite regularly.

I recognized that Hickenlooper was picking up strength. I informed Dirksen of this. On two or three occasions he told me not to worry, that he still thought he had 26 votes for cloture. I told him that I seriously doubted it. From what I gathered, Hickenlooper was picking up votes, and we were in trouble. This proved to be the case.

Finally, as we know, the southerners began to feel that we might get enough votes for cloture. So they wanted to start voting. We refused to vote and held the floor for about a week, simply because we knew we needed a little more time to nail down those cloture votes.

During that period of time, the Hickenlooper group demanded that they have a specified period of time to debate certain key amendments—the jury trial amendment; the FEPC amendment; and some amendments to Title IV, desegregation of public education. After some negotiating we were able to work out a deal wherein each of these amendments would have 4 hours, and we would vote on them all on Tuesday, June 9 [1964].

Prior to my being willing to join in this, I got personal commitments for cloture from [Karl] Mundt [Rep., SD], [Roman] Hruska [Rep., NE], and [Norris] Cotton [Rep., NH]. I felt then Hickenlooper would join with us. I knew that if Hruska would join with us, so would [Carl] Curtis [Rep.,

NE]. So it seemed that we were well on the way. I also gave a commitment, as the record will show, that any of the amendments adopted out of these three would be added to the [civil rights] bill. One of them, the jury trial [amendment, was passed] and was promptly added to the [civil rights bill].

I do believe that this unanimous consent agreement, known as the Hickenlooper Unanimous Consent Package, brought us the extra votes that we needed for cloture. I can recall Senator Russell [the southern leader] complaining quite bitterly that we hadn't cooperated with him when he wanted to vote. I said to him, somewhat in jest, but also in truth: "Well, Dick, you haven't any votes to give us in cloture, and these [Hickenlooper group] fellows do." That was the sum and substance of it.

[The Vote for Cloture]

When we came to the cloture vote, it was a great day. I knew we had the votes. In fact, one hour before the vote was taken, I gave Senator [Philip] Hart [Dem., MI] a note and said we had 69. I thought there was a possibility of one more, and, as the *Congressional Record* shows, we had 71. I had worked very hard, even the night before, to nail down the votes of [Howard] Edmondson [Dem., OK], [Ralph] Yarborough [Dem., TX], and [Howard] Cannon [Dem., NV]. It was doubtful about Cannon, but we were terribly pleased when he came through.

I informed President [Johnson] on Tuesday night at 7:30 that we had the votes. He said he hoped so, but he said it would be very difficult. I told him I was sure of it.

Chapter 4

Thoughts on the Civil Rights Bill

John G. Stewart

John G. Stewart was the top legislative assistant to Senator Hubert H. Humphrey, the Democratic floor leader for the Civil Rights Act of 1964 when it underwent an extended filibuster in the Senate in the spring of 1964. Stewart thus was closer than any Capitol Hill staffer to the inside strategy making that went into gaining the June 10, 1964, cloture vote in the Senate that made passage of the Civil Rights Act of 1964 possible.

In late April 1964, about a month into the filibuster, John Stewart began dictating his thoughts about the civil rights bill. These dictated thoughts were transcribed later by clerical personnel in Senator Humphrey's office on Capitol Hill and routinely filed with Humphrey's other papers on civil rights. Although one of the most powerful and well-known staff assistants in the Senate at that time, John G. Stewart either did not bother or forgot to sign his name to these dictated materials.

Twenty years later, in the mid-1980s, the editor found these anonymous "Thoughts" in the Humphrey papers in the Minnesota Historical Society in St. Paul, Minnesota. Suspecting they were dictated by John G. Stewart, the editor mailed copies to him and he acknowledged authorship in a letter dated September 14, 1983.

John G. Stewart's dictated "Thoughts" constitute the best first-person account available of the mammoth problems that faced those members of the U.S. Senate who were trying to enact a civil rights bill in the spring of 1964.

At the time Stewart began dictating his notes, the 1963-1964 civil rights bill had passed the House of Representatives, been put directly on the Senate calendar (bypassing the Senate Judiciary

Committee), and had survived the "minibuster" over the motion to put it directly on the Senate calendar. The real debate on the bill, and the real southern filibuster, had begun March 30, 1964. Stewart starts his dictation at the point where the filibuster is into its fourth week and the pro-civil rights senators are beginning to make serious strategy for ending it.

THOUGHTS ON THE CIVIL RIGHTS BILL
DICTATED WEDNESDAY, APRIL 21, 1964

Today Senator Humphrey had a very interesting talk with Senator [Everett B.] Dirksen [of Illinois, the Republican leader in the Senate]. The clear burden of the talk was that Senator Dirksen realized the civil rights bill was going to pass and that a good bill was going to pass. He also realized that, for a variety of considerations, it was his duty or at least his position whereby he would have to lend his weight and influence to the bill.

[Dirksen] indicated in his conversation today that he had only one more amendment to offer in addition to the 11 amendments offered to Title VII [equal employment opportunity]. This final amendment would be a minor modification, to use Dirksen's words, to Title II [integration of public accommodations]. Time will tell precisely what this amendment is, but he indicated he would have the amendment by the end of this week.

[Dirksen Cooperative]

In short, Humphrey found Dirksen to be quite cooperative. Dirksen predicted that cloture would not be necessary to pass the civil rights bill. It was his view that the southerners were running to the end of their rope, that there was little more they could say, and that they were convinced the bill would pass largely in its present form. Humphrey disputed Dirksen on cloture, pointing out that perhaps cloture would be the way whereby the southerners could get themselves off a political hook. Dirksen replied that, okay, they would get the votes for cloture. In other words, Dirksen would work with Humphrey toward getting cloture on the bill.

Dirksen also was fully cognizant of the need to move ahead with the bill and predicted that the bill should be pretty much wrapped up by the first week in June. He did not want it in any way to conflict with the Republican [National] Convention or to have repercussions from the bill felt during the Republican [National] Convention.

[The Great Man Hook]

Humphrey has been playing up very strongly the line that this is an opportunity for Dirksen to be the great man of the United States, the man of the hour, the man who saves the civil rights bill. This line has been played up by Humphrey on "Meet the Press" [and in] numerous conversations with journalists. Humphrey instigated Roscoe Drummond's recent article in the Herald Tribune Syndicate pointing up that Dirksen had an opportunity for greatness in the pending civil rights debate. In short, it appears that Dirksen is beginning to swallow the great man hook and, when it is fully digested, we will have ourselves a civil rights bill.

In conjunction with this, Clarence Mitchell [Jr.] of the NAACP [National Association for the Advancement of Colored People] recently had a frank discussion with Senator [Richard] Russell [of Georgia, the leader of the southern filibusterers]. As Mitchell reports this discussion, Russell also knows that the jig is just about up. The main distinction which Russell drew between the situation now and the situation when President [John F.] Kennedy was alive was that they have absolutely no hope of ultimately defeating President [Lyndon B.] Johnson on the bill itself or even gaining any major compromises or capitulations from President Johnson. Interestingly enough, Senator Russell stated that he felt they could have gained major compromises from Kennedy. It would be most interesting to know precisely the basis for this distinction, which Russell drew between Kennedy and Johnson, in terms of the pending civil rights bill.

Returning to Dirksen's conversation with Humphrey, Dirksen also pointed out that he felt it would be a mistake to enforce too stringently the provisions of Rule 19 [requiring that debate be germane to the subject matter of the bill. Dirksen said] the southerners were about to collapse anyway. Therefore, he felt it might only irritate them and perhaps prolong the agony through this irritation. He suggested a reasonable application of Rule 19, not embarrassing anyone but also reminding senators that the rule was there so that the large burden of the day can be spent in debating the substance of the bill itself.

[Dealing with Civil Rights Groups]

In other conversations with Humphrey, it has become increasingly clear that the civil rights groups must be handled with great care and maturity. In short, it is simply impossible to permit the civil rights groups to call all the shots on this legislation. It is also clear that there will come a time when decisions will probably have to be made which the civil rights groups will disagree with. But, as in the House [of Representatives], they will in the end come around and support the bill as it is finally passed and, in fact, claim all the credit for themselves.

In that regard, it is a good object lesson that you must even be willing to go against your strongest supporters when dealing with legislation of such tremendous scope and [comprehensiveness] as the pending civil rights bill. There are enough groups and interests in this nation so that certain accommodations simply have to be made if there is to be a bill. This is a fact which the civil rights groups, looking at the bill from their very narrow perspective, simply cannot comprehend. And, what is even more distressing, is that they immediately interpret any particular change in the legislation as some manner of dastardly sell-out. Clarence Mitchell's bi-weekly eruptions in the leadership meetings only testify to this fact.

It is clearly evident that there must be room for maneuver, that a floor manager of a bill [such as Humphrey] must now close all doors behind him, that he must remain his own man, and not become the captive of any group or particular interest in terms of the legislation. Otherwise he renders himself impotent in the Senate and is seen only as a puppet for the particular interests at work.

[Disagreeing with Friends]

It is easy enough to offend your enemies and to attack them openly at the slightest provocation. It is far more difficult and takes far more courage to disagree with your friends, such as the [Leadership Conference on Civil Rights], and to have to do things which they oppose. But sometimes these are precisely the actions which will give you the ultimate victory.

The outlook for the civil rights bill would seem to be quite good. Senator Dirksen seems to see what the future holds and seems to want to be part of that future. If this report is, in fact, true, then the battle would seem to be almost within reach. But let us reserve final judgment on this kind of report until we see how Senator Dirksen really behaves when the chips are down. That will be the test.

The following day, April 22, 1964, Senator Herman Talmadge of Georgia, one of the filibustering southern Democrats, introduced an amendment that would guarantee jury trials to officials that violated the civil rights act once it was passed into law.

This was a problem to the civil rights forces in the Senate, because it was well known that white southern juries would not be likely to convict white persons for breaking civil rights laws. It was always difficult for civil rights supporters to explain why the jury trial, one of the great protections of U.S. jurisprudence, had to be suspended in civil rights matters.

Notes on the Civil Rights Bill
Dictated April 22, 1964

Action moved forward on a number of fronts today, looking toward the kind of agreement among [Dirksen and Humphrey], the civil rights leaders, the president, etc., that would produce a bill. The Talmadge amendment providing for full jury trials was offered late yesterday evening, and the possibility of a Mansfield-Dirksen substitute incorporating the provisions now found in Title II of the 1957 law was explored with [Mike] Mansfield [the Democratic leader in the Senate] and Dirksen. Obviously, a great deal depends on the timing of the amendments and who offers them.

For instance, if Dirksen and Mansfield could offer a substitute amendment to the Talmadge amendment and, if a vote could be reached on this amendment, it would be a substantial victory for the civil rights forces. It would also serve to bring Dirksen more directly into the ultimate outcome of the bill.

On the other hand, if Talmadge withdraws his amendment for the time being and permits Dirksen to go ahead, then the first amendment which would be voted on would be Amendment 501, relating to the inclusion of hiring halls in the language of Title VII [equal employment opportunity]. This amendment is going to be strongly opposed by the AFL-CIO and might produce a fairly close vote on the Senate floor.

In other words, if the first amendment voted on is Amendment 501, the issue could be close and the civil rights forces might lose. On the other hand, if the first vote could be on the Mansfield-Dirksen substitute for the Talmadge amendment, a substantial victory would result. Which event actually takes place obviously might have some important impact on the ultimate outcome of the bill itself.

[Dirksen and the California Primary]

It is also a fact that Senator Dirksen probably would like to have this bill passed and out of the way before the California [Republican presidential] primary in early June. Otherwise, he might be caught in cross-pressures after [Senator Barry M.] Goldwater [of Arizona] wins that primary, namely, the conservative pressure from the Goldwater people and the more liberal pressure from the House Republican leaders of the civil rights forces. Dirksen could save himself considerable embarrassment if the bill could be locked up prior to the Republican primary in California. In short, Dirksen appears to be moving toward some decision on the issue. He appears to be attempting to coalesce some of his concerns into a package which can produce the votes for cloture on the bill.

[Dirksen Fears Big Government]

In particular, Dirksen's only problems with the bill revolve around the relationship between the federal government and the independent businessman. These are in no way related to the racial problem as such, but to the old fear of so-called big government. If Dirksen can be made to appear the person who attempted to protect the businessman from the evil influences of the federal government, then he should feel reasonably well satisfied. It seems that this kind of problem is far easier to negotiate than problems which get to the central core of the racial problem as such. Thus the discussions will continue at various levels. One should also note that Humphrey and [Thomas H.] Kuchel [the Republican whip in the Senate] did meet with the president today, although I have no idea what they discussed.

There was also a meeting today between [Nicholas] Katzenbach and Burke Marshall [of the Justice Department], senators Clifford Case [Rep., NJ] and Joseph Clark [Dem., PA], and Humphrey and a variety of staff people to go over positions on the Dirksen amendments. No final positions were taken on any of the amendments, but it was decided that substitute language for [some of the] amendments would have to be drafted. If Dirksen could go along with the substitute amendments, then there would be some area to negotiate on other amendments. Tomorrow there will be a meeting with [Representative William] McCulloch [Rep., OH], Kuchel, and senators [Jacob] Javits [Rep., NY] and Case on the bill.

The civil rights forces in the Senate decided to make suspending the jury trial more palatable by providing that jury trials could only be suspended in civil rights cases where the penalty was imprisonment of 30 days or less. This proposal took the form of a Mansfield-Dirksen jury trial amendment.

These Comments on the Civil Rights Bill Are Being Dictated on April 25, 1964

With the introduction of the Dirksen-Mansfield compromise to the Talmadge jury trial amendment, the civil rights forces seemed to take a major step forward by actively involving Senator Dirksen in behalf of the bill. This was accomplished primarily through a series of afternoon and evening conferences on Thursday, April 23. Humphrey appeared to play a major role in these conferences, particularly in regard to keeping the compromise, namely that of 30 days, in the legislation. Dirksen initially proposed ten days and Mansfield agreed, but then Humphrey jacked Dirksen back up to 30 days. The Department of Justice people [primarily Deputy Attorney General Nicholas Katzenbach] were involved at all stages of the negotiations.

[Leadership Conference Excluded]

There has been a studious and somewhat deliberate attempt to exclude the Leadership Conference [on Civil Rights] people from these discussions. It is generally agreed among all concerned that it simply is not possible to discuss each of these various steps with the Leadership Conference people at every stage in the negotiating process. They are informed after the decision is taken, but generally are not at all included in the actual decision-making process.

Our Monday and Thursday morning meetings with the Leadership Conference people have therefore taken on somewhat the aspect of a mock meeting. There is generally a refusal [on the part of the pro-civil rights senators] to answer questions directly, a certain amount of filibustering on behalf of the [Senate] leadership, and I suspect that Clarence Mitchell and others are a little bit disturbed, since they are obviously not being included in the crucial positions. But it is also the judgment of all those concerned that this is the only way one can go about passing the bill. To involve the Leadership Conference at every stage would simply be to invite continual chaos and disruption.

It could also appear at this date that the outlook for the bill is quite good. It will be interesting to see whether this prognosis holds up in the coming week. If a workable package can be worked out with Dirksen, including certain of his amendments on Title VII [equal employment opportunity] and Title II [integration of public accommodations], it should be possible to conclude action on the bill within another 30 days. If Dirksen begins to balk once again, the outlook will of course look quite black.

But there is an increasing feeling that the southerners know they are in deep trouble on the issue this time. They are increasingly sensitive on the floor and do not appear to be as sharp in terms of parliamentary procedure as one has reason to expect. The sharp exchange between Humphrey and Russell—I believe it was Wednesday or Thursday evening—was marked primarily when Senator Russell [the leader of the filibustering southerners] suggested that a point of order was debatable when the rule book clearly demonstrates that it is not. He managed to wiggle out through some advisory opinions from his pal, Howard Cannon (Dem., NV), [who was presiding] in the chair. But the basic point was still clear: namely, that Russell thought a point of order was fully debatable when in fact the rule book says it isn't. Russell is not supposed to make this kind of mistake.

[Catastrophe Avoided]

A certain catastrophe was narrowly avoided yesterday when the Mansfield-Dirksen substitute was submitted to the Talmadge amendment in the improper form. The wording of the substitute amendment had to be quite precise so that it actually did substitute, line by line, for the wording of the Talmadge amendment. The original Dirksen-Mansfield compromise did not do this. Fortunately, however, Charley Watkins [a Senate staffer] tipped Ken Teasdale [a staff adviser to Democratic leader Mansfield] off to this point before anyone else discovered it, and the corrections were made by unanimous consent. If these corrections had not been made, the amendment would not have qualified as a substitute and the parliamentary position which is currently enjoyed by the proponents would have been lost.

It is now impossible to amend the substitute to the Talmadge amendment. However, perfecting amendments to the Talmadge amendment itself would be in order. It will be interesting to see whether the southerners attempt to add any of these perfecting amendments to the Talmadge amendment.

[Southerners in a Quandry]

The southerners clearly are in somewhat of a bind at the moment. If they vote for the Dirksen-Mansfield substitute, they will do so knowing full well that it clearly does not hamper the bill in the way in which the Talmadge amendment would. On the other hand, if they vote against the Mansfield-Dirksen compromise, they will be badly defeated on the first roll call vote of the debate. Psychologically this would not be helpful for them. If, on the other hand, they continue to debate the Mansfield-Dirksen compromise, they run the risk of antagonizing Dirksen and thereby hastening the day of cloture. In short, they seem to be a bit up against the wall at the moment. It will be interesting to see whether they can wriggle out.

I would predict that by Wednesday of next week, namely April 29 or 30, the state of affairs on the bill as a whole should be quite clear. Once we see what Dirksen wants in Title II [integration of public accommodations], we will then know whether or not we can get this bill out of the way promptly or whether we will be in for a long haul through the Republican [National] Convention, or at least up to it.

It is also a thought that Dirksen may very well want to pass the bill prior to the California [presidential] primary. If Goldwater wins this primary, as now appears likely, this will put Dirksen very much in a bind between the radical rightwing around Goldwater and the more moderate and responsible conservatives in the House [of Representatives] who backed the [civil rights] bill solidly. Dirksen's road would be far easier if the bill simply was no longer a question at the time of the California primary, or at least, if the outcome had been assured through cloture or other agreements.

When seeking a cloture vote on a filibuster, it was considered very important that the first attempt at cloture succeed in getting the required two-thirds majority. In the past a failed first cloture vote usually resulted in the civil rights forces losing heart, giving up, and seeking a weakening compromise with the filibustering southerners. In this next section, John G. Stewart becomes very concerned that Everett Dirksen, the Republican leader in the Senate, will seek a cloture vote on the jury trial amendment and lose it. Stewart prefers that cloture only be attempted on the entire civil rights bill, and only when the civil rights forces are certain of a winning two-thirds vote.

Notes on the Civil Rights Bill
Dictated April 29, 1964

After weeks of stagnation, things began to happen quite suddenly yesterday morning and have been moving full steam ahead ever since. Senators Dirksen and Mansfield filed their substitute to the Talmadge amendment. The Mansfield-Dirksen substitute called for jury trials in those cases where the defendant was sentenced to jail for more than 30 days or more than 300 hours in cases of criminal contempt. This seemed to upstage the Talmadge amendment quite dramatically and, if it can be believed, appeared to catch the southerners somewhat by surprise. They immediately went into caucus to find out what their next move should be. They decided that they would oppose the Mansfield-Dirksen substitute for, in the words of Senator Russell, it was only "a mustard plaster on a cancer."

Therefore, it appeared likely that the debate would run throughout this week and possibly next week. At this point, a number of senators began to grumble quite audibly about the length of time spent on civil rights and perhaps that the time had come to take some direct action to seek cloture on the entire bill. At the same time, however, Senator Dirksen early Tuesday morning, April 28, began to talk of filing a cloture petition on the Mansfield-Dirksen substitute [jury trial amendment] itself. Without consulting anyone, Senator Mansfield appeared to agree with this strategy.

[Early Cloture Vote Unwise]

Everyone else with whom we usually work thought this was a most unwise move, as the various memos on this problem will point out in greater detail. . . . [But], all at once, there appeared to be a very strong move underway for filing a cloture petition on the substitute [jury trial] amendment rather than the bill. It was on the way and down the tracks before anyone had time to do much about it. However, by 4 p.m., April 28, a meeting was held in Senator Mansfield's office, attended by Attorney General [Robert F. Kennedy], Katzenbach [of the Justice Department], Larry O'Brien and Mike Manatos [of President Johnson's staff], Senator Humphrey, and Francis Valeo and Ken Teasdale [of the Senate Democratic staff].

At this meeting, [Francis] Valeo outlined the reasons why they ought to attempt cloture on the amendment. Mansfield said nothing. Humphrey then initiated the rebuttal to this position. By the end of the meeting Robert Kennedy, Katzenbach, O'Brien, and Manatos agreed with the Humphrey position. Mansfield said nothing. It was, however, apparent that no firm decision on seeking cloture for the bill or for the amendment was made. Mansfield finally said he would go back and talk to Dirksen some more.

The problem was particularly aggravating because staff people supporting the tougher line [against a cloture vote on the jury trial amendment] were apparently going to be excluded from this meeting. However, I dragged Ken Teasdale down right outside Majority Leader Mansfield's door, and he went in with Humphrey. Through this rather preposterous ruse we managed to get at least one staff person [opposed to cloturing the amendment] into the meeting. So, as the day's events limped to a close, the possibility of cloture on the amendment was still very much alive, although it had not been definitely nailed down. At this point, senators Humphrey and Kuchel went off to the National Interreligious Convocation on civil rights [a meeting in Washington of religious leaders from throughout the nation to support the civil rights bill].

We also held during this day several sessions with Humphrey where Ken Teasdale and I very much urged him to adopt the tougher line, namely, to seek cloture on the bill, to step up the Senate sessions, to seek accommodations with Dirksen on the outstanding amendments, and then bring the whole business to a climax sometime around the middle of May. This still seems to make good sense.

On April 29, the problem was still unresolved. At the early morning meeting of the senators and staff people, attended by senators Humphrey, Clark [Dem., PA], Javits [Rep., NY],and [Philip] Hart [Dem., MI], and appropriate staff people, there was general agreement that the hard line [cloture only on the bill] would be more productive than the softer line for cloture on the amendment. The principal exception to this was Senator Clark, who supported cloture on the amendment. There was also some discussion of Bobby Kennedy's statement concerning the Dirksen amendments: namely, that they were "generally acceptable." This caused all sorts of uproar with Senator Clark and Senator Javits and it took [Deputy Attorney General] Nick Katzenbach some time to pour oil on the troubled waters.

The senators finally met, namely, senators Mansfield, Dirksen, Humphrey and Kuchel, about 4:30 in Dirksen's office.

Prior to this meeting it appeared almost absolutely certain that a cloture petition [would be filed] on the substitute [jury trial] amendment, possibly tomorrow, April 30. That would mean that the crucial vote would take place on Saturday, a nice day for any kind of vote around here. *[Stewart is being sarcastic here. Due to the large number of absentees, Saturday would be a bad day for a cloture vote.]*

It is quite clear that the votes on this matter have not been checked out thoroughly, although Humphrey claims that they would have no trouble getting the necessary two-thirds of those present and voting. The lack of . . . knowledge was . . . demonstrated today when [someone] inquired whether it was 24 or 48 hours after filing of a petition that the vote takes place. Remarkable! *[It is 48 hours.]*

As I dictate this memo, I have not had a chance to discuss the results of the late afternoon meeting with Humphrey to any great degree. He did note briefly that things appear to be going along much better, that he had been pushing Dirksen to get down to the basic problem of the bill itself, and that it was not absolutely sure that a cloture petition would be filed on the amendment. Meanwhile, Senator Russell [the southern leader] was running around madly attempting to work out certain perfecting amendments to the Talmadge amendment which, if adopted, might well avoid a cloture vote.

In other words, Senator Russell appeared to be generally concerned about losing the cloture vote, even if it was on the amendment. Senator [Sam] Ervin, Jr., [Dem., NC] and [southern Democratic staff] were engaged in much uproar and drafting and redrafting in the marble room late this afternoon. Undoubtedly they were working closely with Russell in developing substitute language which they hoped would avoid the vote on cloture. This appeared to be some manner of weakness which should be exploited to the fullest.

[Leadership Difficulties]

I just wish to note briefly the great difficulty there is to maintain control in the present allocation of leadership authority. Mansfield and Dirksen move along in one direction and often do not inform the actual floor captains [Humphrey and Kuchel] of their thinking until the ball has already picked up considerable speed. It is also true that Mansfield seems to follow Dirksen's lead without exception. In other words, Senator Dirksen appears to be acting as the majority leader without assuming any of the responsibilities involved. That is not a bad position to be in.

In summary, the situation, then, is very fluid tonight. There still appears to be a possibility that the tough-line boys [cloture only on the bill] might grab hold of this situation and bring it through to a successful and productive conclusion, but it is by no means guaranteed. Dirksen's motives are still rather obscure, since we had been peddling the line that Dirksen wanted to wind things up in early June, thereby avoiding being caught in a bind between a Goldwater victory in California and the more sensible Republican support for this bill in the House. But if [Dirksen] actively seeks cloture on this amendment, it probably should prolong the entire debate past that deadline.

Perhaps not. But the opportunity for delays clearly can be seen in any such strategy. Finally, one must not leave out President Johnson. The matter was discussed at some length at the Tuesday morning [congressional] leadership breakfast [with President Johnson at the White House]. At that point, Mansfield raised the possibility of using cloture on the amendment and the matter was debated at the breakfast but was not decided.

[Barging into the President's Office]

Subsequently Humphrey took himself down to the White House to see the president unannounced. He kept

McGeorge Bundy [a presidential foreign policy adviser], Secretary [of Defense] McNamara, and others waiting while he barged into the president's office to lay it on the line. In effect, he told the president that the matter was at the point where victory was in sight but that the law had to be laid down here and now. [Humphrey] set forth the reasons why he opposed cloture on the [jury trial] amendment itself. I do not know what Johnson responded. But it has been said that, when Dirksen went to the White House at noon today, he found Johnson in a tough and noncompromising mood. In other words, it appears that Johnson threw the ball back to Dirksen rather than letting Dirksen leave it on the White House stoop. Surely, this was the wise thing to do. So there is much going on, and it will be interesting, to say the least, to see what happens tomorrow.

Notes on the Civil Rights Bill
Dictated April 30, 1964

Today the question of whether or not to seek cloture on the Mansfield-Dirksen substitute [jury trial] amendment or on the bill itself was still before the civil rights leaders. As these notes were dictated, the question still, to the best of my knowledge, was unresolved. The ball more or less rested with Senator Russell [the southern leader] at this point. Would he permit a vote early next week on the Dirksen-Mansfield [jury trial] substitute, or would he force the [senatorial] leaders to seek cloture. It appeared that if he did not permit a vote there would be no alternative but to file a cloture petition on Monday. This would set the stage for a cloture vote on Wednesday, when most of the senators would be in town.

It was reported that the principal reason why Senator Russell had not responded as yet related to the behavior of Senator [Strom] Thurmond [Dem., SC] [one of the most committed southern Democratic filibusterers]. Thurmond would not agree to permit a vote and threatened to filibuster on his own. While this could only last for 24 hours or so, it would, of course, demonstrate a split within the southern ranks. This would not look good and would be a real problem for Russell. Therefore, [Russell] was restrained to a large extent in doing what he felt was the proper course [permitting a vote on the Mansfield-Dirksen jury trial amendment].

[Leadership Conference Restive]

At the meeting of the Leadership Conference this morning it was quite clear that Clarence Mitchell and the other Leadership Conference people were growing quite restive. They felt that the bill was being frittered away and made a variety of threatening or pseudo-threatening statements about the country rising up in wrath. [Mitchell] continued to push his idea about arresting absent senators and seemed unable to grasp why this was not a particularly intelligent suggestion. Humphrey was in a particularly lousy mood during the meeting and responded quite harshly to the suggestion.

The meeting was not a particularly satisfactory one. No decisions were reached to do anything differently than was being done. Humphrey reported that it was likely that Russell would permit a vote before Wednesday of next week and thus the question of cloture on the [jury trial] amendment would no longer be before us. It will be most interesting to see if this is what actually happens.

The rest of the day was devoted to a few meetings. The congressional leaders met with Attorney General [Robert Kennedy], [Deputy Attorney General] Katzenbach, [Assistant Attorney General] Burke Marshall, and [presidential aide] Larry O'Brien in the majority leader's office at 4 p.m. No decisions were, to the best of my knowledge, taken at this meeting. It was primarily just a review of the various options open at the present time. Since the ball rested in

Russell's lap, all anybody could do at this point was wait and see what he decided to do. Once he has made up his mind, then we can take appropriate action. If he does nothing by the middle of the afternoon on Monday, it appears there will be no alternative but to file a cloture petition.

This will bring the first real showdown on the civil rights bill since the vote on the Morse motion at the time the bill was made the pending business. [Senator Wayne Morse (Dem., OR) had proposed sending the civil rights bill to the Senate Judiciary Committee with instructions to report it back, unamended, by a specific date. The civil rights senators opposed this motion and defeated it on the Senate floor.]

Dirksen is still playing his cards rather close to his chest and appears to be in no particular hurry to reach any principal decisions that would wind up the debate on civil rights. So we must be patient and wait and see what happens.

The problem of the Mansfield-Dirksen jury trial amendment took an unusual turn when Senator Thruston Morton, a Republican from Kentucky, presented a perfecting amendment that had the support of the southern Democrats and a number of Republicans. Richard Russell, the southern leader, said there could be a vote on the Morton amendment. The civil rights forces in the Senate thus felt constrained to show their control of the Senate by voting down the Morton amendment and a second perfecting amendment, this one by Senator John Sherman Cooper, also a Republican from Kentucky. Stewart resumes his account just following the Senate votes on these two perfecting amendments.

Notes on the Civil Rights Bill
Dictated Wednesday, May 6, 1964

Today roll call votes were [held] on the Morton amendment to the Talmadge amendment and then on the Cooper amendment to the Talmadge amendment. Both of these were so-called perfecting amendments.

A great deal has transpired over the past 72 hours or so since I last dictated a memo. There is so much to relate that I probably will leave out a great deal. Nevertheless, one must do the best one can in these matters.

The principal development, I suppose, is the reinvolvement of Senator Dirksen in the negotiations toward a final bill and cloture. Once it was clear that the move for cloture on the Talmadge amendment would not be attempted and that some sort of vote would occur today, that is, Wednesday, which it did, the problem of "where do we go from here?" once more reappeared. The staff of friendly [pro-civil rights] senators strongly urged that the pace be accelerated and that a concerted drive for cloture begin.

Senator Dirksen appeared willing to open full-scale negotiations on what would be an acceptable bill. These negotiations opened yesterday, Tuesday, May 4, in Dirksen's office. Present at the Tuesday morning meeting were, among others, Attorney General [Robert Kennedy], Dirksen, Mansfield, Humphrey, Kuchel, [Warren] Magnuson [Dem., WA], [Bourke] Hickenlooper [Rep., IA], [George] Aiken [Rep., VT], Katzenbach and Marshall [from the Justice Department], and assorted staff people. I was not there.

[A Large Number of Dirksen Amendments]

Dirksen unveiled his three tiers of amendments—track A, B, and C. This was somewhat surprising, to put it mildly, since Dirksen had assured Humphrey that he had no more amendments to the bill except a small amendment to Title II [integration of public accommodations].

Apparently his staff changed his mind on that score. A wide variety of amendments were offered. [The Class A amendments were] nearly 40 so-called technical amendments to the entire bill. The Class B amendments were semitechnical, semi-substantive, and the Class C amendments were the more substantive changes which Senator Dirksen would propose for discussion. The session in the morning and the session in the afternoon, which was limited primarily to staff people, were devoted entirely to exploratory discussions of the amendments. No agreements were made on either side. No agreements will be made until the quid pro quo has been established; namely, that we get cloture activity from Dirksen.

But it was interesting to note that in the morning meetings, Hickenlooper made a statement saying that Dirksen was a softie and that [Dirksen] could not speak for Hickenlooper, so it raised the question about what votes Dirksen would be able to produce for cloture, if he decided that cloture is the course.

There is some real feeling that perhaps Dirksen may be overplaying his hand with this grandiose scheme of amendments. It is also possible that Dirksen's staff has presented him with these various changes and that Dirksen is going along with them to see what happens. I would suppose that Dirksen's earlier statement to Humphrey that he had no great number of amendments to offer reflects more accurately Dirksen's true personal attitudes. But we must nevertheless weed through these various proposals and get down to bedrock to what Dirksen really wants. But I must say this weeding process has dragged along for a rather extended period of time.

It should not be overlooked that Dirksen is not totally a free agent in this battle either. He has the Republican Party to be concerned about, and if the Senate is close to voting cloture and Dirksen does not so vote, it will put him in a rather embarrassing and difficult position. So I think we should go ahead on our own as well, in conjunction with the Dirksen negotiations. To assume that only Dirksen holds the key to passage of the bill would, in my opinion, be a serious misreading of our own strength. We do have some strength, in case everyone has forgotten.

Of course the outside groups are getting quite restless with all this activity. They have no idea what's going on and are more or less going nuts. I have suggested to the churches, in particular, that they use May 17, the 10th anniversary of the Brown [vs. Board of Education school desegregation] decision, as a time to rally nationwide support for the bill through telegrams, phone calls, visits, etc. I understand that they will be going ahead with this activity.

[Senate Staff Disorganized]

The votes today were an excellent example of how disorganized the [Senate] leadership staff structure is on the Democratic side of the aisle. There were, to my knowledge, no advance nose counts on the Morton amendment. The wild confusion which prevailed on the floor certainly bears out this feeling. The initial vote on the amendment was tied 45 to 45, which meant the Morton amendment failed. On the motion to table the motion to reconsider, the opponents of the bill won by defeating the tabling motion. They then carried the motion to reconsider. Finally, however, on the second vote on the substance of the Morton amendment itself, they were defeated by a vote of 46-45.

It was quite evident that the majority leader [Mike Mansfield] was totally confused at many points in the process. He was simultaneously paired with both Arkansas senators at one point. He forgot to get Senator [Frank] Moss [Dem., UT] out of the phone booth during the roll call, and Moss subsequently blew his stack and voted with the opponents of the bill for a while to get even with the leadership. In general, it was wild chaos. What a helluva way to run a railroad.

It was also hoped that voting would continue past the Morton amendment. While a vote did take place on the so-called Cooper amendment, about an hour and a half after the final vote on the Morton amendment, the Senate then was unable to continue into the evening on the Mansfield-Dirksen [jury trial] substitute to the Talmadge amendment. Many senators, including Humphrey, believed that the time had come to push into the night in order to get a vote on this amendment but, once again, the majority leader [Mike Mansfield] disagreed, and it now appears that there will be no votes on the Mansfield-Dirksen [jury trial] substitute until Monday or Tuesday of next week.

The southerners like to make deals and then to modify then in various ways, and surely this was one of those instances. Russell agreed to vote on the Mansfield-Dirksen [jury trial] substitute but somehow the Morton amendment became the item that was going to be voted upon. Also, Russell announced that he would be out of town on Friday and that a vote could not occur that day, and so the majority leader acquiesced and the vote will now be on Monday afternoon or Tuesday morning. Once again, a helluva way to run a railroad.

[Civil Rights Forces Lack Direction]

For the record, there is a definite lack of urgency and lack of direction to the civil rights forces at present. Humphrey is frustrated and blocked in by Mansfield. Kuchel is frustrated and boxed in by Dirksen. If there was some way to get this operation off dead center, I believe we could move along in good style. I think the basic strength to pass this bill is in the Senate if it can be activated, focused, and moved along. But at the moment there is no real movement, and there is no real determination to get this movement. How we will get the operation into higher gear is a basic question which should be answered sooner or later. I hope we can have some sort of an answer this week or at least some sort of indication that we will eventually get such an answer.

I think one must fully appreciate the profound difficulties in getting this bill underway and keeping up a head of steam. Nobody really seems concerned except the few committed leaders. The rest seem willing to let the time fritter away until there is no more time. But I will say that it will be somewhat of a major miracle if the pro-civil rights forces can get themselves back in order and push ahead with some degree of resolution and determination. Of course, the southerners have their problems and, in the end, [their problems] are probably even more profound than ours. But right now, ours look pretty profound.

Notes on Civil Rights Bill
Dictated Wednesday, May 13, 1964:
The Big Day of the Deal with Senator Dirksen

I sat through both [the] morning and afternoon sessions where the senators and Attorney General [Robert Kennedy] nailed down the initial compromise package with Dirksen. Attending the meeting were the following senators: Humphrey, Dirksen, [Leverett] Saltonstall [Rep., MA], Aiken, Hart, Clark, [and] Magnuson. The attorney general, [Assistant Attorney General] Burke Marshall, and various staff people were also there.

Prior to this meeting, which convened at 10:30 a.m. at Dirksen's office, the Democrats held a separate meeting in the majority leader's office. Attending this earlier meeting were Larry O'Brien, Attorney General [Robert Kennedy], Mike Manatos, Frank Valeo, and Senator Humphrey. Senator Clark busted into the meeting halfway though, having schemed things along with Senator Javits.

The principal sticking points in the compromise were discussed at the [Democrats'] 9:30 a.m. meeting. These were, in essence, Dirksen's wish to place language for the attorney general's enforcement powers in a separate title, namely [a new] Title XII. Also, there was the relationship between the recommendations of the [Fair Employment

Practices] Commission (FEPC) and the enforcement action which would be undertaken by the attorney general in situations of massive resistance or patterns of discrimination. The general decision was made to take a tough line on the general theory that Dirksen needs our support at this point just about as much as we need his.

[Dirksen's Proposed Procedure]

At the opening of the meeting Senator Dirksen outlined the procedure which he hoped to follow if agreement was reached on the basic points of the various amendments. He suggested that the amendments would have to be mimeographed, that a [Republican] Party conference [of senators] would have to be called, that he would then attempt to secure agreement within the [Republican] Party [senators], and then move directly for cloture. Dirksen expressed the feeling that he would prefer to move on a title-by-title basis, although he did not close out a decision which would result in cloture on the bill itself. Dirksen noted that there was division within the southern ranks and that there were at least six southern senators who believed they should begin voting on amendments now and stop the filibuster as it is currently progressing.

Humphrey noted that the procedure which would be followed on amendments, and agreements which would be reached, if any, would depend largely on subsequent strategy that would be followed on the bill. In short, we want cloture on the whole bill, and we want it soon, and if Dirksen is not willing to go this route then there is really no business to talk to him about his amendments.

[Senator] Saltonstall [Rep., MA] urged the meeting not to consult the House members too carefully on [the proposed new] Title XII at this point. He wanted the Senate to reach consensus and then go to the House to see whether or not this would be acceptable. Clark noted that he felt it was important to have some informal discussions with the

House members, since their role in this legislation is so vital. At this point, Attorney General [Robert Kennedy] sought to get the meeting down to the real problems and suggested that, rather than read through all the various technical amendments that run through all titles, that the various participants at this Wednesday meeting bear down on the areas of substantive disagreement.

[Senator] Aiken [Rep., VT] made the point that the bill at present was "dead." We must therefore seek to resuscitate the bill, and that was in essence what this meeting was supposed to do. He noted that it would be very serious to lose the first cloture vote. Therefore he urged getting cloture on whatever was possible, whether it be the bill, a separate title, or even one amendment.

As the senators began discussing the areas of substantive disagreement, there was first noted by Dirksen his strong hope that there would be a [new] Title XII in the bill containing the attorney general's powers to combat massive resistance. The point was made by Humphrey and others that this might very well be a strategic blunder. You could still have the enforcement powers knocked out of Title XII even though there might be points of reference to the title in Titles II [integrate public accommodations] and VII [equal employment opportunity]. After considerable discussion on this point, Dirksen finally agreed tentatively that there should be located in Titles II and VII language which he had sought to put in [a new] Title XII.

The meeting next turned to the discussion of whether or not the Civil Rights Commission should be made subject to the provisions of the Administrative Procedures Act. Burke Marshall noted that Justice was drafting language which would seek to accomplish the concerns of Senator Dirksen without saddling the Civil Rights Commission with the full scope of the APA.

There was also some discussion on the striking of the voting fraud provision in Title V [continue existence of Civil

Rights Commission and have it investigate vote fraud]. Attorney General [Robert Kennedy] noted that this was a Republican provision added by Republican members of the [House] Judiciary Committee and that he had given his word to support the bipartisan package, of which this was a part. Therefore, unless Saltonstall, Aiken, and Dirksen were able to secure release from [the House Republicans] for this provision, the [Johnson] administration leaders would find it necessary to support this provision and to fight against its deletion. The ball was thrown to Dirksen and Saltonstall to work out whatever they could with their [Republican] brethren in the House.

The same basic disagreements which existed in Title II [desegregate public accommodations] also were found in Title VII [equal employment opportunity], namely the role of the attorney general in seeking enforcement orders in cases of massive resistance or patterns of discrimination. Dirksen's staff people suggested that these recommendations would be informal and private from the [Civil Rights] Commission to the attorney general. Nevertheless, after considerable discussion, Dirksen finally agreed that the [Civil Rights] Commission would have specific authority to recommend enforcement action to the attorney general. [Senator] Saltonstall suggested in addition that the [Civil Rights] Commission should advise and consult with the attorney general, so that the expertise of the Commission could be used fully.

[Senator Clark Walks Out]

Throughout these discussions, [Senator Joseph] Clark [Dem., PA) took a very hardnosed position. This was partially deliberate and planned in advance. He raised all sorts of points, noting the substantial concessions which were being made, and how these could not be viewed as merely technical or as simple adjustments of language. Clark refused to accept the amendments on Title VII [equal employment opportunity] and in the afternoon session finally walked out on the meeting. It was interesting to note that, as soon as [Clark] did leave the session, the spirit of those left picked up immeasurably.

Dirksen emphasized that his objective was to secure as good a bill as he could as quickly as possible. In this light, he urged the particular Indian amendment supported by Senator [Karl] Mundt [Rep., SD] in that it would help deliver his vote for cloture. Dirksen said quite specifically that he hoped to get a bill by the first week in June. It is obvious that there has been some slippage among the Goldwater supporters in the Senate and that this is giving Dirksen a great deal of trouble. The participants agreed that they would then take the disagreed upon language to their respective party caucuses, that they would not come back with added amendments, that they would support the principles agreed upon, and that they were now in business one for all, and all for one.

After this meeting adjourned, Humphrey scheduled a 4:30 p.m. meeting with members of the Leadership Conference, including [Clarence] Mitchell and [Joseph] Rauh. . . . At this meeting, [Assistant Attorney General] Burke Marshall reviewed the general positions that had been taken. The reaction of the Leadership Conference people was guarded. They were not particularly happy but awaited an opportunity to examine the language at first hand. This would take place tomorrow morning, May 14, at 9:30 a.m.

To sum up, the day's events probably were vital to the passage or failure of the bill. It appeared that Senator Dirksen has now fully thrown his weight behind passage of the bill and upon cloture. He did recede on most of the important points today and, as a result, the package does seem to be adequate and effective. Whether or not the various Leadership Conference people will agree remains to be seen. In any event, a great deal was accomplished.

Notes on the Civil Rights Bill
Dictated Tuesday, May 19, 1964

Today the Democrats and Republicans held their respective conferences to discuss the proposed package of Dirksen-Humphrey amendments. I was present at the Democratic Conference and have notes commenting on what occurred there.

[The Democratic Conference]

In summary, there was no general opposition to the amendments among the Democratic supporters of the bill. A number of the southerners were present at the conference and they, of course, expressed various objections. Senator Sam Ervin, Jr., [Dem, NC] carried on in a rather preposterous fashion by voicing all of the standard [anti-civil rights] arguments in the conference. Apparently, he must believe them.

[Ervin] noted that the Volstead Act [prohibiting the sale and use of alcohol for human consumption] had failed because the [U.S.] government could not tell the private individual what he could or could not put into his stomach. Therefore, the Civil Rights Act would fail because the [U.S.] government could not tell the private person what he could or could not put into his mind. The relevance escapes me, but it is interesting to note that Ervin felt it worthwhile to bring it up in the private conference of [Democratic] senators. In short, Ervin made a general ass of himself throughout the conference by raising nitpicking points and by carrying on in a generally ridiculous fashion.

Senator Frank Lausche [Dem., OH] raised a number of points as did Senator [Albert] Gore, Sr. [Dem, TN]. Senator Clark made a very helpful statement by noting that he did not approve this package of amendments but that, on balance, he could in good conscience support the agreements. Senator Hart said the question which senators should ask themselves is: Can I in all good conscience support these changes? Hart announced that he could so support them. Senators Clark, Hart, and Mansfield praised Humphrey at great length and testified to his steadfastness in the past week to ten days.

Humphrey had the floor most of the time and outlined the general changes which would be made in the bill. Copies of the proposed amendments had been distributed that previous afternoon by Majority Leader [Mike Mansfield], and Senator Dirksen's memorandum explaining these changes was distributed at the meeting.

[The Republican Conference]

The Republicans held a separate conference and will resume their meetings this afternoon and tomorrow at 9:30 a.m. They did not discuss Title VII [equal employment opportunity] at any great length. Apparently Senator Hickenlooper has publicly voiced a concern with Title VII as it would stand with the Dirksen amendments, but Dirksen is generally hopeful.

Nick Katzenbach [of Justice] has talked with McCulloch and Celler [in the House of Representatives] and reports that they are in general good shape. However, [McCulloch and Celler] do not intend to make any public statements one way or the other until the Senate has acted. They feel this would only weaken their position and therefore will say little, if anything. But they are in good shape.

The Leadership Conference [on Civil Rights] has had a number of meetings with Humphrey and the Justice Department officials. They have a variety of specific concerns as spelled out in [their] memorandum. But they do not have any basic objections to what has been done. In other words, they are not saying that the roof is falling in, that the bill has been sold out, that there are unacceptable amendments in the Dirksen package. Joe Rauh has told Humphrey privately that if this bill passes, it will be a great victory for the cause of civil rights. In short, the Leadership Conference appears to be in reasonably good shape on this question.

[The Bobby Baker Situation]

This is just a brief note on the remarkable outbursts of senators Case and Mansfield on the [Senate] floor over the Bobby Baker situation. . . . [Senator Case and the Republicans were seeking to extend a Senate inquiry into possible wrongdoing by Baker, a Democratic staffer in the Senate.] I had not dictated any thoughts on this so far. The specific facts on the clash between Mansfield and Case can be found in the *Congressional Quarterly* or the newspapers.

But the interesting point regarding civil rights [is this. Certain senators were very concerned about] Case's inability to make his point of order and personal privilege and appeal the ruling of the Chair. [This concern could make these senators] less likely to vote for cloture on civil rights. In short, this is an interesting example of how one particular incident on the floor, totally unrelated to civil rights, can wash over into the civil rights area and perhaps have an effect there.

It will be interesting to note whether the senators who were allegedly thinking of voting for cloture but now wouldn't will, in the final analysis, carry out this threat. I suppose that they probably will not.

[An Unusual Procedure]

It is also interesting to consider the precise role which the Humphrey-Dirksen-Justice Department meetings assume in the structure of the Congress. This was clearly a group of the senators and their staff acting in a very ad hoc capacity, without benefit of hearings, and with no statutory or legal authority at all. And yet they have apparently come up with what will, in all likelihood, be the Civil Rights Act of 1964. It is worth spending some time thinking about this point and trying to find comparisons in the past. When has an ad hoc group such as this come up with such important legislation? The conversations on the House side were of a similar nature, but the participants were all from the Judiciary Committee. It was, in a sense, an ad hoc subcommittee of the Judiciary Committee that produced the House bill. Now we have an ad hoc committee of the Senate, in a sense, producing the Senate [bill] and probably the final bill, assuming the House accepts the Senate amendments. This is an interesting fact which bears some comment.

[Dirksen Now Fully Supportive]

Now that the Dirksen amendments have been made public, the question relates to whether Dirksen will be able to secure enough votes for cloture and whether President [Johnson] can get enough western Democrats out of town so that cloture can be invoked. As Dirksen indicated in his press conference today, he has the bit in his teeth and is running full steam ahead for cloture on the full bill and passage of the civil rights bill as soon as possible. It will be interesting to restructure the situation as to how Dirksen was brought around into precisely the point where he is today. This was the initial objective which we have all been seeking, and we should not overlook the fact that it has now been achieved. Dirksen is now a complete supporter of the bill and is ready to put all of his prestige and power on the line to secure cloture and eventually passage of the bill itself. I suspect that Russell will see the handwriting on the wall fairly soon.

The strategy now appears to be one of waiting out the days set aside next week for the Kennedy dinners, etc., and then filing a cloture petition early in the month of June. I would hope that the Senate sessions could be stepped up considerably pointing toward the invocation of cloture. But perhaps even that would not be necessary if Dirksen can produce the votes we need. In short, the pieces [are beginning to fall] into place, and if everything goes as it should, we may very well have this bill passed by the Senate by the middle of June. What a great accomplishment that would be.

On June 10, 1964, the Senate passed a motion to cloture the 1963-1964 civil rights bill by a vote of 71 to 29, four votes more than the 67 out of 100 needed. John G. Stewart now records what was required to gain the successful invocation of cloture in the Senate.

A tricky parliamentary situation developed when Senator Bourke Hickenlooper (Rep., IA) wanted to introduce and vote upon three additional amendments. Since none of these three amendments had been included in the Dirksen-Humphrey package of amendments, a "unanimous consent agreement" was required to get them onto the Senate floor for discussion and a vote. A "unanimous consent agreement" requires that every senator present agree to the desired course of action. If there is just one senator who objects, the agreement fails. Stewart shows how, one way or another, the civil rights forces secured "unanimous consent" to allow Senator Hickenlooper and his Republican colleagues to have a debate and vote on three additional amendments.

The civil rights forces also faced an unusual parliamentary situation once cloture was invoked. Any amendment that had been introduced in the Senate prior to cloture could be brought up for a vote on the Senate floor, but no new amendments could be introduced once cloture had been voted. That meant that if a southern amendment were brought up and adopted, and it was discovered later that this amendment was very damaging to the bill, the civil rights forces could not introduce a new amendment to correct the damage done by the southern amendment. Slowly and painfully, the civil rights forces learned they had better defeat every amendment brought up by the southerners in the post-cloture environment.

John G. Stewart

SOME FURTHER NOTES ON THE CIVIL RIGHTS BILL DICTATED JUNE 11, 1964: CLOTURE DAY PLUS ONE

It has been at least a week and a half to two weeks since I have dictated any notes, and I will attempt to recall the more prominent events which have occurred in the interval.

Once the Dirksen package of amendments had been agreed upon by the various principals, these agreements were taken to the respective Democratic and Republican conferences. At that point a variety of additional amendments were proposed and the negotiations resumed. These amendments were largely minor in character, many of them of the nitpicking type made famous by Senator [Jack] Miller [Rep., IA], and did not change in any way the fundamental decisions regarding Titles II [integration of public accommodations] and VII [equal employment opportunity]. These later negotiations primarily were working on things which had not been nailed down at the time the original agreement had been reached.

It is important to note that at this juncture Dirksen was completely involved in the effort to pass the bill.

The principal unresolved question was the date that cloture would be attempted. Initially, Dirksen appeared to think that the third week in June, that is sometime around June 22nd or 23rd, would be the best time. He noted that many senators had made commitments to address the various graduations and commencements, and that these commitments would keep the Senate from acting until the third week in June. It was also suggested that Dirksen was interested in slowing down as much of President [Johnson's] program as possible and that this could be accomplished most effectively by postponing the cloture vote until then.

Humphrey urged Mansfield to urge Dirksen to move the date up as early as possible. Suddenly, with little advance warning, Mansfield and Dirksen announced that the initial vote for cloture would take place on Tuesday, June 9.

This announcement was made on the first or second of June. From that point . . . the efforts went forward to round up cloture votes.

[The Counter-Filibuster]

[But] the southerners suddenly changed tactics and announced that they were prepared to vote on the jury trial amendments. Since a number of our senators were out of town, this immediately transferred to the civil rights proponents the task of maintaining the filibuster, so a so-called counter-filibuster was undertaken to keep the Senate from voting until . . . cloture time had arrived.

This had a bad psychological effect on some senators because it would appear that we were in a position of having to invoke cloture on ourselves. We attempted to set the record straight . . . through a speech by Humphrey where he set forth the delay tactics which had been employed by the South and how we could not be held responsible for the present situation. We also proposed a unanimous consent agreement whereby time would be limited on all amendments and on the vote on the final bill. Russell, of course, had to object to this agreement. These two steps were to transfer some of the burden to the shoulders of the southerners, although dissatisfaction still persisted among some of the middle-western Republicans.

It is also important to note that at this time Dirksen became ill and had to be absent from the Senate much of the time. Also, it should be noted that Governor Nelson Rockefeller [of New York, a liberal, pro-civil rights candidate for the Republican nomination for president], blew the California [Republican presidential] primary on June 2nd. [Senator Barry Goldwater, the conservative, anti-civil rights Republican, won the California primary and thereby gained the 1964 Republican nomination for president.]

To recapitulate, the three events served to shake badly the civil rights proponents' position on this week prior to cloture. Namely, the southerners decision to stop talking and to have several votes on jury trial amendments; Dirksen's illness; and Goldwater's victory in California all served to create a bad environment for the cloture vote.

[The Hickenlooper Revolt]

This came to a head . . . when Hickenlooper led a small rebellion against Dirksen. Hickenlooper announced . . . that he had consulted with about 20 Republicans, and they had decided that several votes had to be held before cloture if they were going to support cloture. This thinking resulted in a unanimous consent agreement propounded by Hickenlooper . . . to the effect that the Senate should agree to four hours of debate on three amendments: a re-offered Morton jury trial amendment with slight modifications; a Hickenlooper amendment to strike the training institutes and grants provision from Title IV [desegregation of public education]; and Cotton's amendment to limit the effect of Title VII [equal employment opportunity] to employers or unions with 100 or more employees or members.

Extensive discussion on this unanimous consent request took place on the floor. . . . Due to Russell's pleadings, the unanimous consent agreement was not decided on Friday but went over to Saturday. On Saturday the unanimous consent request was agreed to by all concerned. We agreed because we could not afford to alienate the Republican support which Hickenlooper had amassed in his small rebellion against Dirksen. In particular, Hickenlooper's move had the support of Cotton, Hruska, Mundt, Miller, [B. Everett] Jordan [Rep., ID], and Hickenlooper himself. Russell could not afford to object because his objection would probably alienate these Republicans and drive them into voting for cloture. So Hickenlooper was clearly the man of the hour Saturday.

The Senate came in on [the following] Monday and began to debate the Morton jury trial amendment in the afternoon. On Tuesday the Senate had four votes on the Morton jury trial amendment, which prevailed by a narrow margin. The vote of 51 to 48 was, however, somewhat closer than had been expected, since many senators indicated their intention to defect to the southern and Republican forces [and support the Morton amendment]. Actually, very few of them did defect, but the combination of Jackson [Dem., WA], Symington [Dem., MO], Long [Dem., MO], and Magnuson [Dem., WA] pushed the amendment through. This was not a real tragedy, however, because it also gave the Republicans something to crow about and made their cloture votes more likely.

The Senate defeated decisively the Hickenlooper amendment. A substitute amendment [then was] offered by Senator Ervin to destroy Title VII [equal employment opportunity]. [This was also defeated, as was] Cotton's amendment on Title VII. These amendments on Title VII were defeated by a substantial margin of 63 or 64 votes against on each one, and this was certainly a good boost toward the historic cloture vote [now scheduled] on Wednesday, June 10.

On Tuesday evening the final tabulations were made as to our strength on cloture. While there had been a number of estimates in the high sixties or low seventies, we could only count 66 votes [of the 67 needed] definitely for cloture on Tuesday evening. There were a number of possibles, and subsequent events showed we were able to recruit most of these. But these facts were not entirely known through the evening. In particular, [Ralph] Yarborough [Dem., TX] and [Howard] Edmondson (Dem., OK) seemed to be likely choices but were still wavering, until the time for the vote. Also, [Carl] Curtis [Rep., NE] was not definitely known, to us at any rate. And [Howard] Cannon's [Dem., NV] vote for cloture was definitely a surprise and must have been the handiwork of President [Johnson].

[Cloture Invoked]

In any event, cloture was invoked and the historic mountain peak had been crossed. Immediately after cloture, Senator [Sam] Ervin [Dem., NC] jumped to his feet and offered a double jeopardy amendment which, if accepted, would have probably gutted the bill. However, in his eagerness to offer the amendment, he offered it to the Talmadge amendment, which was subsequently withdrawn, and therefore the amendment was not a part of the substitute package, even though it had carried by the margin of 49 to 48. Negotiations with Ervin were then undertaken to find some way of modifying his amendment so it did not gut the bill and also arriving at a procedure to include it in the package.

Events on the floor immediately after cloture were extremely disorganized. There was a great emotional letdown after this historic vote, and the leadership seemed to be losing control of their forces. They were able to defeat decisively several votes to modify Title II [integrating public accommodations] and also to strike Title VI [the funds cutoff], but the situation wasn't in hand. There were no basic organizational plans developed to deal with amendments, and everyone was quite pleased to recess at 5:30 p.m. There had also been an earlier recess which ran from about 12:30 to 3:00 to give everyone a chance to recoup and reorganize themselves.

Humphrey was extremely tired at this point and really was not controlling the floor in a very effective fashion. He seemed to be going out of his way to make it up to the southerners, who had been stung so badly with this overwhelming defeat. He was giving sort of general promises that this or that amendment could be accepted, without checking the text of the amendments through, and put himself in several awkward positions.

Today, Thursday, June 11, the thing started off just about as badly. As the *Congressional Record* will show, we soon got ourselves in a major hassle over [Russell] Long's

[Dem., LA] amendment to improve (supposedly) the working of Title VI [funds cutoff] by putting the ban on action in the area of housing into section 601 of the bill. This would have provided some profound constitutional difficulties and could not be accepted. Instead of simply moving to defeat the amendment itself, Humphrey seemed to view himself under some obligation to draft substitute language because he thought we could not defeat the Long amendment. I disagreed, and I believe we could have defeated the amendment.

Nevertheless, we were fortunately able to work things out through some parliamentary good fortune whereby Senator Long was able to modify his amendment in an acceptable way and put some additional wording down in a new Section 605. It seemed to be the feeling of the Justice Department and the civil rights groups that this new wording actually improved the bill somewhat and provided some statutory recognition of President [John F. Kennedy's] executive order [integrating public] housing. Southerners Long [Dem., LA] and Gore [Dem., TN] seemingly did not see it this way [furthering civil rights], since they supported this change, but everyone ended up being satisfied with the result.

[Voting Down All Southern Amendments]

Once this hurdle had been cleared and the language for Ervin's jury trial amendment had been incorporated into the substitute, the steamroller against southern amendments picked up speed. There were 12 roll call votes today. All were successfully dealt with. The southerners lost by substantial margins on almost all the roll calls. By the end of the day, they appeared to be quite dispirited and in a certain state of disarray. Mansfield did them a good turn by permitting the Senate to recess at about 5:45 p.m.

[Richard] Russell seemed quite discouraged, and there was no real sense of organization among the southerners, with various ones offering amendments in no particular order and not really debating them with any particular zest. There definitely seems to be developing the spirit that it's time to get on with other things and to wind up the civil rights bill. It will be interesting to note whether we can, in fact, wind things up next week, or perhaps even early next week.

It always is a marvel how we seem to keep our forces together when there is really no sense of clear organization and so much of it is done on the spur of the moment on an ad hoc basis. Fortunately, there are a large bloc of senators who will vote with you without knowing why, and these are the troops we can fall back on in close scrapes. In any event, the efforts seem to be moving along well, and we hope to make good progress again tomorrow.

At a meeting which was held in Mansfield's office early this morning, there was considerable debate as to how the amendments should be handled and what should be the procedure. Joe Clark [Dem., PA] took a very hardnosed and somewhat acrimonious position that the southerners should more or less be "punished" for their past sins and should be given no consideration whatsoever in this position of cloture. Mansfield and, to a lesser extent, Humphrey, urged a much softer line. [They] pointed out that party unity was essential, that other bills would be coming along, and that we should attempt to be charitable at this point in time.

The principal result of this early meeting was a general agreement to oppose all amendments, unless they were of a minor nature and agreed upon by people on both sides of the aisle, and that we would have to get ourselves organized somewhat better. But unless the southerners put up more of a fight in the coming days, a well-organized force of proponents would not really be necessary. But certainly we would not want to get ourselves back in the situation which prevailed during the initial offering of the Ervin double jeopardy amendment or the Long amendment to Title VI. We were really quite disorganized and unhinged at that point and only escaped through mistakes of the opponents and a certain amount of good luck for ourselves. This is one helluva way to pass a civil rights bill.

At some unspecified point in time, John G. Stewart dictated a final set of notes giving more details about the way in which the civil rights forces in the Senate secured the successful cloture vote on the 1963-1964 civil rights bill on June 10, 1964. Stewart also reviewed the awkward period on the Senate floor following the passage of the cloture motion.

Once cloture was invoked, each senator had only one hour of time to speak for or against the bill. Each senator's speaking time was carefully clocked, and when the hour was up, the senator was told to stop speaking. Many of the southern filibusterers made it a point to use up their full hour and be "silenced," or "gagged" as some of them liked to say, on the Senate floor.

Stewart concludes with a discussion of final passage of the civil rights bill in the Senate on June 19, 1964.

Undated "Final Dictated Thoughts"

These are some final dictated thoughts on the civil rights debate. In particular, these notes will relate to the final week before cloture with an attempt to reconstruct day by day what took place. . . . On Monday, June 1 [1964], we entered the final week before cloture, and we knew that this would be a critical week. We were not sure of 67 votes at this juncture, and we knew that what took place in this week would probably be critical in determining what would happen on the cloture vote. As it turned out, these general thoughts were correct.

On Monday, June 1, Senator Russell, without more than 20 or 30 minutes warning to Senator Mansfield, announced that the time had come to vote on some of the pending jury trial amendments. This presented the proponents of the bill with a real dilemma. We knew the jury trial amendments were extremely popular and, since the initial votes on the Morton amendment, the whole problem of jury trial had received considerable publicity. In short, we were not at all sure of defeating any further jury trial amendments.

A defeat at this point in the strategy would have been a bad psychological blow. In short, we were afraid to permit a jury trial amendment vote, because we would probably lose. On the other hand, the only way to prevent a vote was to initiate a filibuster; that is, to carry along the filibuster through our own speakers. Of course, this had the obvious drawback of putting the proponents of the bill in a somewhat ridiculous position. We would, in effect, be voting on cloture next week to terminate our own filibuster.

This, at least, was the view which would be set forth in the press and would be the view that most senators normally opposed to cloture would assume. Nevertheless, at a meeting in [Majority Leader] Mansfield's office on late Monday afternoon, it was decided to push ahead with the debate and attempt to bull through this week for the scheduled cloture vote on . . . Tuesday, June 9. Humphrey happened to have a rather extensive speech on the jury trial position ready to go [to extend the filibuster], and he was willing to step into the breach on Monday. However, we used the speech on Tuesday, and it was a good speech which seemed to be well received.

[Dirksen's Illness]

It is also important to note that on Monday Senator Dirksen announced he was not feeling well and would have to return home to rest. This is of critical importance since Dirksen's absence was the opening wedge which permitted [Senator Bourke] Hickenlooper [Rep., IA] to carry forth his plans of revolt, which culminated in the unanimous consent agreement offered on Friday, June 5.

On Tuesday, of course, the California primary was held. If Rockefeller had won, that victory would probably have tamped down all further revolts by Hickenlooper, and the waters would have remained unruffled until the cloture vote on Tuesday. However, the [Barry] Goldwater victory appeared to give Hickenlooper additional impetus to carry forth his revolt. In other words, the combination of Dirksen's illness and Goldwater's victory brought to Hickenlooper the opportunity he was seeking to cut back Dirksen's role in the civil rights debate.

[Positive Aspects of the Hickenlooper Revolt]

It is interesting to consider the fact that a [Nelson] Rockefeller victory might have tamped the Hickenlooper revolt which, in turn, means the unanimous consent agreement on Friday would not have been offered, which, in turn, suggests that we might not have had as strong support on cloture as we did. Because, in retrospect, the Hickenlooper unanimous consent proposal was a heaven-sent gift, which certainly assisted the proponents in the final cloture vote. But these last observations are purely speculative in nature, and the answer can never be known.

On Wednesday, as I recall, the debate simply moved along and Russell did not make any great outcries about the filibuster the proponents were not supposedly conducting. But, by Thursday, there appeared to be growing discontent among the ranks of the critical Republicans, namely Cotton, Mundt, Hickenlooper, et al. Something more had to be done, and Ken Teasdale and I decided that perhaps a fairly long and detailed speech setting forth all the facts in the case would be appropriate.

We immediately got to work to prepare such a speech, which Humphrey finally delivered in the middle of the afternoon on Thursday. Dirksen was still not at all well and was unable to make his presentation of the substitute package of amendments. Therefore, Humphrey coupled the comments on the parliamentary situation to a rather exhaustive analysis of the substitute package, which the Justice Department had prepared for Humphrey. It appeared as though this had been a fairly productive afternoon's work, since the talk of revolt and defection had subsided somewhat. But, throughout this week, Hickenlooper and his people were still plotting, and these clandestine meetings culminated with the rapid-fire offensive on Friday, June 5.

On Friday, Dirksen was again in the Senate. Early in the day, by 10:30 a.m., he had conferred with Humphrey and told him that the outlook for cloture was not at all good. Mundt had begun to slip badly, as had Miller, Hruska, and Jordan (Rep., ID). These problems were, of course, due to Hickenlooper's behind-the-scenes activities. On Friday, Cotton delivered a speech where he deplored the parliamentary situation which had existed, castigated the Senate leadership on all sides, and loudly bewailed his position; that is, being unable to vote on any of the principal amendments of the bill prior to cloture. Hruska and Hickenlooper were important onlookers while Cotton delivered his speech, and Russell commended him at its conclusion.

[Hickenlooper Steals the Spotlight]

By Friday afternoon, the Hickenlooper unanimous consent agreement had been prepared and had been brought forward. The tenor of his proposal can best be gleaned from reading Hickenlooper's remarks. This was clearly a direct attack on Dirksen, and everyone interpreted it in that light. However, it also presented Russell with some substantial problems, as he noted Saturday morning. For this brief period, Hickenlooper had actually stolen the spotlight from Dirksen, but it was a very brief and short-lived victory at best. In fact, it served to be the key by which the final votes for cloture were wound up with some to spare.

[Post-Cloture Activity]

These notes will now shift to the general activity which took place after cloture was invoked. Within a minute after cloture had been invoked on Wednesday, June 10, Senator [Sam] Ervin [Dem., NC] was on his feet putting forth a double jeopardy amendment to the bill. Ervin set forth the proposal in a very garbled and unclear way. There was great turmoil in the chamber. Neither the pro-civil rights forces nor the opposition were at all clear as to what was happening in the chamber, and, before anyone knew it, we were having a roll call vote on the Ervin jury trial amendment.

No proponent of the bill had been prepared to reply effectively to this proposal, and it carried by about 8 votes, as I recall. Such senators as Proxmire [Dem., WI], Pell [Dem., RI], Pastore [Dem., RI], Symington [Dem., MO], etc., voted for the double jeopardy amendment. However, Ervin, in his haste to offer the amendment, offered it to the House text and not to the [Mansfield-Dirksen] substitute itself. It was also offered as an amendment to the pending Talmadge amendment.

The chair originally announced that the Ervin amendment had lost and, following that, Talmadge asked unanimous consent to withdraw his amendment. When it was withdrawn, the Ervin amendment was withdrawn with it. After Talmadge made this gesture, the Chair announced they had, in fact, made a mistake, and the Ervin amendment had initially carried. But, even though it carried, it was hanging in space and would have no effect on the ultimate outcome of the substitute once it had been voted upon.

There was considerable hard feeling on Ervin's part at this point, since he felt he had been shortchanged. However,

Humphrey had made no commitment concerning adding amendments to the [Mansfield-Dirksen] substitute once cloture had been invoked. [He] saw no reason why he should simply take the Ervin amendment as originally written and add it to the substitute. There was deep concern that this would actually gut the bill by permitting states to convict or acquit white restaurant owners on spurious and rather meaningless civil rights laws which might be enacted [by the states]. [Under Ervin's double jeopardy amendment, such convictions or acquitals would protect the white restaurant owners] from further prosecution under the federal statute.

In order to accommodate Ervin and to get ourselves out of this mutually disagreeable situation, the Justice Department drafted some additional language which clarified the Ervin amendment. It was then agreed by all parties that this amended version could be offered to the substitute text and added [to the bill]. This was subsequently done. In short, Ervin got his amendment. It did not do substantive harm to the bill, and the problem was laid to rest.

Following the vote on the double jeopardy amendment, . . . Senator Russell called up his amendment which would postpone the enactment of Title II [desegregation of public accommodations] until 1965. This amendment was defeated by a fairly substantial margin. At this point, the leadership wisely recessed the Senate until 3 p.m. so that everyone might reorganize and collect their respective wits.

[Southerners Upset]

The act of invoking cloture had quite an emotional impact on most senators, particularly those from the South, who apparently had believed in their hearts that such a fate could never befall them. Senator Russell seemed particularly upset and disturbed by the fact that cloture had actually been invoked, and then that his amendment to postpone enactment of Title II to 1965 had been defeated. He accused the Senate of acting in the spirit of a lynch mob.

Events had transpired so rapidly after cloture that it was very difficult to even enjoy the fact that cloture had been invoked. It was, in fact, going from the frying pan right into the blooming fire.

Once the Senate reconvened at 3 p.m., Senator [Albert] Gore, Sr., [Dem., TN] offered his amendment to strike Title VI [cutoff of U.S. funds] from the bill. There was substantial debate on this question, which lasted for about two hours as I recall, with Senator Gore's amendment being defeated by a substantial margin around 5 p.m. Once this amendment had been disposed of, the leadership again wisely decided to recess the Senate for the afternoon.

Following the recess, there was a meeting of Justice Department and Leadership Conference people, together with the staffs of the various senators, in the office of the Democratic Policy Committee. One of the topics of discussion at that time was working out acceptable wording for the Ervin double jeopardy amendment. Of even more importance was a discussion of the general position which would be adopted on the many, many amendments which would be called up. At that point, the Senate leadership had not worked out precise details or plans as to how these amendments would be handled, and there was a general disagreement on this score.

Some people, particularly the Leadership Conference types, urged outright rejection of all amendments and to push ahead as quickly as possible. Humphrey disagreed, pointing out that this, in the end, might be a serious mistake, which would lead to retribution on a particular amendment which we hoped to defeat. He noted that you can only push people so far, that you have to take their feelings and desires into account. As it turned out, Humphrey was precisely correct in this attitude. Nevertheless, the Tuesday late-afternoon meeting adjourned with no real decisions being made.

And, oh yes, Humphrey was also very concerned about the various amendments which would be offered to Title VI [cutoff of U.S. funds], particularly relating to housing. [Assistant Attorney General] Burke Marshall and Humphrey got into quite a discussion, at times almost heated, about what Title VI really meant.

[Humphrey Not in Control]

Humphrey seemed to be quite distraught and not really in command of the situation during the next 24 hours. The push for cloture had been a deeply demanding one, and he seemed to let up and relax after the vote had been taken in a way which could not be helpful under the demanding nature of the new circumstances which confronted everyone.

There was a meeting . . . in . . . Majority Leader [Mansfield's] office to try to plot what would be done on the double jeopardy amendment, and also what would be done as to broader policies on amendments in general. . . . The approach to the Ervin double jeopardy amendment was worked out. [Senator] Pastore [Dem., RI] was at the meeting and generally set the tone that something would have to be done with Ervin or else we would have to accept an amendment we didn't really want. It was generally feared that we would lose any double jeopardy amendment that would be subsequently offered.

[Senators] Clark and Mansfield got into almost a shouting match as to the procedures which should be followed now that cloture had been invoked. Mansfield had suggested that perhaps we might want to yield extra time to certain of the principal southern speakers, and Clark said this was ridiculous and got Mansfield sore. As it turned out, the question never really was a live one, since Mansfield soon became convinced that yielding additional time would just be a foolish thing to do with no real pay-off involved.

The Senate convened at 10 a.m., as I recall, and a barrage of amendments immediately were brought up. Humphrey simply was not exercising the kind of leadership which he usually did, and immediately the whole problem of Title VI [cutoff of U.S. funds] broke loose.

This can best be understood by reading the *Congressional Record.* . . . We find ourselves agreeing to work out some sort of compromise language with [senators] Gore [Dem., TN] and Long [Dem., LA] relating to the question of housing. At this point it appeared that this process might be one we would find ourselves engaged in on almost all of the many dozens of amendments which would be offered in this area.

[Policy on Amendments]

In short, the policy of defeating the various amendments which were offered gradually evolved over the early days after cloture, rather than [resulting from] any firm decision on the part of the floor leaders. In fact, no such decision was ever taken, and it was interesting to note that it soon became evident that the best thing to do under the circumstances was simply to defeat amendments as they were brought up. Those few amendments which were adopted after cloture resulted from the persistent efforts of their sponsors and from Humphrey's willingness to be accommodating and helpful wherever he could.

For instance, Long of Louisiana was particularly persistent on several amendments he offered. One was to remove the two words "bona fide" from the category of private clubs under Title II [integration of public accommodations]. He persistently pushed Humphrey on this until some alternate language was worked out which proved to be acceptable to everyone. I think it is fair to say that we gave up absolutely nothing at any point during these hectic days after cloture. On those few instances where we sought to be accommodating, it was always possible to work out language which seemed to satisfy the sponsors of the amendment but which actually did no substantive damage to the bill.

Of course, it was clear that the amendments would probably lose if they were brought to a roll call vote, but we felt it sufficiently in our own interests to accept these amendments in the hopes it would help cut short the calling up of amendments by the opponents of the bill.

The week following cloture was indeed a wild and tumultuous one. The only thing worse than voting on an amendment every 20 minutes is going two months without any votes at all. The various southerners would call up a particular amendment, yield themselves anywhere from 30 seconds to 2 minutes to explain the amendment, and then settle back for the vote. Sometimes we would reply to these amendments but, as debate wore on, the practice became one of simply voting them down regardless. There was no ordered way in which these amendments were brought up, and it appeared that the southerners had no particular plan of strategy either.

The great question which immediately became evident to everyone was how long the southerners would persist in calling up amendments. At one point we felt the drive might end . . . early. . . . However, these hopes proved to be most unfounded.

[No Southern Strategy]

It was also evident that the southerners really had given very little thought to their strategy after cloture. Their amendments were not called up in any particular order, which was a mistake. Had they plotted out precisely which amendments would be called up, they could have scored, perhaps, some impressive victories early in the debate after cloture and therefore opened up the danger of bad amendments being adopted to the bill.

One point should be emphasized. Once cloture has been invoked, only those amendments which have been "presented and read" [prior to the cloture vote] qualify for consideration, except by unanimous consent. Therefore, if a bad amendment carried, there would probably be no way by which this language could be subsequently removed from the bill through another amendment offered by a proponent. This meant that you, in a sense, went to the wall every time an amendment was called up. There was, in short, no room for error at any point in the process.

It was also clear during this period that [Richard] Russell [the southern leader] was having trouble controlling his own troops. . . . It was evident that Russell, [John] Stennis [Dem., MS], [Lister] Hill [Dem., AL], and others of the more moderate southerners were willing to call it quits. But [Sam] Ervin [Dem., NC] and, especially, [Strom] Thurmond [Dem., SC] and [Russell] Long [Dem., LA] were determined to continue. Thurmond said he was going to offer all of his amendments, and Ervin said he would continue to offer amendments as long as Thurmond did. [Richard] Russell clearly was not able to exercise any control over these actions by Thurmond and Ervin.

Mansfield had determined that the sessions would not run too late in the evening in the hopes that the southerners would be reasonable and permit the final vote sometime early in the following week. But as Monday [June 15] passed and no final vote was in sight, it became evident that harsher tactics would be necessary. Therefore, the Senate put in a truly ghastly day on Tuesday, June 16. Over, I believe, 34 roll call votes took place that day, and the previous high in the Senate was allegedly 16 roll call votes in one day. The Senate stayed in session from 10 a.m. until after midnight on that Tuesday. There was a great deal of uproar and grumbling in the chamber all through that day, but the southerners continued to offer amendment after amendment.

[Comedy in the Senate]

As the day wore on into evening on that Tuesday, senators began to get rather well oiled by frequent visits to their respective hideaways around the Capitol. There were some amusing incidents which took place because of this, principally Dirksen's outburst against Russell Long (Dem., LA].

You will recall that we had accepted several of [Senator] Long's minor amendments to the bill, and it was implicitly assumed that the acceptance of the amendments would limit the number of other amendments Long would be offering. But it did not seem to work this way. At one point Long offered an amendment and Dirksen, obviously a little under the weather, jumped to his feet and ran back to Russell [Long], gesticulating wildly, and said something to the effect of, "Goddamn you, Russell [Long], you've broken our agreement. Why you've welshed on our deal."

Long looked absolutely horrified at the specter of Dirksen running up the center aisle of the Senate, and there were a few moments of some concern if not high comedy. Dirksen calmed down, and soon he and Long were striding about the Senate floor, arm in arm.

This was also the time that Senator [James] Eastland [Dem., MS] moved to adjourn the Senate, and there was a yea-and-nay roll call vote on this motion. [Edwin] Mechem [Rep., NM] and [Peter] Dominick [Rep., CO] voted with Eastland, and Dirksen hit the roof on this occasion. He dashed wildly about the chamber and made Dominick change his vote. Mechem had already left the chamber, but Dirksen dispatched a covey of pages to bring him back and thereupon applied the muscle to Mechem as well. Mechem was protesting quite visibly, and Dirksen was also quite visibly telling him he had to change his vote. Finally, [Dirksen] grabbed Mechem by the arm, marched him into the well of the Senate and announced, "Okay, now vote." Mechem did and voted against adjourning.

This was all quite a remarkable performance. Everyone was on the verge of collapse when Mansfield finally decided that it was foolish to continue any further, and the Senate adjourned about midnight.

Wednesday [June 17] was another wild and confusing day. No one knew precisely how long the amendments would continue to be offered, but we had hopes that we could somehow or another get third reading on the bill before the end of business on Wednesday. It was also on this day that Humphrey received the news that his son [Robert] had been operated on for a small cyst on his throat, and the cyst had been found to be malignant. This, of course, upset Humphrey deeply, and it took an amazing act of courage, self-control, and determination to maintain his responsibilities on the floor while he had this knowledge of severe sickness and problems with his son, Robert.

Nonetheless, the pressure was applied, negotiations were held with [senators] Thurmond and Ervin, and it was finally worked out they would offer only a certain number more of amendments. At that point, it was simply a matter of everyone sticking to their guns and of defeating the amendments. By this time the proceedings had truly become a farce. Nobody replied at all to any of the supposed amendments which were offered, and they were just simply defeated by varying margins of 3 to 1, 4 to 1, 5 to 1. There were several close votes, but I would suppose there were really no more than five close votes throughout the period after cloture, where more than 100 roll call votes were held.

[Final Passage]

A third reading finally was secured at the conclusion of business on Wednesday [June 17]. Everyone went home with the knowledge that Thursday would be devoted to final speeches and perhaps a vote on final passage, but certainly this would take place on Friday. Members still had time allotted to them which they could use if they chose to do so, but it was confidently felt that not everyone would use up his full hour of time. The minutes remaining for each senator at the various points in the debate [could] be found by consulting the appropriate copies of the *Congressional Record.*

The last bit of excitement took place on Friday morning [June 19]. Senator [Albert] Gore, Sr., [Dem., TN] had clandestinely, I believe, secured unanimous consent to offer a motion to recommit the bill [to committee] and report out with language relating to Title VI [cutoff of U.S. funds]. [The Gore proposal would prevent] the cut-off of funds from localities which were under a court order to desegregate schools and were following the dictates of that order. Actually, Gore's motion was not in order, since the substance of the amendment, which would be attached [during recommital], had not been presented and read prior to cloture.

When Humphrey learned of the unanimous consent agreement, . . . he considered this to be the highest breach of senatorial ethics, since he had not been informed that the unanimous consent agreement by Gore would be offered on Thursday. If [Humphrey] had been informed, he would have objected [thereby killing Gore's motion to recommit].

So Gore had his last few moments in the spotlight, and the debate, lasting about an hour and one-half, ensued over the question of Gore's motion to recommit. The final vote on this was an overwhelming defeat for Gore, at least partially due to the rather shoddy way he had handled the whole affair. Once the motion to recommit had been defeated, then the final senators marched to the floor for their remarks, with final passage coming on the bill at about 7:40 that evening [Friday, June 19].

Humphrey really was not able to enjoy the great fruits of his victory because he was still quite concerned over the state of his son. We went out and had dinner Friday night, but Humphrey was really quite subdued. Then the party became even more of a drag when the news of the plane crash of senators [Ted] Kennedy [Dem., MA] and [Birch] Bayh [Dem., IN] was announced while we were eating at Paul Young's [Restaurant]. But, in retrospect, everything worked out with [Humphrey's son] Bob [the cancer went into remission] and with Teddy and Birch [who were injured in the plane crash but recovered]. We can all take some solace in having passed a remarkably good civil rights bill, far better than anyone thought we could get.

Chapter 5

The Senate and Civil Rights

John G. Stewart

In 1968, four years after the Civil Rights Act of 1964 was enacted into law, John G. Stewart earned his Ph.D. in Political Science at the University of Chicago. His doctoral dissertation was entitled "Independence and Control: The Challenge of Senatorial Party Leadership." The major portion of the dissertation addressed the question of how political party leaders in the U.S. Senate maintain "control" over a body composed of highly "independent" individual senators.

The concluding chapters of Stewart's dissertation addressed the question of how the party leadership in the U.S. Senate dealt with the herculean task of maintaining political party control during the southern Democratic filibuster of the Civil Rights Act of 1964. In this lengthy description and analysis, Stewart focused his attention on Senate Majority Leader Mike Mansfield (Dem., MT) and Senate Majority Whip Hubert Humphrey (Dem., MN) and their efforts to win the support of Senate Minority Leader Everett Dirksen (Rep., IL) for a cloture vote on the southern filibuster.

This particular first-person account, written after some time had gone by for further research and reflection, emphasizes the way Mansfield and Humphrey were able to work within the established rules of the Senate to move forward a highly controversial and divisive piece of legislation. It is a true "insider" view of the detailed strategic and tactical thinking that goes into moving a major piece of legislation through the U.S. Senate.

Stewart's account of the enactment of the Civil Rights Act of 1964 has been divided into five sections that will constitute the next five chapters of this book. In the first section, Stewart discusses the historical role of the U.S. Senate in dealing with civil rights legislation and the ever-present threat of a filibuster. He next reviews the events that led the Kennedy administration to press for enactment of a major civil rights bill by Congress in 1963. Stewart then traces the bill's tumultuous but steady progress to passage by the House of Representatives in early 1964.[1]

The Impact of the Filibuster

At the root of the party leaders' problems . . . was the fact that a filibuster makes it impossible for a simple majority to conduct the Senate's business.[2] The senators who are filibustering simply refuse to yield the floor to permit any votes on the legislation. The majority, in short, never is given the chance to act.[3]

In these circumstances the party leaders have to choose from among three main alternatives if they desire further action on the bill: (1) produce a *two-thirds* majority to apply cloture and limit debate to one hour per senator, (2) break the filibuster by exhausting the opponents, or (3) concede to the substantive demands of the opponents so the filibuster stops voluntarily. At this point the majority can again assert itself.

Each alternative brings its own problems for the party leaders. The infrequency of cloture being applied on any bill, much less a civil rights bill, suggests the difficulty of this approach. When the Senate voted to invoke cloture during the Communications Satellite debate of 1962, it was the first time since 1927 that a cloture motion had prevailed.[4] In most instances, however, a two-thirds majority is not prepared to vote affirmatively on invoking cloture. When such a two-thirds majority does exist, the filibuster poses no serious threat.

In the process of rounding up the additional votes for cloture, the party leaders must usually give special attention to the group of 8 to 15 senators who generally represent the difference between the simple majority for the bill and the two-thirds majority needed for cloture. Although cloture is strictly a procedural weapon, the ability of these 8 to 15 senators to demand substantive changes in the legislation as their price for cloture tends to link substantive issues with procedure. Since the filibuster cannot be stopped by cloture without the votes of these senators, their bargaining leverage with the party leaders is greatly enhanced. A major effect, then, of any filibuster is to involve the Senate majority leader far more deeply than usual in questions of substance as he struggles to accumulate the two-thirds majority required by Rule XXII [the cloture rule].

The second alternative—attempting to break the filibuster by exhausting the filibustering senators—rarely succeeds because the principal physical burden falls, not on the small group of senators who are speaking, but on the remainder of the Senate, which has to answer quorum calls at any hour of the day or night. Even if the majority leader holds the Senate in session 24 hours a day, the filibusterers can easily divide into teams and arrange their schedules so that each speaker has ample time for rest and recuperation.

Richard Russell of Georgia, the post-World War II leader of the southern Democrats, usually divided his 18 hard-core senators into three teams of six senators each and assigned each team to cover the Senate floor for one day. This provided at least two days rest between assignments, not counting weekends.

Meanwhile their non-filibustering colleagues have been forced to appear on the Senate floor approximately every two hours when the senator who has the floor "suggests the absence of a quorum."[5] These efforts usually end with the filibustering senators ready to continue for weeks and the rest of the Senate near physical collapse.

Extreme proponents of the legislation under siege will often advocate round-the-clock sessions when cloture appears remote or when the substantive price for cloture is too high. "Hold their feet to the fire," these senators demand of their party leaders. But other senators, although not participating in the filibuster, will likely oppose any hasty or summary action. For them, the filibuster represents the Senate's capacity to stand against the immediate demands of a simple majority. Any ill-considered attempt by the party leadership to hinder the exercise of this prerogative may backfire by *increasing* the support which the filibustering senators are able to maintain among their colleagues.

While the alternatives of cloture and physical exhaustion are difficult to execute, the third approach—one of simply conceding what the filibustering senators demand, even if that means abandoning the legislation—becomes increasingly attractive to the majority leader and a large portion of the Senate as the debate drags on. The filibuster, for example, will disrupt the Senate's normal routine in many ways. Procedural shortcuts in the consideration of legislation made possible by unanimous consent of the Senate are sometimes eliminated because one senator will object. Minor Senate business, such as approving the prior day's Journal, can consume hours. Other important legislation backs up on the Senate calendar and in committees. Everyone, except the filibustering senators, is subjected to the repeated inconvenience and annoyance of being summoned to the Senate floor for quorum calls. Tempers are apt to fray and emotions rise in these unpleasant working conditions.

In some cases the filibustering senators will permit all kinds of normal business to transpire since this will tend to lower the frustration level among senators and permit the filibuster to continue unimpaired. One must bear in mind that the filibusterers have only one objective: to prevent votes on the legislation they oppose. Anything else which occurs is to them immaterial. But senators trying to break the filibuster often will object to such unanimous consent requests, thereby hoping to increase the irritation and frustration of other senators against the filibuster.

The flexibility and deference usually paid to the majority leader in scheduling and controlling the conduct of Senate business disappears. And he finds it increasingly difficult to avoid fragmentation of the senatorial party itself. Once a filibuster has begun, differences among contending factions become more difficult to resolve. Senators tend to assume public positions which cannot be compromised easily. Some senators simply get mad at each other. But the fact that a filibuster takes place on the Senate *floor*, the majority leader's domain, means it will be largely his responsibility to somehow bring the Senate through its time of trouble.

These multiple pressures and departures from normal generally create within the Senate a climate ripe for concession or abandonment of the legislation. Senators not identified as strong supporters, usually a substantial majority, frequently are ready to settle for half a loaf, or even no loaf, as the price for ending the misery of a filibuster. The majority leader, moreover, is not likely to expend his limited resources of power and persuasion in an ill-fated drive to apply cloture on a non-compromised bill. Knowing that he must manage the Senate's response to the president's total legislative program, and knowing further that this job will require the cooperation of many senators conducting the filibuster,[6] or representing the deciding cloture votes, the majority leader is likely to eliminate the more controversial sections of the legislation. When this price has been paid and the legislation amended appropriately (or dropped entirely), the Senate can return to its normal procedures of rule by a simple majority.

A filibuster also increases the impact of the president's decision whether to defend the bill under attack. Given the pressures on the majority leadership to concede whatever is necessary to end the filibuster, the president becomes the person best equipped to preserve the controversial parts of the bill. A strong presidential effort to forestall major compromises can on occasion give the party leaders a reason for continuing the fight.

When a filibuster threatens or actually begins, and cloture cannot be invoked easily, the pressures on the majority leader increase rapidly either to compromise the legislation or drop the issue entirely. If neither of these alternatives is acceptable to the president, however, the majority leader is likely to be faced with a difficult decision. Should he lead a legislative battle without even his normal instruments of control or his normal degree of influence? [Under the filibuster, it is the filibustering senators, and not the majority leader, who are in control of what is happening on the Senate floor.]

In 1957 and again in 1960, the Senate passed a major civil rights bill by acceding to certain of the principal demands of the southern Democrats. In 1962, the Senate failed even to consider another civil rights bill when cloture could not be applied to shut off the southern Democratic filibuster.

1963: The Issue Returns to Congress

In 1963 the nation suddenly found itself swept up in a crisis of race relations far surpassing in urgency anything which previously had taken place. In June, 1963, President John F. Kennedy had proposed a new omnibus civil rights bill as a direct outgrowth of the violence and racial strife which gripped Birmingham, Alabama, in April and May of that year. The front-page photographs of police dogs attacking black demonstrators in Birmingham,[7] the reports of high-pressure hoses being used to disperse crowds of black school children,[8] and the bombing of Martin Luther King, Jr.'s, motel room and the home of King's brother dramatized and personalized the demands of the civil rights movement. The key demands were for additional federal legislation to combat the barriers of legalized segregation in education, public facilities, and places of public accommodations, and the need to promote greater equality in employment and voting.

Following several weeks of intensive consultations and drafting by Department of Justice officials and the White House staff, President Kennedy announced his general proposals to the nation in a televised message on the evening of June 11, 1963.

"We are confronted primarily with a moral issue," Kennedy said. "It is as old as the Scriptures and is as clear as the American Constitution. The heart of the question is whether we are going to treat our fellow Americans as we want to be treated. . . . It is a time to act in the Congress, in your state and local legislative body and, above all, in all of our daily lives. . . . I shall ask the Congress of the United States to act, to make a commitment it has not fully made in this century to the proposition that race has no place in American life or law."[9]

June 11, 1963, was also the day of Governor George C. Wallace's unsuccessful attempt to stand in the doorway of the University of Alabama's administration building to block the admission of two black students.[10] And even as the president spoke, a sniper was preparing to assassinate Medgar Evers, the Mississippi field secretary of the NAACP (National Association for the Advancement of Colored People), in the early hours of June 12.[11]

The legislation President Kennedy sent to Congress on June 19, 1963, was drawn primarily to provide legal authority for desegregating places of public accommodation and public facilities, the principal source of the unrest which rocked Birmingham. It also provided additional authority for the federal government to combat discrimination against black voting applicants, to assist in school desegregation suits, and to secure nondiscrimination in the operations of federal programs. Finally, the bill proposed creation of a federal Community Relations Service to assist in mediating racial disputes, a four-year extension of the U.S. Commission on Civil Rights, and statutory authority for the President's Committee on Equal Employment Opportunity, the body charged with securing nondiscrimination in the performance of government contracts.[12] In his message to Congress transmitting the legislation, President Kennedy also called for passage of federal fair employment practices legislation already pending in both the House and Senate.[13]

The House Considers Civil Rights

The obstacles in the Senate which awaited any civil rights bill, much less one of this magnitude, dictated the wisdom of completing action in the House of Representatives before making any attempt to initiate in the Senate. In the Senate there would be a struggle of unknown duration and one whose outcome probably would depend upon whether a southern Democratic filibuster could be defeated. Party leaders projected final House action by middle to late summer, with the Senate hopefully completing its work on the bill prior to adjournment of the first session of the 88th Congress in December of 1963.[14]

This timetable, however, collapsed almost immediately. Subcommittee No. 5 of the House Judiciary Committee, chaired by Emanuel Celler (Dem., NY), had been considering civil rights proposals since May 8, 1963, and promptly scheduled hearings on the new omnibus bill, but the large number of persons and groups seeking to testify made it impossible to adhere to the original time schedule.[15] When the hearings finally concluded on August 2, the subcommittee began the difficult task of evaluating many suggested changes in the bill with a view toward achieving final passage in the House by late September.

But during this period the lobbyists for the Leadership Conference on Civil Rights diligently pressed a number of strengthening amendments upon the civil rights activists on the Celler subcommittee. These subcommittee activists included Peter W. Rodino (Dem., NJ), Byron G. Rogers (Dem., CO), and Robert W. Kastenmeier (Dem., WI). Substantial pressure also was directed against Celler himself.

Throughout the civil rights debate in both House and Senate, the principal lobbyists for the Leadership Conference were Clarence Mitchell, Jr., director of the NAACP Washington Office, and Joseph L. Rauh, Jr., Washington lawyer and counsel to the Leadership Conference. Mitchell and Rauh were joined frequently by Andrew Biemiller, the chief lobbyist for the AFL-CIO labor unions, Jack Conway, executive director of the Industrial Union Department of the AFL-CIO, Arnold Aronson, executive director of the Leadership Conference, and representatives of various service groups, religious instrumentalities and denominations, and other labor organizations.

The efforts of the Leadership Conference paid off handsomely in vote after vote. The subcommittee, dividing largely along party lines, adopted a number of these strengthening amendments[16] and, on October 2, 1963, reported to the full Judiciary Committee a bill that went far beyond the Kennedy administration's position in certain critical areas. It created, for example, an Equal Employment Opportunity Commission with authority to issue enforceable administrative orders. It added the old "Part III" stricken from the 1957 civil rights bill giving the attorney general authority to seek injunctions to prevent violation of any federal right under the Constitution or laws of the United States. It broadened the voting rights provisions to apply both to state and federal elections. It barred discrimination in any business operating under state or local authorization, or if segregation was directly or indirectly sanctioned by the state. All this was coverage far broader than proposed by the administration in its bill.[17]

Party leaders had estimated that approximately 50-60 Republican votes (out of 177) would be needed on the House floor to offset the expected solid opposition of about

100 southern Democrats. Fearing that the bulk of Republicans would never accept the subcommittee's amendments, and that consequently the entire bill was in jeopardy, Attorney General Robert Kennedy, President Kennedy's brother, advocated that the full Judiciary Committee return to the general provisions of the administration's original bill. [Robert Kennedy urged the Judiciary Committee to] begin to hammer out a compromise version in negotiations with Celler, William McCulloch (Rep., OH), ranking Republican on the Judiciary Committee, and Charles Halleck (Rep., IN), minority floor leader.[18]

The fact that a number of southern Democrats on the Judiciary Committee subsequently voted to support the stronger subcommittee bill, apparently believing that it would be easier to defeat on the House floor, gave credence to the administration's concern that the strong subcommittee bill would not survive unless modified.[19]

President Kennedy Intervenes

On October 29, 1963, following several White House meetings where President Kennedy personally enlisted the support of Halleck and McCulloch, the Judiciary Committee approved a compromise bill containing a number of amendments sought by the administration, as well as some advocated by the Republican negotiators. The public accommodations provision was again limited to specific categories of businesses. The attorney general's power under Part III was restricted to authority to intervene in suits brought by private individuals claiming a violation of federal rights on the basis of race, color, religion, or national origin. Court enforcement of non-discrimination orders by the Equal Employment Opportunity Commission was substituted for administrative enforcement. The Community Relations Service was eliminated.[20]

Although the compromise version still was stronger than the administration's original bill in some respects, President Kennedy announced that the Judiciary Committee's action "had significantly improved the prospects for enactment of effective civil rights legislation in Congress this year."[21]

Although the Judiciary Committee formally reported the approved bill (H.R. 7152) to the House on November 20, 1963—three months late according to the original timetable—further action had to await the 2nd session of the 88th Congress, starting January 1, 1964.[22] Two days after the committee's report had been filed, President Kennedy was assassinated in Dallas, Texas. In his address to a joint session of the Congress on November 27, 1963, President Johnson emphasized his determination to press forward on the civil rights front. "No memorial oration or eulogy," he said, "could more eloquently honor President Kennedy's memory than the earliest possible passage of the civil rights bill for which he fought so long. We have talked long enough in this country about equal rights. We have talked for 100 years or more. It is time now to write the next chapter, and to write it in the books of law."[23]

But the delaying tactics of Howard W. Smith (Dem., VA), chairman of the Committee on Rules, in combination with a jammed legislative calendar and the disruptions associated with President Kennedy's death, prevented H.R. 7152 from being cleared for House debate until January 30, 1964, more than seven months after its introduction.

The time had not been wasted. When debate on the House floor finally commenced on January 31, 1964, the bipartisan coalition which had been forged during the difficult negotiations within the Judiciary Committee stood firm against a flood of amendments offered by southern Democrats and conservative Republicans.[24] The Leadership Conference on Civil Rights and the Democratic Study Group, an informal gathering of liberal Democrats, developed an ad hoc communications system which summoned absent representatives to the House floor whenever a crucial vote was about to occur. Possessing the votes, as well as a method of producing them on the floor at the proper time, the managers of H.R. 7152 were able to defeat every amendment which they decided to oppose.[25]

The debate in the House also revealed a determination, particularly pronounced among Republicans, not to accede to any weakening of the bill by the Senate. William McCulloch (Rep., OH), the ad hoc leader of the pro-civil rights Republicans in the House, recalled the events of 1957 when the Senate allegedly jettisoned the House-passed Title III as the price for averting a southern Democratic filibuster. McCulloch vowed he would not be party to any similar operation in 1964. He further indicated that any major change in the Senate would jeopardize Republican support when the bill returned to the House.[26]

On final passage the bill was approved by the margin of 290-130. In this key House vote, 152 Democrats (59 percent of all House Democrats) and 138 Republicans (78 percent of all House Republicans) voted for H.R. 7152, illustrating again the remarkable coalition which had thrown its weight behind the legislation.[27]

During the months of debate in the House, the racial climate in America had grown still worse. Demonstrations and violence in Cambridge, Maryland, forced the governor to call out the National Guard to restore order.[28] Attorney General Robert Kennedy finally helped patch together a shaky peace between black and white leaders in this troubled Eastern Shore of Maryland community.[29] Marches and sit-ins against segregated public accommodations and facilities in Jackson, Mississippi, produced repeated outbreaks of violence and continuing unrest throughout the summer. Civil rights groups in New York City, Chicago, and other northern cities demonstrated against discriminatory membership practices in construction unions.

On August 28, 1963, over 200,000 persons participated in the March on Washington for Jobs and Freedom, implementing the idea first broached in 1941 by A. Philip Randolph, president of the Brotherhood of Sleeping Car Porters, to pressure President Roosevelt into requiring nondiscrimination in government war contracts.[30] Following the partial desegregation of Birmingham's schools in September, 1963, a bomb exploded at the home of a black civil rights lawyer. On Sunday, September 15, another bomb ripped into a black church, killing four young girls attending Sunday school. President Kennedy spoke for millions of shocked and outraged Americans when he expressed "a deep sense of outrage and grief over the killing of children."[31]

Senate Action Necessary

In summary, the continuing deterioration of race relations, coupled with the serious delays in passing the civil rights bill in the House, made prompt action by the Senate highly desirable. Rightly or wrongly, H.R. 7152 was becoming viewed increasingly by the Johnson administration, members of Congress, and the civil rights community as the principal answer to the racial crisis which gripped the nation. In passing the bill in the Senate, however, it appeared necessary to reject any strategy based on compromising essential elements of the bill to avoid or halt a southern Democratic filibuster, the strategy used by Lyndon Johnson in 1957 and 1960.

In 1964, however, this strategy of compromise not only would sacrifice the legislation's capacity to help resolve the current racial crisis, but it would likely insure the bill's rejection in conference by the House of Representatives or even its veto by President Johnson. In fact, the bill probably would never have emerged from a House-Senate conference committee due to the refusal of principal House Republicans to accede to the Senate's changes. Without Republican support in the House Rules Committee and on the House floor, the conference report would be doomed.

If the Senate conferees had backed down and agreed to the House bill, however, the legislation would have been subject to another filibuster when Majority Leader Mansfield moved to accept the conference report in the Senate. If the southern Democrats had been successful earlier in forcing basic changes in the bill, they would have likely prevailed again when the conference committee report was filibustered. Of course, the House might have relented and accepted the Senate's amendments, as it largely did in 1957, but there was no evidence whatsoever to indicate this would have happened.

The Senate thus headed for a truly historic confrontation. Its traditions in support of independent deliberation and opposed to absolute rule by a simple majority were about to run directly into an overwhelming sentiment in the executive branch and among a clear majority of the senators for quick and comprehensive action on H.R. 7152—with a minimum of amendments.

There were, however, mitigating factors in the situation. The president and the principal Democratic leaders in the Senate were publicly committed to passage of the House bill and to work unreservedly to that end. Their prestige and power, however limited it might prove to be in practice, were nevertheless major sources of strength usually denied senators attempting to enact strong civil rights legislation. The severity of the racial crisis in the country, while it increased the pressure on the party leaders to achieve victory, also generated pressure on all senators which might make this victory possible. In the final analysis, however, the outcome in the Senate rested principally on how Majority Leader Mike Mansfield and Majority Whip Hubert H. Humphrey would perform as leaders of the majority senatorial party (the Democrats).

In formulating a strategy capable of handling this delicate legislative situation, the party leaders needed to build a civil rights coalition drawn from the ranks of both parties, one which surpassed the level of Republican support in 1957 and the Democratic strength in 1960. This coalition eventually had to produce enough votes to invoke cloture on the expected southern Democratic filibuster. Past evidence suggested that the crucial senators in this effort would likely be predisposed *against* limiting debate by cloture, especially in its early stages, and more interested in a strategy of compromise and concession as the way to end the debate.

Mansfield and Humphrey began developing the specific components of a strategy to bring the legislation safely through the Senate.

Notes

1. John G. Stewart, *Independence and Control: The Challenge of Senatorial Party Leadership* (Ph.D. dissertation, University of Chicago, 1968). This section is from ch. 4, pp. 136-140, 161-169.

2. For recent comments on the filibuster see Joseph S. Clark, *The Senate Establishment* (New York: Hill and Wang, 1963), pp. 13-14; William S. White, *Citadel: The Story of the U.S. Senate* (New York: Harper and Brothers, 1956), pp. 39-40; Nelson W. Polsby, *Congress and the Presidency* (Englewood Cliffs, N.J.: Prentice-Hall, 1964), pp. 77-78; Donald R. Matthews, *U.S. Senators and Their World* (Chapel Hill: University of North Carolina Press, 1960), p. 248.

3. Standing Rule XIX reads simply: "No senator shall interrupt another senator in debate without his consent." U.S., Congress, Senate, *Standing Rules of the United States Senate*, corrected to January 9, 1963, XIX, sec. 1, p. 21. Charles L. Watkins and Floyd Riddick, *Senate Procedure: Pre-*

cedents and Practice (Washington: U.S. Government Printing Office, 1958), p. 270, note further: "A motion to limit debate is not in order, as it requires unanimous consent. . . .The cloture rule, if invoked, places a limitation on debate on that pending business."

4. *Congress and the Nation* (Washington: Congressional Quarterly, Inc., 1965), p. 1637.

5. According to Standing Rule V: "If, at any time during the daily sessions of the Senate, a question shall be raised by any senator as to the presence of a quorum, the presiding officer shall forthwith direct the secretary to call the roll and shall announce the result, and these proceedings shall be without debate. . . ." U.S., Congress, Senate, *Standing Rules of the United States Senate*, corrected to January 9, 1963, V, sec. 2, p. 4.

6. This was especially true during civil rights debates when many of the filibustering senators were also chairmen of standing committees.

7. *New York Times*, May 4, 1963, p. 1.

8. *New York Times*, May 8, 1963, p. 1.

9. *Congressional Quarterly Almanac—1963*, p. 967.

10. *New York Times*, June 12, 1963, p. 1.

11. *New York Times*, June 13, 1963, p. 1.

12. *Congressional Record*, CIX, pp. 11077-81. On February 28, 1963, President Kennedy had proposed a more limited civil rights bill, dealing only with voting rights, extension of the Civil Rights Commission, and providing federal technical assistance to school districts in the process of desegregation. *Congressional Record*, CIX, pp. 3245-49. These earlier provisions were included in the omnibus bill proposed in June.

13. *Congressional Record*, CIX, pp. 11157-61. These measures, H.R. 405 and S. 1937, 88th Congress, had not been proposed by the Kennedy administration but resulted from congressional initiative.

14. In 1963 the Senate Commerce Committee held hearings on a bill, S. 1732, covering only the public accom-

modations provisions; it was reported favorably to the Senate on February 10, 1964. U.S., Congress, Senate, *Majority Report—S. 1732*, Report No. 872, 88th Congress, 2nd Session, 1964. The Constitutional Rights Subcommittee of the Senate Judiciary Committee also held eleven days of hearings in 1963, which consisted primarily of detailed questioning of Attorney General Robert Kennedy by Chairman Sam Ervin (Dem., NC) on the bill's principal titles. But neither the subcommittee nor the full Judiciary Committee, chaired by Senator James Eastland (Dem., MS), reported any legislation. The Senate Labor and Public Welfare Committee reported S. 1937 on February 5, 1964, dealing with equal employment opportunities. U.S., Congress, Senate, *Majority Report: Equal Employment Opportunity—S. 1937*. Report No. 867, 88th Congress, 2nd Session, 1964. Both S. 1732 and S. 1937 were subsequently abandoned in favor of the omnibus civil rights bill, H.R. 7152.

15. *New York Times*, June 20, 1963, p. 18. Celler said the bill would be reported by the end of July and the House could "easily" pass the bill by "early September at the latest." See also Tom Wicker, "Kennedy's Program," *New York Times*, August 4, 1963, p. E9.

16. The Democrats held a 7-4 majority on Subcommittee No. 5.

17. U.S., Congress, *House Bill 7152*, Committee Print, October 2, 1963.

18. *New York Times*, October 16, p. 1; October 17, p. 1; October 24, p. 1; October 25, p. 1.

19. *C.Q. Almanac—1963*, pp. 348-349.

20. *New York Times*, October 30, 1963, pp. 1, 22. See also Anthony Lewis, "Civil Rights Compact," *New York Times*, October 30, 1963, p. 22.

21. Anthony Lewis, "Civil Rights Compact," *New York Times*, October 30, 1963, p. 22.

22. U.S., Congress, House, *Majority Report: Civil Rights Act of 1963*, Report No. 914, 88th Congress, lst Session, 1963.

23. *New York Times*, November 28, 1963, p. 20.

24. *C.Q. Almanac—1964*, pp. 344-353.

25. For a detailed resume of the system used to control the House floor debate see "Intensive Lobbying Marked House Civil Rights Debate," *Revolution in Civil Rights* (Washington, D.C.: Congressional Quarterly, Inc., 1965), pp. 44-46. One hundred and twenty-two amendments were proposed on the House floor; 28 were accepted by the bill's bipartisan managers.

26. "House Clears Bipartisan 1964 Bill, 290-130," *Revolution in Civil Rights* (Washington, D.C.: Congressional Quarterly, Inc., 1965), p. 43.

27. *Congressional Record*, CX, 2804-2805.

28. *New York Times*, June 15, 1963, p. 1.

29. *New York Times*, July 24, 1963, p. 1.

30. For a summary of racial disturbances in the summer of 1963, see *C.Q. Almanac—1963*, pp. 336-338.

31. *New York Times*, September 16, 1963, p. 1.

Chapter 6

The Civil Rights Act of 1964: Strategy

John G. Stewart

Pro-civil rights senators worked very hard to develop a strategy for defeating the expected southern filibuster of the House-passed civil rights bill. The major leader in this effort was Senator Hubert H. Humphrey of Minnesota, the Democratic whip, ably assisted by his Republican counterpart, Senator Thomas H. Kuchel of California. In this next section of his doctoral dissertation, John Stewart details how the strategy for passing the Civil Rights Act of 1964 in the Senate was debated and developed.[1]

The events of 1957, 1960, and 1962 illustrated the obstacles which the filibuster, or even the threat of a filibuster, imposed upon the Senate in considering civil rights legislation, and the difficulties faced by the senatorial party leaders, particularly the majority leader, in overcoming these obstacles. These earlier battles had revealed the leadership's preference for passing major substantive amendments, or for abandoning the legislation, as the way to free the Senate from the southern Democratic filibuster. In 1964, however, the sentiment in the House of Representatives to reject any significant dilution of the bill by the Senate, coupled with President Johnson's blanket endorsement of the House-passed bill, seemed to foreclose any strategy based on the earlier patterns of the well-timed and substantial compromise.

What strategy did Majority Leader Mansfield devise in these circumstances? For as much as he might have wished otherwise, the Senate had to consider civil rights, the one substantive issue which traditionally had been most difficult to handle. When H.R. 7152 arrived in the Senate on February 17, 1964, Mansfield declared:

> Let me say at the outset that I should have preferred it had the civil rights issue been resolved before my time as a senator or had it not come to the floor until afterward. The senator from Montana has no lust for conflict in connection with this matter; yet this question is one which invites conflict, for it divides deeply. . . . The time is now. The crossroads is here in the Senate.[2]

And in 1964 the president had broadened the issue to include proposals previously deemed beyond the reach of the national government, e.g., guaranteeing equal access to places of public accommodation and equal employment opportunity.

Much of Mansfield's prior three years as Democratic leader had been spent in mopping up legislative proposals left unfinished from earlier congresses and administrations. The majority leader's major task had been to keep the machinery well oiled and functioning, rather than to design elaborate stratagems to rescue hotly contested programs in a narrowly divided Senate. Mansfield's strategy of leadership had been well suited to this earlier environment, with its stress on decentralizing the power and responsibility of party leadership. Individual senators participated more broadly in the legislative process, and the standing committee chairmen assumed major responsibility for guiding legislation on the Senate floor.

With the exception of a marked slowdown in 1963, the Senate had responded well to Mansfield's loosening of the reins and his preference for giving others the spotlight and the publicity.[3] By mid-February, 1964, however, the controversy which surrounded the civil rights bill as it came to the

Senate, plus the extraordinary burden placed on the Democratic party leadership by the likelihood of a southern Democratic filibuster, and the absence of committee personnel to conduct the debate, raised definite questions about the adequacy of the majority leader's usual procedures.

For some months, Mansfield had been quietly preparing the groundwork for this encounter between senatorial norms and procedures and the urgent demands of the civil rights crisis. This advance preparation had reflected in almost all particulars the precepts of leadership which Mansfield followed in less dramatic and controversial legislative situations.

Cooperating with Everett Dirksen

Beginning at least two weeks prior to President John Kennedy's submission of his omnibus bill to Congress on June 19, 1963, Mansfield, on his own initiative, had been striving to establish a common front with Minority Leader Everett Dirksen (Rep., IL) in responding to what the president was likely to propose. Two factors appeared relevant to Mansfield's conduct at this point in early June, 1963. Given the southern Democrats' certain opposition to whatever the president would propose, it was clear that the legislation could be approved only with the support of a broad bipartisan coalition, surpassing in solidity and depth anything which had existed in prior civil rights battles. Without Dirksen's enthusiastic participation in this coalition, it could never function effectively. As summed up later by a member of Mansfield's staff: "If success [was] possible only on a bipartisan basis, then political initiative and any resulting credit which might develop therefrom should also be bipartisan. It was therefore essential that the bipartisan efforts be emphasized from the very beginning."[4]

Beyond this obvious factor, however, Mansfield's early negotiations with Dirksen were fully in accord with his normal modus operandi. The majority leader seemed always to consult in the most meticulous way with the minority leader on all leadership decisions. While part of Mansfield's motivation for these regular consultations with Dirksen undoubtedly stemmed from the need to line up support for the legislation at hand, he also appeared to act out of a deeply held conviction that the Senate, as an independent and autonomous body, had a vital institutional responsibility to exercise in responding to the president's legislative agenda.

In Mansfield's view, a sense of trust and mutual respect between the leaders of the respective parties, and hopefully between the parties themselves, was an essential ingredient in the Senate's orderly and responsible execution of its role in the governmental structure. This relationship could not endure if the normal differences between the senatorial parties were tinged with personal distrust, bitterness, or an attitude of victory at any price. Partisanship, while always a factor in the conduct of the Senate, had to be balanced with a sense of "institutionalism."

In this spirit, and benefitting from the good relations with Dirksen and most other Republicans which he had built up over the preceding three years, Mansfield sought out the minority leader to explore what areas of the omnibus civil rights package, if any, could be sponsored jointly by the leadership of both parties. At a minimum Mansfield also hoped to tone down Dirksen's initial reactions to the administration's program and avoid any flat condemnation which would make later negotiations more complex and difficult. To these ends informal discussions between the party leaders and their staffs first took place during the week of June 3, 1963. In the late afternoon of Thursday, June 13, Mansfield requested a meeting in the minority leader's office to identify specific areas of agreement and disagreement.[5]

Prior to this session, and in addition to his consultations with Mansfield, Dirksen had conferred on several occasions with President John F. Kennedy and his brother, Attorney

General Robert Kennedy. Dirksen had been kept generally informed of the administration's thinking on the substance of its civil rights proposals. Attorney General Robert Kennedy met with all Republican senators on June 10, 1963.[6] President John F. Kennedy then discussed the legislation with Republican leaders on June 11.[7] Finally, Attorney General Robert Kennedy met again with Dirksen for a 45-minute conversation on June 12.[8] These conferences reportedly resulted at least in part from a strong recommendation from Vice President Lyndon Johnson to consult closely with the Republican congressional leadership before sending the legislation to Capitol Hill.

As a result of these earlier deliberations, Dirksen on June 13, 1963, affirmed to Mansfield his support of all aspects of the administration's omnibus bill with one major exception: the enforceable provisions guaranteeing equal access to places of public accommodation.[9]

Hoping to resolve this crucial disagreement, the party leaders directed their staff assistants to spend the weekend attempting to draft a compromise proposal that both could accept. Dirksen appeared to favor either a totally voluntary public accommodations section, or one based on the 14th Amendment to the Constitution, rather than the commerce clause (Art. I, sec. 8) as proposed by the Kennedy administration.[10] Dirksen also stressed that his sponsorship of the other provisions would be subject to the approval of the Republican Conference (all the Republican senators meeting together to discuss proposed legislation).

These efforts to develop a mutually acceptable formula for dealing with segregated hotels, restaurants, lunch counters and gasoline stations did not, however, succeed. On Monday, June 17, 1963, Dirksen emerged from a bipartisan meeting of congressional leaders with President Kennedy to announce his opposition to the administration's public accommodations proposals. He also indicated his willingness to join with Mansfield in sponsoring the other sections of the bill.[11]

The next morning Mansfield summoned Majority Whip Humphrey to his office to review plans for receiving the administration's civil rights bill the following day.[12] Emphasizing the importance of maintaining a common Mansfield-Dirksen front at every step of the Senate's consideration of the legislation, Mansfield enumerated a three-pronged scheme for introducing the bill which he hoped would minimize the danger of forfeiting Dirksen's cooperation permanently and would also strengthen the leadership's control of the legislation in committee.

First, he and Dirksen would sponsor jointly a bill containing all the administration's proposals except Title II (integration of public accommodations). The majority leader, however, planned to declare his personal support of the public accommodations section. Mansfield also planned to acknowledge the problem of perfecting the most desirable approach for implementing Title II and that he intended to continue seeking a formula which both leaders could accept.

Second, Mansfield would introduce in his capacity as majority leader the administration's complete omnibus bill, but he asked Humphrey, in collaboration with Thomas Kuchel (Rep., CA), the minority whip, to assume primary responsibility for organizing senators to speak in favor of the bill when it arrived and for securing additional cosponsors. This arrangement would permit Mansfield greater restraint in his advocacy of the administration's total package, a posture more likely to engender a productive relationship with Dirksen.

Third, the majority leader and Warren Magnuson (Dem., WA), chairman of the Committee on Commerce, would introduce a bill limited solely to the public accommodations title (Title II) of the omnibus bill. Since the commerce clause of the Constitution served as the basis for the administration's proposals on public accommodations, Magnuson's Commerce Committee would normally receive a bill limited to that one provision, whereas the omnibus bill, as well as the Mansfield-Dirksen version, would normally be referred to the Judiciary Committee, chaired by Mississippi's James Eastland, a pro-segregation southern Democrat.

While Magnuson's committee could be counted on to hold hearings and report the Title II bill favorably, a far less hospitable reception awaited the omnibus bill in the Judiciary Committee. Indeed, few persons believed the legislation would reappear once it came under Senator Eastland's jurisdiction. Moreover, when the Magnuson public accommodations bill reached the Senate calendar following its approval by the Commerce Committee, other titles of the omnibus bill could be offered as amendments.

By dividing the administration's civil rights package into three elements, Mansfield hoped to retain maximum control of the legislation without jeopardizing his ties to Dirksen. Mansfield's plan illustrated the procedural options open to the majority leader, options which affected not only the *way* a particular bill was considered but also the substantive outcomes which might be achieved.

On Wednesday, June 19, 1963, President Kennedy sent his Civil Rights Bill of 1963 and an accompanying message to Capitol Hill.[13] Mansfield initiated the tripartite plan of introduction. He sponsored the omnibus bill (S. 1731)[14] but left to Humphrey and Kuchel the role of major advocates. He and Magnuson sponsored the public accommodations title in a separate bill (S. 1732).[15] And, later in the afternoon, following a conference of Republican senators where Dirksen discussed his plans with his party colleagues, the majority and minority floor leaders jointly sponsored a bill containing all the administration's proposals but Title II (S. 1750).[16] All senators were invited to cosponsor any or all of the three bills.

Shortly after the Senate convened, Mansfield described his collaboration with Dirksen: "If those who agree that something must be done do not, at the final moment, agree on something that can be done, there will be no bill. . . . It is in the attempt to approach this agreement on means that Senator Dirksen and I have worked together, in consultation with the president of the United States on this bill. We are not in accord on every point, such as the provisions dealing with public accommodations; but we are still constantly working toward agreement."[17]

During the eight months which intervened before the Senate again turned its attention to civil rights, Mansfield, awaiting the outcome of the House debate, made no further overtures to Dirksen. He did, however, explore with his staff possible procedures for retaining Dirksen's cooperation, even if they were unable to resolve their differences over public accommodations. The majority leader, for example, considered a scheme where he and Dirksen would collaborate in seeking to apply cloture on a Mansfield-Dirksen substitute bill, containing everything on which the two leaders could agree, but where Mansfield, after the application of cloture, would submit the issue of public accommodations to the Senate for a separate vote without Dirksen's support. Although a number of factors eventually militated against this procedure, it is noteworthy that Mansfield continued to think in terms of sustaining a common front with Dirksen regardless of the minority leader's position on Title II, then considered to be the heart of the bill.[18]

In summary, the early negotiations and maneuvers surrounding the introduction of the civil rights bill, and the subsequent discussions between Mansfield and his staff, laid the foundation for developing the bipartisan coalition which would be needed to overcome the southern Democratic filibuster. The factor of party affiliation was deliberately submerged in an effort to secure an effective institutional response. Despite the unique character of the civil rights bill, these initiatives by the majority leader did not represent a special ad hoc tactic designed for the moment, but rather were a predictable result of his basic strategy of leadership.

Encouraging a Fair and Reasoned Debate

The second major tenet of Mansfield's strategic response to the civil rights bill, which the majority leader initiated prior to the legislation's arrival in Congress, concerned his effort to insure the fair and reasoned conduct of the debate itself. Mansfield emphasized the importance of guaranteeing the southern Democrats' opportunity to oppose the legislation without fear of reprisal or sudden parliamentary maneuvers by the party leader.[19]

On February 17, 1964, Mansfield said: "The majority leader will propose in procedural matters, but it will rest with the Senate to dispose. . . . Even if there were parliamentary tricks or tactics, . . . the majority leader would not be inclined to employ them. I can think of nothing better designed to bring this institution into public disrepute and derision than a test of this profound and tragic issue by an exercise in parliamentary pyrotechnics."[20] As with his campaign to win Dirksen's support, Mansfield's motivation seemed to arise from a fortuitous combination of his beliefs as to the general conduct of the majority leadership and a more direct self-interest in passing this civil rights bill.

Mansfield believed he should strengthen the credibility of the Senate's independence in the legislative process. One factor in achieving this credibility, a factor over which he had some control as majority leader, was the character and conduct of the floor debate. Given his assumptions of the Senate's independent role in the governmental system, Mansfield believed that a controversial issue merited a searching and deliberate examination by all contending factions. Raw emotion, personal invective, or parliamentary slight-of-hand could only detract from the atmosphere of decorum and dignity of the debate. Recognizing that civil rights surpassed all other issues in its potential for discord and strife within the Democratic Party, and indeed within the Senate generally, the majority leader redoubled his efforts to avoid the debate's degeneration into an acrimonious encounter of name calling and chaos.

On February 17, 1964, Mansfield said: "I would devoutly hope that no senator will cast the first stone. I would devoutly hope that no senator will assume for his state a superior enlightenment on this issue. . . . There is moral perfection on this issue in none of us and in no place—North, South, East, or West—in the land."[21]

He also maintained that any attempt by the bill's proponents to steamroller the southern Democratic opposition by tactics such as round-the-clock sessions would only backfire. The southern Democrats would withstand the assault, and the sympathy of uncommitted Republicans holding the balance of power on cloture might be irretrievably sacrificed. Recalling then-Majority Leader Lyndon Johnson's predicament in 1960 when neither 24-hour sessions nor cloture could dent the filibuster, Mansfield determined at the outset that a major step toward victory would be achieved when the legitimacy of the southern Democratic opposition had been called into question.

When, and if, it became apparent that the southern Democrats had received full opportunity to debate the legislation on its merits, and when they had made their case to the Senate and the public at large, Mansfield believed that a further continuation of the filibuster would begin to appear as simple obstructionism to otherwise sympathetic senators. In an atmosphere where each senator had been able to pursue his particular concerns or interests, Mansfield hoped that cloture would become more of a viable alternative to the crucial senators, especially to the Republicans led by Everett Dirksen.

A staff memorandum to Senator Mansfield noted: "If there is any lesson to be learned from reading the history of the 1957 and 1960 civil rights experiences, it is that the slowest, fairest and most openhanded methods available should be used from the outset. In this regard there should be open and frank communication at all times, advance warning on major steps to be taken insofar as possible, and the use of purely standard procedure."[22]

Mansfield let the southern Democrats know at the outset that he would keep them fully informed of the Senate leadership's decisions on the civil rights bill. As soon as the Kennedy administration's general approach to the forthcoming legislation had been agreed upon, Mansfield asked Attorney General Robert Kennedy to brief the southern Democrats privately before all the specific provisions had been nailed down.

On Monday, June 10, 1963, Robert Kennedy met with Richard Russell and his southern colleagues in the Capitol. The attorney general stressed the administration's desire to draft a moderate statute, but one capable of averting further disorders such as took place in Birmingham, Alabama. Although Robert Kennedy had no illusions about the certainty of the southern Democrats' opposition to the bill, he attempted to allay their fears that the legislation would be punitive in nature. He suggested that passage of these relatively moderate proposals might avert more extreme measures by Congress or the administration if the racial unrest continued unchecked. The meeting between Robert Kennedy and the southern Democrats reportedly was free of personal invection or bitterness. Each side apparently understood the political forces which compelled the other.[23]

During the summer and fall of 1963, Mansfield continued to emphasize privately the importance of keeping lines of communication open to the southern Democrats and avoiding the use of unusual or questionable parliamentary tactics. He raised with his staff the wisdom of using the Senate Rule XIV procedure for placing the civil rights bill passed by the House directly on the Senate calendar and bypassing the Judiciary Committee. This was the parliamentary device first used by William Knowland (Rep., CA) and Paul Douglas (Dem., IL) in keeping the 1957 civil rights bill out of James Eastland's committee. Mansfield feared that the Democratic leaders' use of this unusual tactic would render them vulnerable to the charge of shortcircuiting the legislative process.

Several alternative methods for bringing the civil rights issue before the Senate were developed, although Mansfield postponed any final decision on the matter until the House had completed its work on the bill.[24] Indeed, until the substance of the House bill was finally determined, these investigations by Mansfield had to remain speculative. They did, however, shed light on Mansfield's desire to take whatever steps were possible to maintain good relations with the southern Democrats and, in general, to foster a spirit of respect and tolerance among all senators during the forthcoming debate.

Selection of Humphrey as Floor Manager

As the House of Representatives neared the end of its work on the civil rights bill, Mansfield decided to ask his majority whip, Hubert Humphrey, to assume the job of floor manager for the legislation when it reached the Senate. Usually this crucial and time-consuming task fell to the chairman of the committee or subcommittee that considered the legislation, or to someone designated by the chairman. In the case of the civil rights bill of 1964, however, the Judiciary Committee almost certainly would not report legislation to the Senate. The aversion of its chairman, James Eastland of Mississippi, to assuming the job of floor manager was exceeded only by the administration's determination to keep the bill out of his hands.

Humphrey, on the other hand, seemed to be an excellent choice. His long-standing involvement in the struggle for civil rights legislation was balanced by an informed and realistic view of the legislative process. His credentials with outside civil rights groups were impeccable. And, as majority whip, he had participated fully in the White House discussions during the bill's preparation and the subsequent meetings of congressional leaders during its debate in the House. Designating the whip as floor manager would also tend to reinforce the leadership's control of this complex and highly controversial bill.

The choice of Humphrey made sense to Mansfield for several other reasons. In addition to the majority leader's normal aversion to an assignment which would involve sustained public attention, he believed that his most effective contribution to the conduct of the debate could be in keeping up his frequent and off-the-record visits with Everett Dirksen in the hopes of gradually winning him over. To the extent that Mansfield could avoid defending the controversial sections of the legislation publicly, these relations with the minority leader stood to prosper. Or, alternatively, to the degree which Mansfield became identified as the measure's principal defender in the Senate, his relations with Dirksen and other uncommitted senators would be more strained. This posture, in short, would hamper his possible usefulness as mediator between the Senate and the president of the United States when crucial decisions had to be made.[25]

Hubert Humphrey subsequently noted in a memorandum: "Mansfield gave me all possible cooperation. He wanted to be at liberty to work closely with Dirksen and not be too directly involved with the day-to-day details on the floor. . . . He was more or less a free man, able to contact Dirksen at will, while I was in charge of the routine day-to-day details on the floor of the Senate."[26]

Mansfield also had no desire for repeated confrontations with 18 southern Democrats, many of them chairmen of important standing Senate committees. He needed their cooperation and support on countless items of Senate business each session. He also wanted to preserve as high a level of party stability as conditions would permit. Although the majority leader had made clear his support for a strong civil rights bill, he sought to avoid exacerbating his personal relation's with the southern Democrats by constant exposure on this bitterly contested issue.

In his regular duties as majority whip, Humphrey had demonstrated a great flair for the tactical details of floor leadership: nose counting, procedure, stalling for time, timing of amendments, debating ability, switching votes, and the like. In a real sense he had assumed a good portion of that tactical burden, which Lyndon Johnson deliberately made the sole province of the majority leadership during his tenure in the office. This talent, a peculiar mixture of intuition, diligence, and reliable sources of information, seemed an essential attribute for the person serving as the bill's floor manager.

Finally, Humphrey wanted the job. He viewed the forthcoming struggle as a culmination of 15 years of agitation within the Senate to pass civil rights legislation of this scope and significance. Humphrey later wrote: "This assignment was one that I appreciated, and yet one that I realized would test me in every way."[27]

The majority leader also asked three other senators to work with Humphrey: Warren Magnuson (Dem., WA) to manage the debate on public accommodations; Philip Hart (Dem., MI) on voting and other judicial questions; and Joseph Clark (Dem., PA) on equal employment opportunity. Mansfield announced these appointments on the Senate floor on February 17, 1964, the day H.R. 7152, the administration civil right bill, arrived from the House of Representatives.[28]

Organization of the Civil Rights Forces

Recognizing fully the importance and difficulty of this assignment, Humphrey began fleshing out the leadership's strategy. Humphrey was in full agreement with Mansfield's emphasis on maintaining a dignified debate, one which avoided acrimonious disputes with the southern Democrats and permitted them every opportunity to make their case against the bill. Humphrey subsequently noted:

> I made up my mind early that I would keep my patience. I would not lose my temper, and that if I could do nothing else, I would try to preserve a reasonable degree of good nature and fair play in the Senate. I had good working relationships at all times with the southerners, even on some of the more difficult days. . . . I also knew that it would hurt me politically and reflect adversely upon the Senate if we got into an acrimonious, bitter name-calling debate. And therefore at all times I tried to keep the Senate on an equilibrium with a degree of respect and friendliness.[29]

Humphrey also saw the need for considerable strengthening of the pro-civil rights forces in and outside the Senate. Mansfield's deliberate decentralization of procedures for controlling floor debate meant, in effect, that Humphrey had to recentralize certain functions in the hands of the party leaders for the duration of the civil rights debate. With the general approval of the majority leader, Humphrey set about taking a number of specific actions which Mansfield had neither the desire nor the aptitude to initiate.

As a member of the civil rights bloc which had suffered so many humiliating defeats and disappointments in the past, both in its efforts to amend Rule XXII (the filibuster rule)and to pass substantive legislation, Humphrey was determined to eliminate the disorganization and internal bickering which had characterized all earlier efforts. Indeed, he considered the question of whether the civil rights forces could sustain a coordinated offensive for a period of months as probably decisive in passing an acceptable bill. Such a convincing and spirited demonstration would have to include answering quorum calls promptly, defeating all compromise amendments opposed by the bipartisan leadership, and offering a reasoned defense of the bill's merits on the Senate floor. It meant, in short, generating confidence among the bill's supporters that victory was possible and fighting the normal pressures for concession and compromise that were bound to spring up once the filibuster had run for several weeks.[30]

Evidence of weakness, disorganization, or discouragement would, conversely, increase the probability of losing the support of those senators holding the balance of power on cloture and embolden those who sought major concessions. Dirksen, in particular, could be expected to assess carefully the desire of the civil rights forces to match their stirring words on behalf of racial justice with specific deeds. His judgments on cloture and the substance of the legislation could not help but be influenced by the commitment and tenacity demonstrated by the supposed advocates of the bill.

Humphrey went out of his way to establish good relations with Everett Dirksen. He recorded in a memorandum: "On my first TV appearance I praised Senator Dirksen, telling the nation that he would help, that he would support a good civil rights bill, that he would put his country above party, that he would look upon this issue as a moral issue and not a partisan issue. I did so not only because I believed what I said, but because we also needed him. . . . We couldn't possibly get cloture without Dirksen and his help."[31]

If at some point in the debate the legitimacy of the southern Democratic filibuster began to be questioned by the uncommitted senators, Humphrey believed that the usual pressures for concession and compromise might be transformed into pressures for applying cloture. This crucial shift in sentiment, however, appeared unlikely to develop until the civil rights forces established their ability to sustain the fight indefinitely, to outlast the southern Democrats no matter how long it took. Humphrey vowed that for once the senators supporting civil rights would be organized as effectively as those in opposition.

Following Mansfield's announcement of his appointment as floor manager, Humphrey conferred with senators Hart, Magnuson, Clark, and others about their organizational plans. He also communicated promptly with Thomas Kuchel of California, the minority whip, whom Dirksen had chosen as floor manager for the Republicans. During this period, Department of Justice personnel, led by Nicholas Katzenbach, the deputy attorney general, and Burke Marshall, the assistant attorney general for civil rights, spent many hours briefing Humphrey on the bill's substance, as well as discussing strategy. By Friday, March 6, 1964, Humphrey, Magnuson, Hart, and Clark had agreed on the following plan of action.[32]

The Strategy for Stopping the Filibuster

1. Additional "captains" would be appointed to manage each title of H.R. 7152. In addition to Hart's responsibility for Title I (voting rights), Magnuson's for Title II (integration of public accommodations), and Clark's for Title VII (equal employment opportunity), Humphrey designated Wayne Morse (Dem., OR) in charge of Title III (desegregation of public facilities and the attorney general's powers); Paul Douglas (Dem., IL) of Title IV (school desegregation); Edward Long (Dem., MO) of Title V (Civil Rights Commission); John Pastore (Dem., RI) of Title VI (cutoff of federal funds); and Thomas Dodd (Dem., CT) of Title VIII, IX, X, and XI (Community Relations Service and miscellaneous provisions). These senators would present their respective titles on the Senate floor and generally assist Humphrey in their defense.

Not only did this arrangement relieve Humphrey and his three principal assistants of the burden of mastering the details of the entire bill, but it also involved a broader cross section of the senatorial party in the leadership's offensive. Given the penchant of many of these senators for public advocacy, Humphrey considered it prudent to provide such opportunities at the outset.

In a memorandum Humphrey later noted: "When each senator had a chance to debate the bill, title by title, they also had an opportunity to get some good press for themselves. This was good not only for the issue itself, but also for the senators and their public relations. . . . It involved them also in active floor duty, in constant and in sharp debate with the opposition. They became ever more committed."[33]

2. A special whip system would be established to help senators respond promptly to quorum calls. The Democrats agreed to keep at least 35 senators in Washington each day to answer quorums. The Republicans promised 15. Whenever a senator had been assigned to "quorum duty," he or she had to produce a replacement if he or she could not be present as scheduled. The Democratic Policy Committee maintained a master chart to record on a daily basis the whereabouts of all non-southern Democrats. Staff assistants of six senators—Frank Church (Dem., ID), Edward Kennedy (Dem., MA), Thomas McIntyre (Dem., NH), Patrick McNamara (Dem., MI), Edmund Muskie (Dem., ME), and Gaylord Nelson (Dem., WI)—each agreed to telephone the offices of five or six additional senators to alert them to impending quorum calls. These special arrangements had but one objective: to produce 51 senators as quickly as possible whenever a filibustering southern Democrat "suggested the absence of a quorum."

3. Senators would be assigned on a rotating basis to monitor the Senate floor throughout the debate. They would guard against any sudden parliamentary maneuvers by the southern Democrats and occasionally pepper the fili-

bustering senator with questions. It was assumed that most senators not on duty would rarely spend time on the floor, appearing only to answer quorum calls. But Humphrey insisted that a corporal's guard had to be present at all times. He also planned to spend several hours each day personally debating the bill.

4. The civil rights forces would publish a daily newsletter. This mimeographed single sheet would be distributed each morning to friendly senators, providing them with a schedule of the day's activities on the Senate floor, a list of the day's floor monitors, rebuttals to southern Democratic arguments, and generally serve to dramatize the impression of organization and effectiveness which the civil rights forces were attempting to create.[34]

5. A staff meeting would be held in Humphrey's whip office approximately 15 minutes before the Senate convened each day to discuss current plans and problems with title captains, their staff assistants, and Justice Department officials. Twice a week the lobbyists from the Leadership Conference on Civil Rights would be invited to attend these meetings. These sessions would serve to keep the various leaders in close touch and would help identify potential trouble before it reached the crisis stage. Additional meetings would also be necessary to handle the more crucial developments.

Maintaining Republican Support

Having agreed with his Democratic colleagues on a scheme of organization, Humphrey turned his attention to firming up relations with the Republican advocates of a strong civil rights bill. Operationally this group numbered between 6 and 12 senators, depending on the issue at hand. Although there was little doubt about these senators supporting the basic concepts of H.R. 7152, several issues threatened the effectiveness of the bipartisan coalition needed to pass a strong bill. Indeed, so much attention had been paid to Everett Dirksen and his more conservative colleagues in the Republican Party that few persons recognized the problems between Republican and Democratic proponents of civil rights. If relationships among the civil rights activists in the two parties could not be harmonized, what hope existed for winning the support of the less-committed Republicans?

Beginning in the mid-1950s and continuing up to 1963, a bipartisan core of civil rights proponents introduced in each Congress a series of activist civil rights bills, usually patterned after the recommendations of the U.S. Commission on Civil Rights. In these years congressional action on these proposals was highly unlikely. By early 1963, however, this informal civil rights coalition was experiencing certain stresses. The Republicans had few compunctions against advocating a number of strong legislative remedies to the growing civil rights crisis and did not hesitate to criticize President Kennedy when his civil rights messages did not include these far-reaching proposals. But the Republicans also continued to seek Democratic cosponsorship of their bills, a move which at least indirectly would have implied criticism of President Kennedy by senators of his own party.

In March, 1963, Humphrey, Douglas, Clark, and Hart, the Democrats' principal civil rights activists, met to consider their course of action in these delicate political circumstances. Although they personally favored a more vigorous posture by the Kennedy administration, they agreed unanimously to advocate these policies within the councils of the administration and to avoid any public action which might be interpreted as criticism of the president. They agreed to support President Kennedy's civil rights proposals of February 28, 1963, and attempt to build a broader base of support among their Democratic colleagues. They would also withhold their names from bills sponsored by Republicans. In sum, the Republican and Democratic civil rights factions would have separate packages of legislation. The common front of the past few congresses had been broken.[35]

The subsequent events in Birmingham, Alabama, and the president's decision to submit a new omnibus bill altered this situation considerably. Legislation of the magnitude advocated by the Republican activists had been proposed by the Democratic administration. A restoration of bipartisan unity appeared essential for these proposals to pass.

The Democrats' reawakened concern for good relations with the Republican backers of civil rights was first demonstrated when President Kennedy's omnibus bill came to the Senate on June 19, 1963. Humphrey, who upon Mansfield's request was coordinating the introduction of the administration's complete omnibus bill (S. 1731), sought to limit additional cosponsors to an equal number of Republican and Democratic senators, approximately nine from each party. Since many more Democrats than Republicans sought to cosponsor the omnibus bill, Humphrey hoped to prevent a heavy imbalance of Democrats. But Humphrey soon discovered that Democrats who favored the bill were unwilling to withhold their names in the spirit of bipartisanship, and his plan collapsed before the end of the afternoon. When the Senate adjourned, 42 senators were listed as cosponsors. Only eight were Republicans.[36]

The political instincts which opened the schism between the Democrats and Republicans in early 1963 did not simply vanish upon submission of the omnibus legislation. The Republicans, in particular, saw President Kennedy, and later President Johnson, walking off with the major accolades for proposing and passing the legislation, despite earlier efforts of the Republican activists to promote stronger civil rights action.

Partisan sniping broke out soon after the House passed the administration civil rights bill. On February 16, 1964, Republican senators Hugh Scott (Rep., PA) and Thruston Morton (Rep., KY) said they suspected a "deal" had been engineered by the Johnson administration to gain southern

Democratic votes for the tax reduction bill, recently passed by the Senate, in exchange for weakening of the civil rights bill.[37] Humphrey denied the charges the following day. "The only deal needed in the Senate," he said, "is a deal between the Republicans and the Democrats to carry into action the provisions of the Emancipation Proclamation."[38]

A week later Senator Jacob Javits (Rep., NY) said cloture could only be invoked if "President [Johnson] puts the same kind of strength behind it as he is credited with putting behind the tax bill."[39] And on February 27, 1964, Javits joined his fellow New York Republican, Kenneth Keating, in opposing the Democratic leadership's decision to pass the wheat-cotton bill before moving on to civil rights. They argued that the southern Democrats' interest in the cotton legislation might compel them to expedite the civil rights bill if the latter were taken up first.[40] Scott put the issue more bluntly when he addressed a Philadelphia civil rights rally. He charged the Democratic leaders in the Senate with putting "cotton before people."[41]

These rumblings by no means indicated an open break between the Republican and Democratic civil rights supporters. But they did disclose the potentiality for partisan warfare with the bipartisan civil rights coalition being destroyed in the process.

The Democratic leadership was especially fearful that a break with the Republicans might occur over attempts to strengthen still further certain provisions of the House bill. The Republican civil rights supporters in the Senate, principally Kenneth Keating (Rep., NY), Jacob Javits (Rep., NY), Hugh Scott (Rep., PA), Clifford Case (Rep., NJ), and Thomas Kuchel (Rep., CA), talked of offering various amendments to remedy alleged weak spots in the House bill. Regardless of the motives involved, such strengthening amendments placed the Democratic leadership in a dilemma. If they opposed the amendments, they opened themselves to criticism from the civil rights movement. If they supported the amendments, they jeopardized further the likelihood of gaining the support of the uncommitted senators holding the balance of power on cloture.

Beyond this difficulty, however, loomed an even more troublesome consideration. The adoption of any strengthening amendment would violate President Johnson's stated policy, one supported by the Democratic leaders, of passing H.R. 7152 essentially intact. If this were done, the House could be persuaded to agree to the minor Senate amendments and the bill would go to the White House for the president to sign into law. If the Senate made major changes, however, there would be a conference with the House of Representatives to resolve differences in the two bills. Since taking the bill to conference also gave the troublesome House Committee on Rules another opportunity for delay, as well as the southern Democrats in the Senate another opportunity to filibuster the conference report, the Democratic senatorial leaders wanted to preserve the House text of H.R. 7152.

For example, on the TV news program, "Meet the Press," March 8, 1964, Humphrey said: "I think it would be desirable for us to take the work that has already been completed in the House and pass it in the Senate. That would avoid, sir, going back through the House again, through conference and bringing it back to the Senate."

Humphrey also believed that any sign of dissension within the bipartisan ranks of the civil rights senators over strengthening amendments would encourage the diehard southern opponents to prolong the struggle. For all of these reasons, he felt it vital to establish stable working relationships with the Republicans before any of these problems became more acute.

Fortunately, Humphrey enjoyed a warm personal relationship with Kuchel, the Republican floor manager for the civil rights bill. Upon learning of their respective assignments to direct the floor debate of H.R. 7152, the two senators began discussing informally ways to promote bipartisan unity. On February 28 and March 9, 1964, Humphrey met with Kuchel to review the general organizational plan developed by the Democratic leadership.

Humphrey sought full participation by the Republicans. Kuchel endorsed the idea of the title captains making an affirmative presentation once the bill became the Senate's pending business. Dirksen had already announced Republican counterparts to the Democratic title captains. They included Kenneth Keating (NY) for Title I, Roman Hruska (NE) for Title II, Jacob Javits (NY) for Title III, John Sherman Cooper (KY) for Title IV, Hugh Scott (PA) for Title V, Norris Cotton (NH) for Title VI, and Clifford Case (NJ) for Title VII.[42] Hruska and Cotton subsequently declined to serve and were never replaced.

Instead of relinquishing the Senate floor to the southern Democrats, the usual procedure in past filibusters, Humphrey and Kuchel believed a thorough title-by-title presentation by bipartisan teams would help discredit the argument of the bill being rushed through the Senate. It would also provide an opportunity to refute some of the serious misrepresentations of the bill's effects and would generate favorable news. This might partially blunt the opening attack by southern Democrats.

Kuchel also agreed to collaborate in publishing the daily civil rights newsletter and to invite Republican title captains to the daily staff meetings in Humphrey's office. In meeting their daily quota of 15 senators to answer quorum calls, however, the Republicans declined to use the Democrats' master chart maintained by the Democratic Policy Committee.[43]

The crucial question of strengthening amendments remained unresolved. Although Humphrey and Kuchel recognized the dangers in changing the House bill, neither could suggest a way to prevent determined senators from offering amendments. Neither whip possessed the sanctions to enforce such an edict. In fact, Kuchel himself had already raised publicly the possibility of strengthening H.R.

7152 by making Title I (voting rights) applicable to state as well as U.S. elections and by stiffening the provisions of the public accommodations section.[44] He repeated these suggestions on the Senate floor several weeks later.[45] Senators were simply encouraged to check all strengthening amendments with Humphrey or Kuchel, but this proposal was never implemented in practice.[46]

Humphrey could only keep the situation under surveillance. If senators introduced strengthening amendments and attempted to call them up for a vote, further steps would then have to be considered. Although this major problem of Democratic-Republican relations remained unsettled, the Humphrey-Kuchel discussions resulted in shared responsibility for the pending measure and a general commitment to work together in the coming debate. Whether this tenuous alliance would survive the strains and pressures of the coming weeks could not be predicted by either floor manager.

Organization of Outside Support

While the pro-civil rights forces were drawing up their organizational plans, Humphrey began coordinating these efforts with the activities of the Leadership Conference on Civil Rights and other friendly groups and individuals. Relations between the Democratic leadership and the Leadership Conference lobbyists were also less secure than one would have normally suspected.

In early 1963 Leadership Conference members were disappointed that President Kennedy limited his civil rights proposals essentially to the field of voting rights. For example, on May 28, 1963, Clarence Mitchell of the NAACP told Celler's Judiciary subcommittee: "I have been around here long enough to know that if you start off with a program that emphasizes voter registration and legislation to protect the right to vote you will wind up not only with that but also it will be a watered down version of what you started out with.... The main thing that is needed is something like Part III [giving the U.S. attorney general the power to intervene in civil rights disputes]."[47]

Several months later, a major bulwark of the Leadership Conference, the AFL-CIO, expressed dismay over the reported omnibus bill under preparation in the White House. A memorandum transmitted to the president's staff stressed the absolute necessity of an equal employment opportunity provision and strengthening other sections. The memorandum concluded by noting that "the labor movement cannot itself afford to settle for less than strong, forthright legislation. Any bill which does not include the provisions listed herein . . . will have to be termed inadequate by the AFL-CIO."[48] This AFL-CIO memorandum was taken to the White House by Senator Humphrey during the drafting sessions which preceded the bill's submission to Congress on June 19, 1963.

Finally, the forceful lobbying activities of the Leadership Conference membership had produced a greatly strengthened bill as reported by the Celler subcommittee in the House, a version which the administration moderated in a number of respects before the bill came to the House floor.[49]

With these events providing a backdrop to the Senate debate, the Leadership Conference members were determined to stop any massive compromises of H.R. 7152 as the price for passage. Their approach to the problem was simple and straightforward. Hold the Senate in session until a noncompromised bill passed, all year if necessary. Institute round-the-clock sessions if the filibuster continued. Arrest absent Senators who failed to answer quorums. And under no circumstances consider approving any legislation less stringent than the bill approved by the House. In particular, do not sacrifice Title VII (equal employment opportunity) or dilute the enforceability of Title II (public accommodations) in order to win the cooperation of Everett Dirksen. Moreover, the Leadership Conference lobbyists were deeply suspicious that Mansfield and Dirksen would unexpectedly unveil this kind of secret deal and that Humphrey and Kuchel would be unable to prevent such a catastrophe.[50]

The chief Leadership Conference strategists, Joseph L. Rauh, Jr., and Clarence Mitchell, Jr., were especially fearful of an early effort by Mansfield to apply cloture. In their view, any attempt for cloture in the early weeks of the debate was bound to lose. This loss would make the legislation vulnerable to major concessions as the way to extricate the Senate from the grip of the southern Democratic filibuster. These fears of an early cloture effort were reinforced by a visit Rauh and Mitchell paid to Majority Leader Mansfield during the closing days of the House debate. They promptly began circulating the phrase, "cloture means compromise," and sought methods to pass the bill without cloture.

In addition to exhausting the southern Democratic speakers by round-the-clock sessions, Rauh and Mitchell proposed that Mansfield and Humphrey enforce Rule XIX strictly, the provisions which specified: "No senator shall speak more than twice upon any one question in debate on the same day without leave of the Senate." Rauh and Mitchell reasoned that if the Senate recessed each day instead of adjourning (thereby preserving the same legislative, as distinct from calendar, day), the southern Democrats would eventually exhaust their two speeches and the filibuster would necessarily terminate.

Fearing a sellout in the Senate, stressing the dangers of relying on cloture, and proposing the two-speech rule as the best way to overcome the southern Democratic filibuster, Rauh and Mitchell came to Humphrey's office on February 28, 1964, to review strategy with the majority whip and Kuchel, his Republican counterpart.[51] Humphrey reviewed briefly his ideas for organizing the civil rights forces in the Senate. He and Kuchel emphasized the important role which church-related groups could play in dramatizing the moral dimensions of the civil rights struggle. In response, Rauh and Mitchell outlined the plans of the Commission on Religion and Race of the National Council of Churches, the National Catholic Welfare Conference, and several Jewish religious groups for bringing state delegations of clergy and laymen to Washington and for organizing extensive grassroots campaigns in critical states, especially in the Midwest.

The floor managers cautioned against any blatant attempt to pressure senators like Dirksen into supporting the bill. Such tactics, they stressed, would likely have the opposite effect and make their cooperation even harder to secure. The Leadership Conference could, however, usefully urge senators to answer quorum calls promptly and to remain in Washington whenever they were listed for quorum duty. Residents of the senators' states could tactfully remind absent members of their primary obligation to stay in Washington until the civil rights bill passed.

In closing, Humphrey and Kuchel discussed their desire to keep emotion and acrimony to a minimum and declared flatly their opposition to any tactic such as arresting absent senators, which would increase bitterness and hard feeling. They discussed the prospects of using the two-speech rule and pointed out the principal defect in the Rauh-Mitchell proposal. Since two speeches could be delivered by each senator on every *amendment* as well as on the bill itself, the southern Democrats could offer as many amendments as were necessary to continue the filibuster indefinitely.

Humphrey and Kuchel pledged, however, that cloture would not be attempted until its application was certain and that the Senate leadership would settle for nothing weaker than the House bill. The meeting ended with a promise to conduct the civil rights campaign in the Senate on a bipartisan basis and to consult frequently with the Leadership Conference lobbyists.[52]

Rauh and Mitchell left Humphrey's office feeling somewhat more optimistic about the floor leaders' determination to fight for a strong bill and their willingness to work closely with the civil rights organizations. Yet their concern about a secret deal between Mansfield and Dirksen had not been allayed.[53] In fact, Humphrey and Kuchel recognized that conditions could develop in such a way that concession and compromise would appear as the only way to end the debate. In these circumstances they would be relatively powerless to stop a compromise between Mansfield and Dirksen and the southern Democrats. If Mansfield and Dirksen followed Lyndon Johnson's 1957 formula, and if the southern Democrats bought the deal, the compromisers would have gained the decisive edge.

Relations with President Johnson

In 1964 the person best situated to head off such a repetition of Lyndon Johnson's strategy of 1957 was, of course, President Lyndon Johnson. The leaders of both senatorial parties knew his unwavering support would be needed to invest their efforts with the unity, coherence, and momentum that could ward off any sudden capitulation to the southern Democrats.

The civil rights battles of 1957, 1960, and 1962 demonstrated the effect of marginal presidential support during a filibuster or if a filibuster was threatened. In 1957, for example, President Eisenhower undercut his congressional leaders when they were fighting to preserve "Part III." Three years later he made no public effort to discourage the close collaboration between Majority Leader Johnson and Minority Leader Dirksen in turning back all attempts to restore to the Civil Rights Act of 1960 certain provisions deleted by the House of Representatives.

In 1962 President Kennedy offered little resistance to the abandonment of his literacy test legislation after it was blocked for three weeks by a southern Democratic filibuster. Alternatively, President Kennedy's forceful advocacy of the Communications Satellite proposal in 1962, coordinated closely with the joint efforts of Mansfield and Dirksen to impose cloture, brought that debate to a successful conclusion without the adoption of any major substantive amendments. Although presidential support, standing alone, could not transform a lost cause into victory, it might determine the actions of the senatorial party leaders in a closely contested situation when the pressures for compromise were rising in the heat of a filibuster.

President Johnson never wavered in his commitment to the Civil Rights Act of 1964. He had taken an active role during the bill's preparation, counseling President Kennedy on the need for Republican support and the importance of organizing external groups supporting the legislation. Later he stressed the urgency of prompt congressional action in his November 27, 1963, address to the joint session of Congress following President Kennedy's assassination. He renewed this commitment in his first State-of-the-Union address. "Let this session of Congress," Johnson said, "be known as the session which did more for civil rights than the last hundred sessions combined."[54]

Following passage of the bill by the House of Representatives, rumors abounded of President Johnson's alleged willingness to compromise the enforceability of the public accommodations section in order to insure the bill's passage in the Senate. For example, on February 16, 1964, the *New York Times* noted a story carried the previous day on CBS News that President Johnson had told two southern senators he was willing to limit the public accommodations section of the bill.[55] The report was denied by the White House press office the next day.

As noted above, several Republican senators made similar accusations [of a possible Johnson sellout]. But at his press conference of February 29, 1964, the president again spelled out his position on the issue: "The civil rights bill that passed the House is the bill that this administration recommends. I am in favor of it passing the Senate *exactly in its present form*. . . . We stand on the House bill."[56]

Johnson was no less adamant in private. He personally assured Clarence Mitchell and Joseph Rauh of the Leadership Conference of his determination to stand solidly behind the House bill and to oppose vigorously any effort to weaken the bill in the Senate.[57] He brought the same message to Mansfield and Humphrey and indicated his willingness to wait months until the Senate passed the kind of bill he wanted, even if this jeopardized other important parts of his legislative program. The president also pointed out to his Democratic leaders that the southern Democrats were much less prepared physically to repeat their performance of 1960. He urged the application of unremitting pressure, round-the-clock sessions if necessary, as the surest and swiftest way of bringing the debate to a successful conclusion.[58]

But aside from reinforcing his support for the House bill and urging Mansfield and Humphrey to get tough with the southern Democrats, President Johnson did not become deeply involved in the detailed planning and negotiations. In his memorandum on the Senate debate, Humphrey noted: "We did not bother the president very much. We did give him regular reports on the progress of civil rights over at the Tuesday morning breakfasts. But the president was not put on the spot. He was not enlisted in the battle particularly."[59]

The Democratic leaders kept the president fully informed of the bill's progress and met with him informally from time to time. The president also relied heavily on the judgment and skill of the Department of Justice personnel, including Attorney General Robert Kennedy, Deputy Attorney General Katzenbach, and Assistant Attorney General Burke Marshall, who were working closely with Mansfield and Humphrey at every stage of the debate. The White House legislative staff, directed by Lawrence O'Brien, kept in touch with both the Department of Justice officials and the congressional leadership.

President Johnson's posture of total support for H.R. 7152 undoubtedly had important political implications. He may have sought to erase the final vestiges of doubt about his commitment to the cause of racial justice.[60] But regardless of motive, his unqualified endorsement of the bill had an even greater impact on Capitol Hill. It provided the Democratic leadership with an absolute mandate to wage the struggle in terms of total victory. And as the debate droned on inconclusively, this level of presidential support proved vital in sustaining an effort which otherwise might have fallen victim to the normal senatorial pressure for concession and compromise.

The Southern Democratic Strategy

Following a strategy conference of southern Democratic senators, Richard Russell of Georgia, generalissimo of the forces opposing the civil rights bill, summed up their plans concisely: "We intend to fight this bill with all the vigor at our command."[61]

In senatorial shorthand, this one line pronouncement translated into a guarantee of many weeks debate by the southern Democrats until the atmosphere became ripe for major concessions. On March 29, 1964, immediately after the Senate refused to send H.R. 7152 to the Judiciary Committee, Russell spelled out the other crucial element of his plan: "We shall enter into the battle next week with the earnest hope and prayer that we may find the means and strength to bring the facts of the issue to the people of this self-governing republic before it is too late."[62]

Planning once again to use his battle-tested three-platoon system, Russell confidently believed his forces could forestall for months any major votes on the bill. During this period of "extended debate," the southern Democratic leader banked on public sentiment rising against the bill so that cloture could not be invoked without major surgery to the legislation. Various factors were seen contributing to this anti-civil rights sentiment: (1) continued racial unrest and disruptions throughout the country; (2) the entry of Alabama's governor, George C. Wallace, in the Wisconsin, Indiana, and Maryland primaries; and (3) the national campaign against the bill being carried forward by the Co-ordinating Committee for Fundamental American Freedoms.

Russell also believed that the proponents of the legislation would end up fighting among themselves. The southern Democratic leader hoped that the over-zealous church and civil rights groups would over pressure and eventually lose the support of the crucial, uncommitted senators, particularly Everett Dirksen. Dirksen soon responded in precisely this fashion to zealous picketing by members of the Congress of Racial Equality (CORE). On February 17, 1964, he said on the Senate floor: "If the day ever comes when, under pressure, or as a result of picketing or other devices, I shall be pushed from the rock where I must stand to render an independent judgment, my justification in public life will have come to an end."[63]

Recognizing the improbability of totally blocking the legislation, Russell knew that the adoption of major amendments would provoke a parliamentary crisis when the bill returned to the House of Representatives. The Republican House leaders had announced their refusal to accept any significant concessions made by the Senate. This potential deadlock, when compounded by the possibility of further complications arising out of the national political conventions scheduled for the summer, gave Russell hope that, at a minimum, the most offensive provisions of the bill could be excised. Another possibility, less likely, was that the legislation could become mired by disagreements between the House and Senate and ultimately abandoned.[64]

The arithmetic of the situation gave credence to Russell's strategy of extending the debate until major changes were achieved. If he could convince just 15 senators drawn from the ranks of conservative Republicans and border and far-west Democrats to withhold their support for cloture, this number, in addition to his southern contingent of 19 (including Republican John Tower of Texas), would be sufficient to keep the filibuster alive indefinitely.

Appearing on the CBS news program "Face the Nation," Russell developed a thesis that seemed likely to attract the support of many of these senators whose votes were essential to applying cloture. "The public accommodation section, as severe as it is," he stated, "is not the worst provision in the bill." Instead, Russell pointed to Title VI (cutoff of U.S. funds) and Title VII (equal employment opportunity) as being "much more damaging" to the American economic and governmental system.[65]

Russell soon expanded this thesis on the Senate Floor: "The bill is the answer to a bureaucrat's dream. It is the realization of a bureaucrat's prayers. . . . I honestly believe that no bill has ever been submitted to the American Congress that poses a greater threat to our forms of government, that threatens to substitute a government of men—men clothed with an official title but operating without the restraint of law—that is posed by the pending measure."[66]

Russell faced one major obstacle in determining his tactics of opposition. As demonstrated by Strom Thurmond's (Dem., SC) one-man 24-hour filibuster at the conclusion of the 1957 civil rights debate, there existed among the southern Democrats varying degrees of anti-civil rights commitment and realism which Russell had to take into account. It seemed likely that Thurmond might prove equally obstinate in blocking votes on compromise amendments or other tactical moves by the southern Democrats designed to drain off pressure for cloture.

Russell's problems were not unlike those faced by any party leader having to adjust his strategy and tactics in accordance with the demands of influential party members. Since Russell and his southern colleagues could not afford politically to appear less opposed to the civil rights bill than Thurmond, their strategy became one simply of prolonging the debate, avoiding cloture, and banking on the usual pressures for compromise to destroy any chance of passing the bill intact.[67]

A number of observers saw the southern Democratic strategy for defeating the 1963-1964 civil rights bill as pedestrian and unimaginative. Humphrey later noted in a memorandum: "Frankly, I was rather surprised at the southern tactics. . . . It seemed to me that they lost their sense of direction and really had little or no plan other than what they used to have when filibusters succeeded."[68]

Richard Russell knew he could expect no help from his former protege, Lyndon Johnson. Russell also knew he was facing an organized bipartisan coalition of civil rights activists and that he was in for the battle of his career. But he could see exploitable weak spots in his opponents' armor, and he meant to exploit them in ways which could not be written off simply as prejudice or defense of legalized segregation.

The Pro-Civil Rights Strategy

In preparing for the considerable task of leading the civil rights debate, Mike Mansfield initiated in June, 1963, two components of the strategy which the Democratic senatorial leadership ultimately developed: (1) winning the support of Minority Leader Everett Dirksen and (2) encouraging a reasoned and searching debate of the bill itself. Both of these components reflected Mansfield's general belief that the Senate's participation in the legislative process was worth taking seriously and that he, as the majority leader, had an institutional responsibility to see that its credibility as an independent participant was preserved.

Under the direction of the bill's floor manager, Hubert Humphrey, two more strategic dimensions were developed: (1) organization of the civil rights forces in the Senate to enable them to survive the rigors of a southern Democratic filibuster for months, if necessary, and (2) coordination of this offensive with the outside groups and individuals supporting the bill. Humphrey had also taken steps to involve actively a number of senators in the Senate leadership's planned offensive. This was not going to be a one-man show. The four prongs of this strategy were, however, highly interdependent. Success or failure on any one front would affect the outlook on the other three.

Humphrey, and to a lesser degree, Mansfield, had conceived the leadership's initial strategic objective in the following terms: Maintain unremitting pressure to pass a substantively acceptable bill in the face of organized southern Democratic resistance in a manner that eventually would destroy the legitimacy of the filibuster in the eyes of those senators holding the balance of power on cloture. If the southern Democrats could be tagged with blatant obstructionism, and if this could be coupled with the refusal of the civil rights forces to back down, the leaders might then channel the normal pressures for compromise of the bill's substance into pressures for invoking cloture without prior debilitating concessions. Once cloture had been invoked, the simple majority in favor of H.R. 7152 could assume control.

However persuasive this strategy might have appeared conceptually, a study conducted by the Democratic Policy Committee staff revealed the severe obstacles to its execution. In the memorandum summarizing the results of this tabulation, the staff emphasized that "the success of a cloture attempt is precarious at best even with the support of Senator Dirksen. It should therefore not be attempted until all are exhausted and until the leadership has used every strategy . . . to ensure the greatest chance of its success."[69]

In the Democratic Policy Committee study, the performance of every member of the Senate in 1964 was tabulated on all cloture votes since the atomic energy amendments of 1954. On the basis of this analysis, 55 senators were considered ready to invoke cloture on H.R. 7152 in the form it passed the House. Thirty-three senators were labeled as "reasonably sure against." This category included the bloc of 19 southern Democrats, all of whom were unquestionably against.[70] Finally, 12 senators were identified as "crucial."[71] This group included nine Republicans and three Democrats, and on their votes was thought to hang the question of cloture.

Summing up, the challenge confronting Mansfield and Humphrey could be understood by realizing that cloture on H.R. 7152 would require the affirmative vote of *every senator* identified in the Democratic Policy Committee study as "crucial," assuming no favorable votes were cast by the senators rated as "reasonably sure against" and all 100 senators voted.

The magnitude of this task, plus the simple fact that the Senate had never invoked cloture on any measure remotely associated with civil rights, stimulated considerable speculation that a compromise deal with the southern Democrats would be the only way to end the debate. But President Johnson's equally well-known opposition to such a solution, a position also taken by the crucial Republican members of the House, further clouded the outcome of the debate.

Mansfield, Humphrey, and Kuchel, the principal party leaders supporting the bill when the Senate began its debate, knew they faced a stiff test of legislative leadership. The difficulty of their assignment was summed up with this question: Could they control the debate in a manner which permitted senators, both collectively and individually, to exercise independent judgments on the controversial issues without sacrificing the substantive objectives which President Johnson and the House of Representatives considered essential?

NOTES

1. John G. Stewart, *Independence and Control: The Challenge of Senatorial Party Leadership* (Ph.D. dissertation, University of Chicago, 1968). This section is from ch. 5, pp. 170-205.

2. *Congressional Record*, CX, p. 2774. All page citations from the *Congressional Record* in chpts. 5, 6, 7, 8, and 9 are from the daily edition.

3. For a more detailed analysis of Mansfield's strategy of leadership and the performance of the senatorial party under his leadership, see John G. Stewart, *Independence and Control: The Challenge of Senate Party Leadership* (Ph.D. dissertation, University of Chicago, 1968), pp. 42-57.

4. Staff memorandum, Democratic Policy Committee, August 18, 1963.

5. Memorandum by Senator Mansfield on conference with Senator Dirksen, Washington, D.C., June 13, 1963.

6. *New York Times*, June 11, 1963, p. 20.

7. *New York Times*, June 12, 1963, p. 1.

8. *New York Times*, June 13, 1963, p. 13.

9. The areas of agreement included voting rights, extension of the Commission on Civil Rights, school desegregation, statutory authority for the President's Committee on Equal Employment Opportunity, and a comprehensive "Powell amendment" barring use of federal funds in segregated or discriminatory activities. Although the matter was not discussed specifically, Mansfield also believed that Dirksen would support a voluntary community relations or conciliation service to mediate racial disputes. Memorandum by Senator Mansfield on conference with Senator Dirksen, Washington, D.C., June 13, 1963.

10. Author's notes, June 30, 1963, Washington, D.C.

11. *New York Times*, June 18, 1963, pp. 1, 21.

12. The results of the meeting are enumerated in a staff memorandum of June 18, 1963.

13. *Congressional Record*, CIX, pp. 11157-11161.

14. *Congressional Record*, CIX, pp. 11077-11081.

15. *Congressional Record*, CIX, pp. 11081-11082.

16. *Congressional Record*, CIX, pp. 11161-11165.

17. *Congressional Record*, CIX, p. 11076.

18. Staff memoranda to Senator Mansfield, August 15, 1963, Washington, D.C.

19. *Congressional Record*, CV, pp. 2882-2884.

20. *Congressional Record*, CX, p. 2775.

21. *Congressional Record*, CX, p. 2775.

22. Staff memorandum to Senator Mansfield, October 30, 1963, Washington, D.C.

23. *New York Times*, June 11, 1963, p. 20.

24. Staff memoranda to Senator Mansfield, October 30, 1963, and November 14, 1963, set forth some of the alternatives to the Rule XIV procedure. For example, the Commerce Committee could report its bill two weeks before the House bill was expected to come to the Senate. The majority leader would move to take up the Commerce bill. If the southern Democrats filibustered the motion to take up, the need for Rule XIV would then be established by the time the House bill arrived. If, however, the southern Democrats permitted the Commerce bill to become the pending business, various amendments based on the House text could be offered to it. The staff noted, however, that Rule XIV might still be needed to enable the Senate to pass the same bill sent from the House. If the congressional leaders wished to avoid returning the bill passed by the Senate to the House Rules Committee, the Senate had to act on the identical bill approved by the House. Otherwise, the Rules Committee could not be bypassed and further delays might ensue.

25. These conclusions are based primarily on the author's personal observations and a number of informal conversations on the question with senators, staff assistants and reporters at the time of Humphrey's appointment as floor manager.

26. Hubert H. Humphrey, undated memorandum on Senate consideration of the Civil Rights Act of 1964, Hubert H. Humphrey Papers, Minnesota Historical Society, Senatorial Files, 1949-1964, Legislative Files, Civil Rights, 1961-1964, C[ivil] R[ights] Diary, Box 150.B.12.2F.

27. Hubert H. Humphrey, undated memorandum on Senate consideration of the Civil Rights Act of 1964.

28. *Congressional Record*, CX, p. 2774.

29. Hubert H. Humphrey, undated memorandum on Senate consideration of the Civil Rights Act of 1964.

30. Author's conversation with Senator Hubert H. Humphrey during development of pro-civil rights strategy, as recorded in the author's notes on March 10, 1964, Washington, D.C.

31. Hubert H. Humphrey, undated memorandum on Senate consideration of the Civil Rights Act of 1964.

32. On February 28, 1964, Humphrey met with Kuchel to develop common guidelines for conducting the debate. On March 6 he reviewed the plans with the Democratic title captains and met again with Kuchel on Monday, March 9, the day Mansfield moved to make H.R. 7152 the pending business. Those specific meetings were, of course, supplemented by many telephone conversations and discussions on the Senate floor. Notes on civil rights debates prepared by author, March 9, 1964, Washington, D.C.; staff memoranda of meetings, February 28, 1964, March 6 and 9, 1964, also summarized plans of bipartisan leaders. See also the description of the civil rights forces in operation provided by Theodore H. White, *The Making of the President 1964* (New York: Atheneum Publishers, 1965), pp. 183-184.

33. Hubert H. Humphrey, undated memorandum on Senate consideration of the Civil Rights Act of 1964.

34. These newsletters were reprinted from time to time in the *Congressional Record*. Numbers 1-25, *Congressional Record*, CX, pp. 7245-7254; number 26, *Congressional Record*, CX, p. 8105; numbers 27-76, *Congressional Record*, pp.

13966-13981. The newsletter also produced an amusing confrontation on the Senate floor between Humphrey and the southern Democrats described on p. 220.

35. Memorandum by Senator Humphrey describing the meeting, March 12, 1963, Washington, D.C.

36. *Congressional Record*, CIX, p. 11173.

37. *New York Times*, February 17, 1964, p. 14.

38. *Washington Evening Star*, February 17, 1964, p. 14.

39. *Washington Post*, February 24, 1964, p. A1.

40. *Congressional Record*, CX, pp. 3850-3854.

41. *Washington Post*, March 2, 1964, p. A8.

42. *Congressional Record*, CX, p. 3197.

43. The Humphrey-Kuchel agreements were summarized in a staff memorandum, March 9, 1964, Washington, D.C.

44. *Washington Post*, February 24, 1964, p. A1.

45. *Congressional Record*, CX, pp. 6348-6349.

46. Staff memorandum of Humphrey-Kuchel meeting, March 9, 1964, Washington, D.C.

47. U.S. Congress, House, Subcommittee No. 5 of the Committee on the Judiciary, *Hearings on Miscellaneous Civil Rights Proposals*, 88th Congress, 1st Session, 1963, p. 1266.

48. AFL-CIO memorandum, "Labor Views on Administration Civil Rights Package," June, 1963.

49. See pp. 158–159.

50. These views were expressed to the author and other staff of Democratic senators in a series of meetings and telephone conversations with Leadership Conference representatives, principally Joseph L. Rauh, Jr., and Clarence Mitchell, Jr., between February 10 and 28, 1964. Author's notes.

51. Author's notes.

52. The author's notes and "Minutes of Civil Rights Meeting," February 28, 1964, as prepared by the staff of the Democratic Policy Committee, summarized the principal points of discussion and agreements between Humphrey and Kuchel and Leadership Conference representatives.

53. The Leadership Conference lobbyists were to raise this concern from time to time in the pre-session staff meetings in Humphrey's Capitol office and in private conversations, see below, p. 262. This option had, moreover, been raised in certain staff memoranda prepared for the majority leader, e.g., October 30, 1963, November 14, 1963, and again on April 9, 1964.

54. *CQ Almanac—1964*, p. 862.

55. *New York Times*, February 16, 1964, p. 20.

56. *New York Times*, March 1, 1964, p. 44 (emphasis added).

57. Evans and Novak report in some detail the various private meetings between civil rights leaders, including Rauh and Mitchell, and President Johnson where he pledged his determination to fight for a strong, noncompromised bill. See Rowland Evans and Robert Novak, *Lyndon B. Johnson: The Exercise of Power* (New York: New American Library, 1966), p. 378.

58. Evans and Novak, *Lyndon B. Johnson: The Exercise of Power*, p. 379.

59. Hubert H. Humphrey, undated memorandum on Senate consideration of the Civil Rights Act of 1964.

60. Evans and Novak, *Lyndon B. Johnson: The Exercise of Power*, p. 379.

61. *Washington Post*, March 6, 1964, p. A6.

62. *Congressional Record*, CX, p. 6245.

63. *Congressional Record*, CX, p. 2776.

64. For a description of Russell's strategy, see "Strategy Leading to Enactment of Rights Bill Analyzed," *Revolution in Civil Rights*, p. 52; E. W. Kenworthy, "Civil Rights: Bill Moves on to Tougher Senate Battleground," *New York Times*, February 9, 1964, p. E3; E. W. Kenworthy, "The Coming Filibuster," *New York Times*, February 23, 1964, p. E10; Robert C. Albright, "A Rights Bill 'If It Takes All Summer,'" *Washington Post*, March 8, 1964, pp. 1, 16; "Once More to the Filibuster over Civil Rights," *National Observer*, March 9, 1964, p. 1.

65. "Face the Nation" broadcast of March 1, 1964.

66. *Congressional Record*, CX, pp. 4576, 4584.

67. See "Strategy Leading to Enactment of Rights Bill Analyzed," *Revolution in Civil Rights*, p. 52.

68. Hubert H. Humphrey, undated memorandum on Senate consideration of the Civil Rights Act of 1964.

69. Staff cloture study, Democratic Policy Committee, February 20, 1964, Washington, D.C.

70. It would not be accurate to suggest that senators categorized as "reasonably sure against" were written off by the Democratic leadership. Indeed, several came to figure prominently in the leadership's plan for cloture, e.g., Hruska (Rep., NE), Curtis (Rep., NE), Monroney (Dem., OK), and Edmondson (Dem., OK). The Democratic Policy Committee memorandum also suggested that the leaders continue seeking the support of these senators in the "reasonably sure against" category. See staff cloture study, Democratic Policy Committee, February 20, 1964, Washington, D.C.

71. The "crucial" senators were as follows: Hayden (Dem., AZ), McGee (Dem., WY), Walters (Dem., TN), Carlson (Rep., KA), Dirksen (Rep., IL), Hickenlooper (Rep., IA), Smith (Rep., ME), Williams (Rep., DL), Jordan (Rep., ID), Mechem (Rep., NM), Miller (Rep., IA), and Pearson (Rep., KA).

Chapter 7

The Civil Rights Act of 1964: Tactics I

John G. Stewart

John Stewart now turns his attention to the tactical problems faced by the pro-civil rights Senate leaders in carrying out their elaborate strategy for defeating the filibuster. This section of Stewart's dissertation covers the surprisingly tough southern resistance to the "motion to consider" the civil rights bill on the Senate floor. Once that obstacle is out of the way, Stewart describes Hubert Humphrey's elaborate efforts to convince Senate Republican Leader Everett Dirksen of Illinois to support a cloture vote to end the filibuster and thereby enact the Civil Rights Act of 1964 into law.[1]

For both the civil rights forces and the southern Democrats, the time had passed for strategy conferences and planning meetings. At the outset of the debate, however, no one knew whether the Senate would prove equal to the crisis of confidence in representative democracy engendered by the civil rights upheavals. And people were not sure what painful course of events might develop if the Senate failed to sustain the essential parts of the decisions already made by the president and the House of Representatives. Some persons forecast violence and disorder in the nation's capital. Others talked of a possible revolution within the Senate itself.[2] Fully aware of this involvement in a momentous legislative encounter, and with no firm assurance of what the future might hold, the senators in mid-February, 1964, finally faced on the Senate floor the issue that was to command their time, attention, energy, and courage until early summer.

THE MOTION TO CONSIDER H.R. 7152

Nothing illustrated more graphically the importance attributed by each side to the civil rights battle than the six weeks of maneuvering which were necessary to make H.R. 7152 the Senate's pending business. To proceed to the consideration of any legislation on the calendar, the Senate must approve a motion to this effect, a motion usually offered by the majority leader.[3] This preliminary procedural step is usually quite routine. In a few seconds the Senate passes the majority leader's motion without debate or dissent. But in 1964 the Senate labored with this and several prior procedural steps from February 17, the day H.R. 7152 arrived from the House, until March 26, when Mansfield's preliminary motion of consideration was finally approved.

This opening period also demonstrated anew the wide range of procedural options available to the majority leader in bringing legislation before the Senate. These options, despite their procedural character, were nevertheless restricted by contending forces within the senatorial party, by various institutional restraints, by pressures from outside the Senate, and by the substantive objectives to which the party leadership was generally committed. This multitude of contending, and often conflicting, pressures focused directly on Majority Leader Mansfield in his early conduct and direction of the civil rights debate.

Although Humphrey and Kuchel had been designated floor managers for the legislation, Mansfield made it clear that he intended to remain visibly in charge until H.R. 7152 was actually the pending business of the Senate. The process of getting the legislation to this point in the parliamentary process was the prerogative, indeed, the responsibility, of the majority leader, and Mansfield intended to exercise it. A memorandum to Senator Mansfield from his staff noted: "There is some misunderstanding as to who would be out in front until bill is pending. Kuchel and Humphrey do not understand that majority leadership will be in charge until bill is pending."[4]

The process of securing this preliminary procedural objective also brought to light certain major strategic differences between the majority leader and the floor managers, differences which were to reappear from time to time later in the debate.

Before Mansfield could even offer the motion to proceed to the consideration of H.R. 7152, the House-passed bill had to be placed on the Senate calendar, from where it could be motioned up, rather than referred to Senator James Eastland's (Dem., MS) Judiciary Committee, where it would more than likely remain for the rest of the session. As discussed in the previous chapter, Mansfield hoped to follow normal parliamentary practices as closely as possible, not only to minimize the chances of alienating the uncommitted senators but also because he personally preferred to run the Senate that way.[5] But bypassing a standing legislative committee was distinctly abnormal. It was a step requiring the use of the Rule XIV procedure executed by Knowland and Douglas in the civil rights debate of 1957.[6] Mansfield viewed the prospect reluctantly. He had instructed his staff to explore all other possibilities for bringing the civil rights issue before the Senate, such as calling up a bill already reported by a committee and amending it to correspond to H.R. 7152.[7]

There were, however, a number of factors militating against this more normal approach. Given President Johnson's announced policy of opposing all amendments to H.R. 7152, the parliamentary situation would be simplified considerably by working with the identical text passed by the House. Moreover, given the precedent of Knowland's successful use of Rule XIV in 1957, the civil rights proponents among the Democrats would have been most distressed if Mansfield declined to follow a similar course in 1964. The Leadership Conference would have been equally vocal in their displeasure. Finally, the advantage of the leadership maintaining a firm grip on the House bill at the outset by directing it to the calendar outweighed the danger of offending the procedural sensibilities of uncommitted senators.[8]

So by the time the legislation was ready to be carried by messenger from the House to the Senate chamber, Mansfield knew that his personal misgivings had to yield in this instance to these other considerations, both substantive and political. The Rule XIV procedure was dusted off and made ready.

Bypassing the Senate Judiciary Committee

On February 17, 1964, Mansfield initiated the complicated series of parliamentary moves outlined in Rule XIV by objecting to the usually perfunctory second reading of the bill. He noted at the time that "the procedures which the leadership will follow are not usual, but neither are they unprecedented. And the reasons for unusual procedures are too well known to require elaboration."[9] The bill then remained at the presiding officer's desk until Wednesday, February 26, 1964, when the majority leader took the final steps in guiding H.R. 7152 to the sanctuary of the calendar, safe from the parliamentary booby traps and land mines of the Judiciary Committee.[10]

In the interim Mansfield had completed as much urgent business as possible, primarily the adoption of the conference report on the Revenue Act of 1964. After H.R. 7152 was placed on the calendar on February 26, 1964, Mansfield held off the civil rights debate for almost two additional weeks to permit passage of the wheat-cotton legislation (the planting season was rapidly approaching) and the military procurement authorization bill.

At this point Hubert Humphrey sought to defend more explicitly the leadership's decision to use Rule XIV: "It was designed for extraordinary circumstances. . . . I repeat that civil rights legislation did go to committee. The problem was that it did not come out of committee. . . . I have been around here long enough to know that the only way civil rights legislation can really be gotten before this body is through extraordinary, but legal means. Now, one of the extraordinary means is Rule XIV. It is legitimate, it is valid."[11]

But Richard Russell, vehemently disputing the legality of the procedure, made the point of order that Rule XXV, which established the jurisdiction of committees, required in addition the referral of all legislation to the appropriate committee.[12] Wayne Morse (Dem., OR), often a stickler on such procedural matters, agreed with Russell and announced his intention to move the referral of H.R. 7152 to the Judiciary Committee for a specified period of time once the bill became the Senate's pending business.[13] Russell had made the same point of order in 1957 (just as Morse had offered the same motion), only to have it rejected by the Senate on a roll call vote.

This time the presiding officer, Lee Metcalf (Dem., MT), citing the earlier 1957 precedent as controlling, simply overruled Russell, instead of following the more accepted practice of referring the question to the Senate for its decision.[14] The southern Democratic leader, visibly annoyed as much by Metcalf's failure to refer the issue to the Senate for its decision as by the substance of the ruling itself, appealed from the decision of the chair. After several additional hours of debate on Russell's appeal, Mansfield moved to lay it on the table. The tabling motion carried by the comfortable margin of 54-37.[15] With this, H.R. 7152 went to the calendar.

At this juncture, however, Majority Leader Mansfield's concern for fair and orderly procedure suddenly reasserted itself. With a minimum of advance notice to Humphrey and Kuchel, he asked unanimous consent that "House bill 7152 be referred to the Judiciary Committee with instructions to report back, without recommendation or amendment, to the Senate not later than noon, Wednesday, March 4."[16] Javits (Rep., NY) immediately jumped to his feet to object, thereby blocking the majority leader's request for unanimous consent. Javits suggested, however, that Mansfield make the request again the next day when he would have had more time to consider it.

Mansfield explained that he wanted to permit the committee an opportunity to hold hearings on H.R. 7152, especially on those provisions added on the House floor. "By this arrangement," the majority leader said, "at least some of the procedures which have been objected to, legitimately, could be given consideration."[17]

The following day Mansfield offered the request again. This time, however, Judiciary Committee Chairman Eastland objected and made this observation: "The net result would be that we would be handcuffed. . . . I will not be a party to sending a bill to that committee when it cannot amend it and cannot make a recommendation. . . . Therefore, . . . I object."[18] If Eastland had not objected, Javits and Keating subsequently announced they were prepared to do so.[19]

Little more than a pro forma bow to the Judiciary Committee and to those senators who dissented from the use of Rule XIV, Mansfield's unexpected unanimous consent request revealed the narrow line he was attempting to follow in deciding these tactics over procedure, a line which ran between providing adequate protection to H.R. 7152 and paying appropriate deference to established senatorial practices. And given the special parliamentary problems caused by the filibuster, these two objectives often could not be reconciled. This curious mixture of the regular and the extraordinary represented Mansfield's attempt to keep everyone reasonably satisfied.

On Monday, March 9, 1964, Mansfield offered his motion that the Senate proceed to the consideration of H.R. 7152. He thereby initiated the first sustained confrontation between the bipartisan civil rights forces and the southern Democrats.[20] Since the preliminary motion to consider was debatable, Richard Russell and his troops elected to begin the filibuster immediately. If, and when, the motion to consider H.R. 7152 passed, a second filibuster could then be launched against the bill itself.[21]

Introduction during the "Morning Hour"

Prior to making the motion to consider, however, Mansfield again had to decide between following regular procedure, a move certain to insure the southern Democrats' opening filibuster, or to attempt another unusual parliamentary maneuver with possible short-run advantages for the civil rights forces. This time the majority leader decided in favor of established practice. Under the rules a motion to take a bill from the calendar which is made during the "morning hour," i.e., before 2:00 p.m., is *non-debatable*. "Morning hour" includes a number of routine activities, e.g., reading of the Journal, presentation of petitions and memorials, reports of standing and select committees, introduction of bills and resolutions, plus other activities, such as insertion of material into the *Congressional Record* and taking up without debate bills and resolutions from the calendar.[22]

Offering the motion to consider in these circumstances (during the "morning hour") would have necessarily foreclosed to the southern Democrats their chance to begin the filibuster on the preliminary motion. But the southern Democrats usually preserve their opportunity to filibuster by preventing the majority leader from offering the motion in the nondebatable circumstances of the morning hour. By holding the floor until the morning hour expires at 2:00 p.m., the southern Democrats compel the majority leader to offer the motion to consider when the morning hour is over and the motion is again debatable.

The southern Democrats usually accomplish this feat by having the previous day's Journal read in full, instead of dispensing with this routine task by unanimous consent, as is usually done, and then offering and debating amendments to the Journal until the hour of 2:00 p.m. is reached. On March 9, 1964, southern Democratic leader Richard Russell followed precisely these tactics to block Mansfield from calling up H.R. 7152 in non-debatable circumstances.[23]

Mansfield's staff, however, had developed some complicated parliamentary moves which seemed to permit his presenting the motion during the morning hour, regardless of the obstructionist tactics used by the southern Democrats. But Mansfield considered these maneuvers too "tricky," especially since he had already resorted to Rule XIV to place H.R. 7152 on the calendar.

Mansfield resolved instead to offer his motion whenever he could get the floor after 2:00 p.m., even though this decision guaranteed a filibuster on the motion to consider.[24] On March 9, 1964, therefore, the majority leader made no effort to hinder Russell's performance in holding the floor until the morning hour was over. Mansfield then obtained the floor and expressed the hope that eventually the Senate would have a chance to vote H.R. 7152 up or down.

"There is," Mansfield said, "an ebb and flow in human affairs which at rare moments brings the complex of human events into a delicate balance. At those moments, the acts of governments may indeed influence, for better or for worse, the course of history. This is such a moment in the life of the Nation. This is that moment for the Senate." He then offered the motion to consider.[25]

During this opening skirmish Mansfield also decided to recess the Senate each evening, rather than adjourn, in order to maintain the same "legislative day," a parliamentary term denoting the time between adjournments. An adjournment would have automatically brought a new legislative day and another "morning hour," thereby forcing the southern Democrats to repeat their dilatory amending of the Journal. But the majority leader concluded that the minor advantage which might accrue to the civil rights forces, e.g., embarrassing the southerners, was not worth the ill-feeling and bad publicity for the Senate which would accompany such a maneuver.[26]

The question raised by Mansfield's motion to consider was strictly procedural: "Should the Senate proceed to the consideration of H.R. 7152, the Civil Rights Act of 1964?" Immediately after Mansfield's remarks, Lister Hill of Alabama, Russell Long of Louisiana, John McClellan of Arkansas, and Sam Ervin of North Carolina took the floor and the filibuster began.[27]

The Filibuster of the Motion to Consider

The southern speakers initially stressed the procedural injustice that allegedly would be perpetrated if the Senate considered the bill without its prior referral to the Judiciary Committee, and they attempted to build support for the motion of referral which Morse had announced he would offer if the bill became the pending business.[28] Before long, however, the southern Democrats shifted the focus of the debate to more substantive matters and began a comprehensive attack on the controversial parts of the legislation, particularly Title I (voting rights), Title II (integration of public accommodations), Title VI (cutoff of U.S. funds), and Title VII (equal employment opportunity). Although the civil rights forces had planned originally to withhold their affirmative arguments of support until the bill itself was pending, Humphrey decided to take on the southern Democrats without delay in order to avoid a blackout of news favorable to the bill.[29]

On March 10, 1964, for example, Humphrey questioned Sparkman of Alabama and Stennis of Mississippi during their attacks on the public accommodations provision of the bill. In replying to Stennis's assault on the constitutional basis for Title II, the majority whip took special pains to emphasize that his disagreements were not personal.

Humphrey observed: "He (Stennis) is speaking in a responsible, thoughtful and informed manner. I believe these arguments should not fall upon an empty chamber." Humphrey then launched his counterattack and the exchange continued for the better part of an hour.[30]

On March 11, 1964, Humphrey managed to extract from Ellender of Louisiana the admission that, yes, "in many instances the reason why the voting rights were not encouraged is that the white people are afraid they would be outvoted. Let us be frank about it."[31]

The appearance of the daily civil rights newsletter elicited a spirited exchange between Stennis and Humphrey. "I should like to ask," inquired Stennis, "who writes these mysterious messages, which come to senators before the *Congressional Record* reaches them, and in them attempts to refute arguments made on the floor of the Senate." Pleased with the opportunity to publicize the organizational efforts of the civil rights forces, Humphrey readily admitted the newsletter's parentage.

"There is no doubt about it," Humphrey said. "The newsletter is a bipartisan civil rights newsletter. . . . For the first time, we are putting up a battle. Everything will be done to make us succeed. . . . I wish also to announce that if anyone wishes to have equal time, there is space on the back of it for the opposition."[32] A number of other pro-civil rights senators joined the debate in these early days, including Javits, Hart, Kuchel, Keating, Clark, Case, Cooper, Ribicoff, Douglas, and Pastore.

Although disagreements among senators were frequent, invective and personal attacks were kept to a minimum. In fact, exhibitions of friendly regard were not uncommon. Nearing the point of recess of March 12, 1964, for example, Willis Robertson of Virginia, having just ridiculed every title in the bill, walked over to Humphrey and proffered a small confederate flag for his lapel.

Humphrey accepted the flag graciously and praised Robertson for his "eloquence and his great knowledge of history and law, but also for his wonderful . . . gentlemanly qualities and his consideration to us at all times." Robertson then delivered the southerners' ultimate compliment: "I told the senator (Humphrey) that if it had not been for the men from Wisconsin and Minnesota, when Grant finally came down into Virginia, we would have won, but they formerly belonged to Virginia. We could not whip them."[33]

Arm in arm, Humphrey and Robertson retired to the majority whip's Capitol office for some early evening refreshment.

But despite these spirited exchanges on the floor, days passed without revealing any significant progress toward reaching a vote on Mansfield's motion to proceed to the consideration of H.R. 7152. The civil rights forces had hoped initially that, after a week's debate, the southern Democrats would permit a vote. The first week passed without any indication, formal or informal, that the opponents' speeches would end voluntarily in the foreseeable future. In these circumstances, the bipartisan leadership faced a crucial tactical decision. Should cloture be attempted as a means of bringing Mansfield's motion to a vote? And how would such a maneuver affect the likelihood of invoking cloture on the bill itself?

Cloture the Motion to Consider?

On March 17, 1964, the *New York Times* reported that Mansfield, Dirksen, Humphrey, and Kuchel had agreed to seek cloture the following week if the southern Democrats continued to debate the motion to consider H.R. 7152.[34] In fact, the two floor leaders were far more disposed to this tactic than either Humphrey or Kuchel. The floor managers, thinking largely in terms of their strategy of withholding cloture until it could be invoked on the entire bill, considered the motion to consider far too early a point in the battle to attempt such a difficult move.

Although some senators were becoming exasperated with the southern Democrats' stalling on the preliminary motion, Humphrey and Kuchel knew that the 12 crucial senators needed for a two-thirds majority were far from convinced. To attempt cloture and to fail would seriously cripple the civil rights forces in their campaign to generate confidence and momentum behind the legislation. And those senators who voted against cloture once would be that much more difficult to win later in the debate. Both senators, moreover, wanted to avoid defaulting on their pledge to the Leadership Conference that cloture would be used only when its application against the entire bill was certain.[35]

Humphrey and Kuchel proposed instead that various steps be initiated to dramatize the obstructionism of the southern Democrats. Mansfield could make daily unanimous consent requests to vote on the motion to consider. The floor captains could generally tighten up on parliamentary procedure, e.g., by objecting to various types of unanimous consent requests by individual senators, they could dramatize in more personal ways the consequences of the southerners' unwillingness to permit a vote on the preliminary motion. The floor managers also stressed that simply the *threat* of cloture might convince Russell of the risks he was running in continuing to block the Senate from taking up the bill.[36]

Mansfield agreed to hold off for the time being on the cloture effort, and the matter was not pursued further. But the fact that it even came up testified to a greater inclination by both Mansfield and Dirksen to think in terms of a compromise settlement. For there was little disagreement among the party leaders that, once cloture had been tried and had failed, the bill would then become far more vulnerable to major concessions in the pattern of earlier civil rights debates.

From Mansfield's perspective, however, this possibility was much less of a disaster than it would have been for Humphrey or Kuchel. Partially due to a less intense involvement over the years in the civil rights effort, and partially due to a perspective which necessarily considered the civil rights bill as one among many bills that would have to pass under his general direction, Mansfield gradually emerged as less of an absolute proponent than either floor manager, less willing to think only in terms of demolishing the filibuster as the essential step toward total victory. But at least for the time being, cloture was held in reserve.

The Initial Filibuster Ends

The Humphrey-Kuchel approach (allow no early vote on cloture) was made more credible by the relatively good record achieved by the civil rights forces in responding to quorum calls and, consequently, their ability to maintain pressure on the southern Democrats. Quorum calls were averaging just over 20 minutes, although there were some exceptions. On March 11, 1964, 60 minutes were required to produce 51 senators. On March 16, 1964, 67 minutes were needed.[37]

Richard Russell also concluded at this juncture that he was beginning to push his luck in continuing the filibuster against the motion to consider. He obviously wanted to avoid provoking senators into the successful application of cloture so early in the game. Recognizing that to continue the filibuster further would eventually incur those risks, Russell passed the word quietly to Mansfield that a vote on the preliminary motion could occur towards the end of the second week of debate, probably on Thursday, March 26, 1964. Both sides, in short, concluded that it was in their respective best interests to avoid a showdown over cloture at this stage in the debate.

Under these circumstances, Russell did not announce his decision publicly. The southerners just stopped talking and the vote took place. The bipartisan leaders had not the slightest desire to discuss such delicate matters (the southerners voluntarily ending the filibuster of the motion to consider) on the floor. To do so would have embarrassed Russell and probably forced him to continue the filibuster regardless of the consequences. Indeed, the principals to the decision talked little about it even in private.[38]

Without fanfare, the Senate convened at 9:00 a.m. on March 26, 1964, and promptly voted, 67-15, to proceed to the consideration of H.R. 7152. Only southern Democrats cast votes in opposition.[39]

Referral with Orders to Report?

As he had announced earlier, Senator Wayne Morse (Dem., OR) then moved to refer the bill to the Judiciary Committee with instructions to report it back to the Senate not later than April 8, 1964. Morse defended his motion on two major grounds: (1) the committee would have an opportunity to hold hearings, and (2) the committee could file a majority and minority report on the legislation which, in Morse's opinion, would be needed by the courts in determining the bill's legislative history.[40]

In opposing Morse's motion, Mansfield pointed out that he had attempted earlier to refer the bill to the Judiciary Committee. The majority leader then remarked: "It ought to be abundantly clear by this time that the majority leader is not a procedural radical. . . . The majority leader prefers to stay as close as possible to usual procedure and still move the business of the Senate. . . . But there is a higher responsibility to see to it that whatever can be done by the leadership, and it is not much, is done, to the end that proper and pressing business of the Senate is faced and disposed of by the Senate. . . . The procedure may be a very unusual one but it is entirely in order."[41]

Mansfield also noted that the bill, upon its return from the Judiciary Committee on April 8, 1964, would have to be motioned off the calendar, providing the southern Democrats with still another opportunity to filibuster the motion to take-up. On this basis, the majority leader moved to lay Morse's motion on the table. Although the press carried reports that this vote would be close, Mansfield's tabling motion carried easily, 50-34.[42] The last impediment to the Senate's consideration of the bill itself had been overcome.

The Procedural Role of the Majority Leader

What had these opening weeks of debate demonstrated? In general terms, they revealed that the majority leader's prerogative to initiate tactics of procedure was an important source of his power and influence within the senatorial party. His decisions on procedure were accepted by a substantial portion of both senatorial parties. Mansfield's shifting back and forth between regular and irregular practices also suggested that procedural initiative could not be divorced from substantive ends or insulated from the various forces striving to achieve those ends.

The majority leader, for example, had to consider the interests of (1) senators, primarily Republicans, who were not irreconcilable opponents of its provisions and who wanted the bipartisan leaders to move with deliberation and restraint, and (2) senators, primarily Democrats, who supported the bill enthusiastically and wanted to proceed as expeditiously as possible. And there existed at all times Mansfield's personal dislike of using any procedural device, however "legal" in the sense of its possessing some foundation in rules or precedent, which stood outside normal senatorial practices.

The resulting patchwork pattern of procedural steps had the one redeeming feature of avoiding any major defeats or irretrievable defections in the early weeks of the battle. Mansfield ended up maintaining the leadership's control of the bill and buying time in which to push forward the more ambitious plans for eventually winning cloture on the full bill.

Cloture Still Far Away

These opening weeks also indicated how far removed the civil rights forces were from this objective of cloture. Everett Dirksen, for example, had continued to display serious reservations about crucial parts of the legislation. During his speech supporting the Morse motion of referral, the minority leader propounded a series of detailed questions about alleged ambiguities and weaknesses in the bill. He paid special attention to Title VII (equal employment opportunity) and also announced his intention of offering at a later date a complete substitute for Title II (integration of public accommodations).[43]

The performance of the 12 senators rated as "crucial" by the Democratic Policy Committee staff was also disheartening. Only 4 of these senators[44] voted with the bipartisan Senate leadership in opposing the Morse referral motion (that is, they voted in favor of Mansfield's motion to table). Of the 8 others, 7 voted for or were paired in favor of referral[45] and one neither voted nor announced his position.[46] Although a vote on this motion did not necessarily reveal a senator's eventual position on invoking cloture, the low level of support did suggest that a long and probably indecisive period of probing and sparring lay ahead before the question of cloture could be successfully handled.

On the more favorable side, however, Humphrey and Kuchel were generally satisfied with the performance of their civil rights forces during this initial confrontation with the southern Democrats. Their scheme of organization had functioned successfully. The floor had been well patrolled. Most of the quorum calls had been answered in good order. The impression was abroad in Washington that this time the civil rights forces were organized and meant business. For example, one analyst noted: "Civil rights forces, not to be out-done by southern opponents, have thrown up their own well-manned command post in the Senate. . . . As militarily precise as the southerners' three-platoon system, the Humphrey forces are organized down to the last man."[47]

The Leadership Conference on Civil Rights and the various religious groups across the country were beginning to generate encouraging support for the bill. For example, the Leadership Conference was now bringing delegations of constituents to visit with the uncommitted senators in Washington. Lobbyists also helped round up pro-civil rights senators for quorum calls, especially on Saturdays. The Commission on Religion and Race of the National Council of Churches had dispatched members into the states of crucial midwestern senators to stimulate interest and help organize support for the bill.[48] Humphrey had met with leaders of the three major faiths to plan an interreligious convocation in Washington for later in the debate.[49]

These efforts were needed. The Coordinating Committee for Fundamental American Freedoms, the group coordinating lobbying against the bill, and funded in part by the Mississippi State Sovereignty Commission, was generating large quantities of mail in opposition to the legislation.[50]

For his part, Russell had only to maintain the 34 votes he achieved on the Morse motion to frustrate indefinitely the efforts of the civil rights proponents to apply cloture. Having no real reason to be discouraged by his double defeat on March 26, 1964, the southern field general declared to the press: "We have lost a skirmish. . . . We shall now begin to fight the war."[51]

A Mid-April Lull

"It is our intention," Hubert Humphrey announced on April 9, 1964, "to step up the tempo of the debate, in the hope of being able to bring about an orderly disposition of the bill through the legislative process."[52] The proponents of H.R. 7152 had just completed their ten-day explanation and discussion of the bill's 11 titles, a project they initiated after the legislation became the Senate's pending business on March 26, 1964. But Humphrey soon discovered that April was not the month for orderly disposition or accelerated tempos. Indeed, these weeks were to be remembered as a time of continued uncertainty and frustration for all participants, a time of probing, testing, and anxious waiting.

Beginning on March 30, 1964, with Humphrey's three-hour-and-ten-minute exposition of the full bill, followed by a similar, although somewhat shorter, presentation by Kuchel, the captains appointed by Humphrey and Dirksen occupied the Senate until April 9 with a title-by-title discussion of H.R. 7152.

This exercise seemed worthwhile for several reasons. It put the proponents' case on the public record. It replied to many of the charges leveled by the southern Democrats. It continued to generate news favorable to the civil rights cause and thereby encouraged the people working in behalf of the legislation outside of Congress. Most importantly, however, it gave the proponents an opportunity to debate its controversial and complex provisions in a public forum where opponents could challenge the affirmative case.

If the uncommitted senators were likely to stress at some future point the importance of the Senate exercising its independent judgment on the bill's major provisions, Humphrey and Kuchel hoped to demonstrate at the outset their respect for this position and their willingness at least to listen to their arguments. And, at a minimum, the floor managers hoped their ten-day affirmative presentation would eliminate a possible excuse which uncommitted senators might later use to justify a negative cloture vote: namely, that the Senate was being forced to act on H.R. 7152 without adequate debate and deliberation.

During this period, however, the proponents were rarely challenged. The southern Democrats seemed content to bide their time until they had to resume the burden of carrying the debate. The uncommitted Republicans simply stayed away from the floor.

In addition to the speeches on the various titles of H.R. 7152 delivered by the appointed title captains, other pro-civil rights senators delivered speeches in favor of the legislation. In this period, Edward Kennedy (Dem., MA) delivered his maiden Senate speech on April 9, 1964. He closed with these words: "My brother was the first president of the United States to state publicly that segregation was morally wrong. His heart and soul are in this bill. . . . It is in that spirit that I hope the Senate will pass this bill."[53]

The tempo lagged badly on Saturday, April 4, 1964, when 51 senators failed to answer a quorum call for the first and only time of the debate. Describing the situation as "a sham and an indignity upon this institution," Mansfield recessed the Senate until Monday.[54] After a quorum had reported on Monday, the majority leader called together all non-southern Democrats and stressed that the outcome of the debate depended primarily on their behavior. Sounding a familiar theme, Mansfield emphasized the limits to his authority as party leader, how he possessed no more power than the most freshman senator to compel their attendance, and how he neither sought nor particularly enjoyed the responsibilities of the majority leadership. He closed his lecture by noting: "We have leaned over backwards to accommodate senators in this debate; now you have to meet us halfway."[55]

In addition to Mansfield's dressing down, Humphrey turned the Leadership Conference operatives loose to impress upon negligent senators the importance of their making future quorum calls. Representatives of the AFL-CIO carried most of this burden. For the remainder of the debate, the civil rights forces never again failed to produce a quorum.

Other factors contributed to the indecisiveness and fluidity of this period in mid-April. Senator Dirksen began to unveil bundles of amendments which weakened the bill in a number of crucial respects.[56] The minority leader, however, noting the hostile reaction of the civil rights forces, also continued to revise his proposals. "If you don't get a whole loaf of bread," he observed, "you get what you can."[57]

The bipartisan leaders doubted the wisdom at that juncture of talking seriously with Dirksen to see whether a common ground for joint action could be developed. What else might he propose? What were his ultimate objectives? Was he working secretly with Senator Russell? And what about President Johnson's "no amendments" edict? Under what conditions could it be withdrawn? Lacking firm answers to any of these questions, the bipartisan leaders dipped into their reservoir of patience and did nothing.

Senator Russell talked in general terms about the possibility of the Senate voting on certain amendments in a week or two, but no firm arrangements were made.[58] The southern leader also pondered the impact on the civil rights debate of George C. Wallace's showing in the Wisconsin presidential primary. The segregationist Alabama governor lost to President Johnson but received 25 percent of the vote. Perhaps this demonstration of white opposition to the cause of civil rights would reinforce the doubts of the uncommitted Republicans.[59]

Most senators watched with great interest the public reaction to the threatened "stall-in" sponsored by the Congress of Racial Equality (CORE) on the parkways leading to the New York World's Fair. Proponents feared this civil disturbance would endanger public support for the bill. Indeed, the southern Democrats hoped for precisely this result.

"CIVIL WRONGS DO NOT BRING CIVIL RIGHTS"

Largely to counteract this growing aversion within the Senate to various forms of demonstrations and civil disobedience, Humphrey and Kuchel on April 15, 1964, issued a statement wherein they stated: "Civil wrongs do not bring civil rights. Civil disobedience does not bring equal protection under the laws. . . . Illegal disturbances . . . strike grievous blows at the cause of decent civil rights legislation."[60]

The Leadership Conference lobbyists fretted quite openly about the danger of the bipartisan leadership falling victim to Dirksen's early amendments. They feared a quick sellout. Joseph Rauh and Clarence Mitchell of the Leadership Conference also disagreed with Mansfield's continued refusal to hold round-the-clock sessions or enforce the rules more strictly. For example, southern Democrats often were granted unanimous consent to continue a speech at a later date which, in effect, granted them an additional speech under the terms of Rule XIX. These dissatisfactions were voiced frequently in the pre-session strategy sessions in Humphrey's whip office.[61]

Mansfield talked publicly about the possibility of the filibuster lasting until the fall.[62] He also received a deeply pessimistic evaluation of cloture from certain of his staff advisers. These advisers claimed the civil rights forces lacked about 10-12 votes, an evaluation which recommended an *early* attempt at cloture to be followed by negotiations with Dirksen to produce whatever compromises would be necessary for passage of the bill.[63] Since this memorandum recommended precisely the strategy which Humphrey and Kuchel opposed, the floor managers could not help but worry that at some later date the majority leader might strike a bargain with Dirksen which would be unacceptable to the president, the House of Representatives, and the civil rights groups.

Humphrey, the majority whip, reviewed the analysis prepared by Mansfield's staff and asserted that, in his opinion, the outlook for cloture was much brighter. Humphrey estimated on April 16, 1964, that they lacked only 4-5 votes. He urged strongly adhering to the initial strategy of holding back on cloture until its application was assured.[64]

Humphrey began to advocate publicly a tightening up of procedures on the Senate floor and raised the possibility of holding round-the-clock sessions.[65] On April 20, 1964, he attempted to invoke Rule XIX (the two-speech limit) against George Smathers (Dem., FL), a southerner who was about to commence his third speech on the pending motion. Dirksen interceded and recommended that Humphrey refrain from enforcement of the rules that evening. Humphrey agreed but said they would be enforced in the future. The matter never came to a decision. All senators subsequently were credited with two more speeches when the southerners introduced and called up a jury trial amendment.[66]

The filibuster, as in earlier battles, was beginning to erode the confidence and enthusiasm of those supporting the bill. With no break expected to develop in the foreseeable future, an atmosphere of uncertainty and doubt was beginning to envelop the proceedings.

The Talmadge Amendment

Then Richard Russell decided to act. Late in the evening of April 21, 1964, Herman Talmadge (Dem., GA) introduced and called up an amendment to extend the right of trial by jury to persons accused of criminal contempt of the federal courts.[67] In the civil rights debate of 1957, the Senate, after considerable controversy, had passed a similar amendment. A subsequent compromise with the House, however, provided for a jury trial in criminal contempt cases where the judge fined the defendant more than $300 or sentenced him to more than 45 days in jail. Convictions with lesser sentences could be handed down by the judge.[68]

Most northern supporters of civil rights had opposed the absolute guarantee of a jury trial, but Lyndon Johnson had been successful in recruiting support for a jury trial amendment from several Democrats with unquestioned civil rights credentials (for example, Kennedy, Green, Mansfield, and Pastore). For these senators, the importance of jury trials per se in criminal cases apparently outweighed the possibility that the provision might be used in the South to avoid compliance with the law.

This aspect of the issue was not always unspoken in 1964. On May 1, 1964, Javits of New York and Russell of Georgia engaged in a heated and bitter exchange. Russell accused Javits of impugning the integrity of southern juries. Javits denied it. It stood as one of the bitterest moments of the debate.[69]

Given the history of 1957, Mansfield, Humphrey, and Kuchel recognized at once that Russell had played one of his strongest cards. The Talmadge amendment appealed to all southern Democrats as a way of limiting the federal government's role in enforcing the bill, but at the same time the amendment would likely win significant support among Republicans and some northern Democrats by its attractiveness as a civil liberties issue. The pro-civil rights Senate leaders frankly doubted their ability to defeat the Talmadge amendment on a straight up or down vote.[70]

Their principal worry, however, was not over the substantive damage the amendment might do to the bill. Rather, they primarily wanted to avoid the psychological lift that would redound to the southern Democrats if they won the first major substantive test of the debate and the accompanying blow to the confidence and momentum of the civil rights forces. Absorbed in the context of the disappointing progress of the prior three weeks, such a blow might fatally impair the Senate leadership's four-pronged strategy, which still seemed to offer the only hope of passing an acceptable bill. The Talmadge amendment, in short, represented a substantive issue likely to affect the distribution of forces within the Senate, a distribution which ultimately might decide the entire contest.

The Mansfield-Dirksen Substitute Amendment

It was a test the Democratic leadership could not afford to lose. They immediately began to devise a countermove. Although this meant abandoning the oft-declared policy of passing the House bill without change, Mansfield and Humphrey decided to propose a substitute amendment that hopefully would command enough Republican and northern Democratic support to capture this first major vote and deny to the southern forces this vital tactical advantage. Since the jury trial formula developed in 1957 had already been included in Title II (integration of public accommodations) of the 1964 bill, the leaders decided simply to propose extending this provision to other appropriate sections of H.R. 7152.[71]

They also saw another possibility. Why not convince Dirksen to cosponsor the substitute jury trial amendment with Mansfield? This arrangement would add valuable support for the substitute on a roll call vote. More importantly, it would also for the first time involve Dirksen actively with the civil rights leadership in seeking a common tactical objective. When Mansfield went to Dirksen with this proposal, he found him surprisingly ready to do business. He, too, was becoming restless with the lack of action on the Senate floor.

On Thursday, April 23, 1964, the Mansfield-Dirksen substitute jury trial amendment was hammered out in a series of meetings between Humphrey, Kuchel, Dirksen, and representatives of the Justice Department. Dirksen first proposed a maximum penalty of a $300 fine and 10 days imprisonment that could be imposed without a jury trial. Humphrey, however, advocated applying the 1957 limit of

$300 and 45 days to all appropriate sections of the bill. The negotiators compromised at $300 and 30 days.[72]

Mansfield, continuing his studied policy of deferring to Dirksen, urged the minority leader to take the lead in offering the substitute in the Senate. Dirksen assented and confidently introduced it the next day, Friday, April 24, 1964. "I trust," he intoned, "it will be agreeable to everyone when it is finally called up for a vote."[73]

The bipartisan leadership had put the southern Democrats on the defensive with the introduction of the Mansfield-Dirksen substitute jury trial amendment. Those senators who wanted to demonstrate in some way a degree of independence from the precise formula passed by the House and supported by the president had been given a relatively innocuous opportunity to do so. The joint sponsorship by the two floor leaders broadened the amendment's appeal within both senatorial parties, isolating the southern Democrats and consolidating the non-southerners of both parties. The bipartisan leaders seemed fully in control.

Despite the fact that introduction of the Mansfield-Dirksen substitute jury trial amendment violated the Johnson administration's policy of "no amendments," the incident generated little comment in this light. Primarily this reflected the fact that the amendment simply applied an existing procedure to the entire bill and did not affect the bill's major substantive provisions.[74]

Under Senate procedure, moreover, the Mansfield-Dirksen amendment as a substitute would be voted on first and, if passed, would replace the Talmadge amendment in its entirety. If the southern Democrats voted against the Mansfield-Dirksen substitute, they would probably pass up their one chance to go on record in support of some jury trial provision. But if they supported the substitute, they would, in effect, be surrendering to the flanking action by the party leaders. Their opposition might also end all possibilities of future cooperation with Dirksen and drive him into the eager embrace of Mansfield, Humphrey, and Kuchel. Expressing the new feeling of optimism which swept through the civil rights camp with these developments, Humphrey left a Thursday meeting with Dirksen to announce: "Things are looking great. All last week's stomach aches are gone."[75]

Under the circumstances, Richard Russell decided to continue stalling. Despite a general expectation within the Senate that votes on the jury trial issue were likely to occur early the next week, probably on Monday, April 27, or Tuesday, April 28, 1964, the southern Democrats maintained their filibuster without a break. In the face of this renewed opposition, Mansfield could do no better than express "hope that at some time early next week, we will be able to come to a vote, perhaps on Tuesday, or thereabouts."[76]

On Monday, April 27, 1964, Russell left a conference of southern senators to denounce the Mansfield-Dirksen substitute as "a mustard plaster on a cancer."[77] He noted additionally their intention to discuss the substitute at length. The Senate, in short, would not be voting in the foreseeable future.

At this point a number of senators began to grumble openly about the obstructionism of the southern Democrats. Humphrey said he detected "a growing restlessness among the senators."[78] Even Dirksen could declare that it was time to stem the flow of southern talk and start voting. Momentum for cloture seemed to be building in precisely the manner hoped for by the civil rights command.

An Early Cloture Proposal

So it was with great distress that Humphrey and Kuchel learned on Tuesday, April 28, 1964, that if the southern Democrats did not permit a vote by Tuesday, May 5, 1964, Mansfield and Dirksen had agreed to seek cloture on the jury trial amendments alone, not the entire bill.[79] In a procedural dispute quite similar to the one which arose over Mansfield's abortive move to apply cloture on the motion to take-up, Humphrey and Kuchel continued to believe that cloture should be the ultimate weapon used to destroy the filibuster completely, not to cripple merely a segment of it. It should not be attempted until its application was certain. Indeed, failure would hand the southern Democrats a major victory just when the tide seemed to be turning in favor of the civil rights cause. Furthermore, failure to get cloture could possibly open the door to major compromises in substance.

Even the successful application of cloture would produce a vote on nothing more than a relatively minor amendment. Moreover, success might also bleed off the rising pressure and frustration which otherwise could be directed to end the filibuster permanently. Whatever happened, it would alter significantly the basic strategy of cloture which Humphrey and Kuchel had been following from the outset and make it more difficult to forestall piecemeal amendments which could weaken and perhaps emasculate the bill.

Mansfield, however, saw no way of refusing to cooperate with Everett Dirksen. The majority leader had gained his active support in proposing cosponsorship of the substitute. Now the minority leader wanted to vote on it. Given the adamant position against voting adopted by the southern Democratic forces, cloture on the amendment seemed to be the only viable alternative. Dirksen had no interest at present in applying cloture on the entire bill until his various amendments had been given careful attention by the bipartisan leadership.

Mansfield felt he could not jeopardize his relations with Dirksen on this bill, or on future matters of mutual concern, by refusing to cosponsor the cloture petition. These internal considerations outweighed for Mansfield any obligation to adhere strictly to the original cloture strategy devised by Humphrey and Kuchel, the Leadership Conference, and the other civil rights activists in the Senate. If his minority counterpart wanted cloture, Mansfield concluded he had to go along.

With Dirksen having already announced to the press the decision to attempt cloture,[80] an emergency meeting of Democratic strategists convened in the majority leader's office late Tuesday afternoon, April 28, 1964. Principals at the meeting included Mansfield, Humphrey, Attorney General Robert Kennedy, Deputy Attorney General Nicholas Katzenbach, and Lawrence O'Brien, chief legislative strategist for President Johnson. Humphrey argued strongly against attempting cloture at that time and limiting its application to the jury trial amendments. He stressed that it would require abandoning the entire plan of action for passing a bill acceptable to the president and the House of Representatives.

Mansfield remained silent while a member of his staff pointed out that Dirksen seemed likely to go ahead anyway. His cooperation on the remainder of the bill might depend on achieving prompt approval of the jury trial substitute. The executive branch officials generally agreed with Humphrey's position, but they had few suggestions about how to divert Dirksen from his present course. Mansfield, however, agreed to go back to the minority leader to see whether the cloture drive might be postponed for several days. In the interim, Richard Russell might change his mind about blocking all votes.[81]

In fact, alarms were running through the southern Democratic ranks. If Humphrey and Kuchel were concerned that the cloture effort might fail, Russell was again worried that it might succeed. From his perspective this would attach Dirksen even more firmly to the civil rights coalition. Then cloture on the entire bill would simply be a matter of time. It had also been reported that Russell was having difficulty in convincing certain southern senators, Strom Thurmond of South Carolina in particular, of the danger of continuing the filibuster on the jury trial issue. The danger was that a refusal to permit any votes might produce the application of cloture.

Russell's difficulties were reported in the *New York Times*: "It appears from statements by the Senate leaders and Mr. Russell that both sides were engaged in a war of nerves. . . . He (Russell) said, he is not trying to make Mr. Dirksen invoke cloture; he hoped he would not do it; he did not rule out a vote some time next week, and he would be glad to talk about this with Mr. Dirksen next Monday. . . . But, Mr. Dirksen went on, Mr. Russell could not give this assurance (to vote) because Senator Strom Thurmond . . . was absent. Nobody, he (Dirksen) said, can be sure of what Mr. Thurmond might do."[82]

The Morton Amendment

But if Russell could offer a "perfecting" amendment to the Talmadge Amendment, capable of attracting majority support, he could justify to his southern colleagues a brief suspension of the filibuster in order to vote on the perfecting amendment.[83] This, in turn, would probably dissipate the immediate pressure for cloture.

The Democratic and Republican Senate leaders gathered in Dirksen's office late in the afternoon of Wednesday, April 29, 1964, to continue their discussion of the advisability of cloture. As the same time, Richard Russell, Sam Ervin (Dem., NC) and Thruston Morton (Rep., KY) were meeting off the Senate floor in the Marble Room, reportedly preparing a perfecting amendment to the Talmadge amendment. Word of Russell's activity soon reached the senators in Dirksen's office and, given the basic differences over cloture between Dirksen and Mansfield, on the one hand, and Humphrey and Kuchel, on the other, this intelligence provided a good excuse to postpone again a final decision on whether to seek cloture immediately on the Mansfield-Dirksen substitute.[84]

By Friday, May 1, 1964, the cloture crisis had again disappeared.[85] Russell's perfecting amendment had been drawn up, and the southern Democrats had agreed informally to permit a vote. Mansfield, Dirksen, and Russell gathered on the Senate floor to exchange expressions of faith that a vote would take place on Wednesday, May 6, 1964. This discussion substituted for any more formal agreement, a step certain southerners, particularly Thurmond, would have found difficult to let pass unchallenged.[86]

Morton, then working closely with Russell, introduced the perfecting amendment, which restricted the right of jury trials to criminal contempt cases arising solely from the provisions of H.R. 7152.[87] Since a moderate Republican was formally sponsoring the amendment, the civil rights forces could not attack it solely as an effort to impair the effectiveness of the legislation. Moreover, given the historical attractiveness of the jury trial issue under any circumstances, the vote on the Morton perfecting amendment seemed likely to be close.[88] Russell, in short, had made an impressive recovery in countering the tactical advantage assumed by the civil rights forces upon the introduction of the Mansfield-Dirksen substitute.

With both sides agreed to a showdown over the Morton amendment, and fully aware that the vote would be close, the time had arrived for the bipartisan leaders to take every precaution necessary to guarantee victory. Yet the reduction of the Democratic party leadership's capacity to direct events on the floor, an outgrowth of Mansfield's efforts at [leadership] decentralization, almost handed the decision to Russell and Morton. Four roll call votes were required ultimately to settle this one issue of the Morton amendment and defeat the coalition of Republicans, southern Democrats, and western Democrats supporting it.

The initial vote produced a 45-45 tie. Needing a clear majority, the amendment had failed.[89] But when Dirksen moved routinely to table Mansfield's routine motion to reconsider, the civil rights forces, including Dirksen, were defeated, 44-47.[90] The Senate then voted immediately on the motion to reconsider the Morton amendment and again the civil rights coalition lost, 46-45.[91] Finally, the floor leaders pulled themselves and their forces together and managed to defeat the Morton amendment on its reconsideration, 46-45.[92]

Commotion on the Senate Floor

At times during the four-vote sequence the majority and minority leaders barely maintained control of their forces. Commotion on the floor reached such a pitch that all staff members were ordered into the cloakrooms to reduce the noise level. Accurate surveys of the vote had not been taken in advance, and the leadership's apparatus for notifying senators functioned poorly. Frank Moss (Dem., UT), for example, missed the first vote entirely because the Democratic cloakroom staff failed to summon him from a phone booth. He then voted against the leadership on the motion to table out of spite.[93]

Mansfield also had pledged to Russell that McClellan and Fulbright, both of Arkansas, would receive "live pairs," i.e., two pro-civil rights senators would withhold their votes on the roll calls to cover the absences of the two southern Democrats. On the first vote, Mansfield, in the confusion, found himself paired with both senators and Humphrey had to give a "live pair" to Fulbright.[94]

The incident only narrowly avoided becoming a debacle of major dimensions. The party leaders could take scant pride from their ragged performance. The votes illustrated dramatically a principal weakness of Mansfield's leadership strategy: the lack of a reliable system for marshalling the senatorial party behind the party leadership in a closely fought and crucial vote.[95]

On balance, the southern Democrats in defeat looked better than the civil rights coalition in victory. It was just the kind of showing which could strengthen the southerners' will to resist and cause uncommitted senators to doubt the sense of purpose of those supporting the bill.

No More Votes

Hubert Humphrey and Thomas Kuchel, therefore, were all the more eager to vote promptly on the Mansfield-Dirksen substitute itself and hopefully settle the question of jury trials in their favor. Time for additional voting had been discussed in the Republican cloakroom with Russell. The two floor leaders had received the impression that a vote on the Mansfield-Dirksen substitute would be possible. Russell, however, denied such an understanding and announced that no further votes were likely for the remainder of the week.[96]

The question of whether Russell, in fact, agreed to more votes continued to recur over the following days. Most pro-civil rights senators believed he had made this pledge, but Mansfield eventually denied it on the Senate floor: "The distinguished senator from Georgia is a man of honor. . . . When he gives his word, it is as solid as gold."[97]

Following Russell's decision not to allow a vote on the Mansfield-Dirksen substitute, Humphrey summed up the feeling of many senators when he said: "I would be less than honest if I said I was not unhappy. This is not what I would call a 'happiness house'. . . . Occasionally it is a quorum of frustration."[98]

The frustration deepened when the southern Democratic forces on May 11, 1964, called up another perfecting amendment introduced by George Smathers (Dem., FL). Now a vote on the Mansfield-Dirksen substitute had to await the disposal of the Smathers amendment. The southern Democrats apparently had resumed the strategy of total obstructionism.[99]

To be sure, the bipartisan civil rights forces had defeated the Morton amendment. They had also averted a probable southern Democratic victory on the Talmadge amendment. Sensing its appeal to many senators who otherwise were favorably disposed to the civil rights bill, the leaders had used the substantive issue of jury trials to devise a parliamentary situation which brought them into joint action with Dirksen for the first time and, however briefly, shifted the tactical initiative in their favor.

And, as they had done on the motion to consider, Humphrey and Kuchel, with a well-timed assist from Russell, had resisted successfully a move to apply cloture to that limited section of the bill. But the incident revealed again the different interests which propelled Mansfield more readily to accommodate Dirksen on such tactical matters, even if that threatened a strategy designed to produce cloture on a substantively acceptable bill.

The Frustration Continues

During the frustrating weeks of April and early May, the civil rights proponents had continued to produce quorums and generally maintain pressure on the filibustering senators. The Leadership Conference also had been busily at work bringing delegations to Washington to lobby for the bill as well as beating the drums for favorable mail and telegrams. Finally, there had been a discernable increase in the frustration of many senators over the inability to make sustained progress on the bill, although the poor showing on the Morton amendment did little to generate the image of confidence and strength which Humphrey, in particular, felt was essential in accumulating the two-thirds majority for cloture.

The four votes on the Morton amendment also revealed that most of the senators evaluated in February as "crucial" to applying cloture still were not aligned with the civil rights forces. Indeed, 8 of the 12 "crucial" senators opposed their party leaders on the vote, 3 were favorable and 1 senator was absent.[100] Even though the jury trial issue was extraneous to the substance of the bill itself, these continued defections could not be overlooked, especially since Dirksen's involvement had produced no visible impact on the behavior of the "crucial" Republicans.

Through all of these hectic maneuvers, President Johnson had remained remarkably aloof. Kept fully informed by Lawrence O'Brien and the senatorial leaders, he nevertheless appeared to feel that his personal involvement at this juncture could only hinder the successful management of the bill. The major change in policy concerning amendments to the House-passed bill occasioned by the introduction of the Mansfield-Dirksen substitute jury trial amendment went by without comment by the White House. The president knew precisely why that countermove was essential to block passage of the Talmadge amendment.

Although it could not be appreciated fully at the time, the refusal of the southern Democrats to permit further votes on the jury trial issue proved to be a major factor in convincing Dirksen to cast his lot with the civil rights forces and to advocate a bill which could be accepted without qualms by the president and the House of Representatives. As business on the Senate floor in effect ground to a halt due to the inability to continue voting, the battle for the Civil Rights Act of 1964 shifted into the rear of Dirksen's chambers on the second floor of the Capitol. On May 5, 1964, the day before the vote on the Morton amendment, the minority leader had agreed to open full-scale negotiations with the bipartisan supporters of H.R. 7152 and Justice Department officials. Under discussion were an imposing series of amendments which Dirksen had brought forward for consideration and over which both sides were now willing to bargain seriously.

As these negotiations commenced, two questions were uppermost in the minds of Humphrey and Kuchel. Would it be possible to evolve amendments which met Dirksen's demands but which did not impair any of the bill's major provisions, especially those dealing with enforcement? And would it then be possible to amass a two-thirds majority behind these changes in order to invoke cloture? Deeply frustrated by their lack of progress on other fronts, the bipartisan leaders could only hope that somehow the answers to these questions would be in the affirmative.

The Dirksen Amendments

Even prior to President Kennedy's submission of his omnibus civil rights bill in June, 1963, the Democratic leadership in the Senate, particularly Majority Leader Mansfield, recognized the crucial role likely to be assumed by Minority Leader Dirksen when the legislation finally reached the Senate. The single fact that cloture hinged on Republican votes guaranteed to Dirksen a position of commanding influence. As stated previously, Mansfield sought diligently to structure an environment where communication with the minority leader could be maintained, despite Dirksen's initial opposition to the enforcement provisions of the public accommodations title.[101]

The imposing support for H.R. 7152 developed among Republican members of the House, and the decisive leadership exercised by William McCulloch (Rep., OH) within the House Judiciary Committee and on the House floor, complimented Mansfield's efforts significantly. Given the major Republican investment in the bill that emerged from the House debate, Dirksen would have found it difficult to shoulder major responsibility for the emasculation or death of H.R. 7152 in the Senate. After all, in the House, 78 percent of the Republicans voted for H.R. 7152, and 11 of the 12 members of the Illinois Republican delegation in the House voted in the affirmative. The 12th member, Hoffman, failed to vote.[102]

Thus it was that, given the problems of recruiting a two-thirds majority for cloture, the minority leader possessed more influence and leverage than any other senator in determining the outcome of the debate, assuming he could deliver the votes of a substantial portion of the uncommitted Republicans.

On February 17, 1964, the day H.R. 7152 arrived from the House of Representatives, Dirksen's remarks on the floor left little doubt that he intended to make the most of this unusual leverage. And he also dropped some broad hints of his desire to stamp the final product with the Dirksen imprint. "Already some amendments have occurred to me," he observed. "I shall try to shape them. I shall try to put them in form. If I think they have merit, I shall offer them."[103]

Dirksen subsequently opposed Mansfield's efforts to place H.R. 7152 directly on the calendar under the provisions of Rule XIV.[104] On the Morse motion to refer the bill to the Judiciary Committee, he not only voted in favor of its referral but also distributed to every senator a memorandum setting forth a number of questions and alleged ambiguities which he had detected in the bill and which he believed could be clarified by committee action. He also spoke of his intention to propose later in the debate a substitute amendment for Title II (integration of public accommodations).[105]

In sum, during these early weeks the minority leader labored studiously to reinforce his independence vis-a-vis the bipartisan civil rights forces and to strengthen his position as the decisive factor in the battle. He emphasized in his public statements a desire to cooperate in helping the Senate discharge its duties in considering the legislation "within the limitations of the convictions that I hold."[106]

For their part, Mansfield, Humphrey, and Kuchel went out of their way to stress the vital role that Dirksen would assume in the Senate's consideration of H.R. 7152 and that how, when the chips were down, the minority leader would respond affirmatively to the rising civil rights crisis and use his considerable influence to enact meaningful legislation.[107] They were, in short, setting the stage for Dirksen to play a fully visible and crucial role in defeating the southern Democrats and passing an acceptable bill.

Dirksen knew that, as with all senatorial party leaders, his influence in deciding the outcome of the debate would be no greater than the support he would receive for his final position within the Republican senatorial party. The minority leader could command the support of his party colleagues no more readily than the majority leader could command his. Divergent interests would have to be taken into account and interested senators would have to be given an opportunity to have their say. Moreover, the range of opinion among the Republicans on crucial sections of H.R. 7152 spanned an ideological spectrum almost as broad as existed within the Democratic Party. But whereas Mansfield had written off the possibility of ever winning affirmative support from the southern Democrats, Dirksen had to spread his net wider, hopefully to include most of the Republican senators found between the extremes of liberal Jacob Javits of New York and conservative Barry Goldwater of Arizona.

The efforts of Mansfield and Humphrey to maintain an environment hospitable to Dirksen's gradual evolution toward support of the civil rights bill was also deemed to be a significant factor in determining the minority leader's final position. They sought to protect Dirksen from internal and external pressures which might either solidify his opposition to Titles II (integration of public accommodations) and VII (equal employment opportunity) or separate him prematurely from the uncommitted members of his own party. Some of the more outspoken advocates of the bill who came to Washington as lobbyists were diverted to other senators less crucial to the outcome of the battle. And the Democratic leaders reminded their more impatient colleagues in the Senate and the Leadership Conference lobbyists that Dirksen's vote, standing alone, meant nothing in the context of a filibuster. Without the votes of the "crucial" Republicans, Dirksen would simply be part of a frustrated and helpless simple majority.[108]

In the early weeks of the debate, even before H.R. 7152 became the pending business, Dirksen's staff began drafting a package of amendments to Title VII (equal employment opportunity).[109] The minority leader then began the formidable task of accommodating the widest possible cross section of the Republican Party as these and other proposals were refined and developed, a process that was destined to continue until early June.

The Republican Policy Committee

On Tuesday, March 31, 1964, Dirksen set forth the essential details of these amendments at the weekly luncheon meeting of the Republican Policy Committee.[110] The forum of the Policy Committee's weekly luncheon had several advantages. It was more informal than a full-dress Republican Conference. It was recognized as the principal power base of the more conservative members of the party. Bourke Hickenlooper of Iowa was chairman. The Republican Policy Committee provided an easy, accessible procedure for Dirksen to build his necessary base of support over a period of weeks.

Dirksen decided to bring subsequent modifications of these amendments to the next three consecutive Policy Committee luncheons. The fact that he did this prior to the introduction of the amendments on the Senate floor suggested the degree of difficulty he encountered in developing a broad base of support within the Republican senatorial party. Dirksen, in reporting "considerable" support following the March 31 meeting, also acknowledged the need for additional refinements and winnowing.[111]

By April 7, 1964, at the next luncheon, the minority leader distributed mimeographed copies of his amendments to each Republican senator in preparation for their discussion at a full-dress Republican Conference on Thursday, April 9. In general terms, Dirksen proposed shifting the burden of enforcing the equal employment standards in Title VII from the federal Equal Employment Opportunity Commission, as specified in H.R. 7152, to the individual complainant. He also provided that state agencies with authority to deal with job discrimination would be accorded, upon their request, full jurisdiction in such cases.[112]

Dirksen Amendments Extensive

Since Dirksen had taken pains earlier to portray his amendments as being primarily technical and clarifying in nature, it was with surprise and some dismay that civil rights activists among the Republicans realized their full impact. Kenneth Keating of New York told reporters that the amendments would "seriously weaken the effectiveness of the bill."[113] Clifford Case of New Jersey announced his inability to vote for any civil rights bill containing such proposals, a sentiment shared by Keating and Jacob Javits of New York. There were also reports of dismay among Republican leaders in the House.[114]

Expecting much milder medicine, the bipartisan leaders were shocked and confused by Dirksen's initial proposals, but they were willing, for the time being at least, to adopt the theory that Dirksen was still engaged in a testing and probing operation within his party. They still believed that Dirksen was less wedded to the substantive specifics of his Title VII (equal employment opportunity) proposals than to a more general desire to leave his distinctive mark on the bill. They remained reasonably confident, moreover, that his interests as Republican floor leader could not in the end be served by being saddled with responsibility for the bill's defeat in the Senate or its rejection by the House.

A memorandum written following a bipartisan leadership meeting summed up the situation this way: "It is absolutely essential that we not make any concession to Dirksen at this time. . . . At the same time, it was agreed that in order to get cloture, we must get Dirksen."[115]

The Democratic leaders deferred to their Republican colleagues, principally Kuchel, Javits, and Case, in the job of moderating the unacceptable aspects of the Dirksen amendments. The minority leader, demonstrating again his flexibility on the subject, promptly agreed to continue his efforts to develop provisions acceptable to the pro-civil rights Republicans.[116] The Leadership Conference lobbyists were anxious to mount a full-scale attack against Dirksen, but Humphrey and Kuchel persuaded them to maintain a discrete silence while the Republican negotiations proceeded.[117] Humphrey told the press he would await the outcome of these discussions before commenting specifically on the Dirksen proposals. But he also noted: "We don't intend to let any crippling amendments pass."[118]

For the third consecutive week, Dirksen took his redrafted amendments to the Policy Committee luncheon on April 14, 1964. In the interim certain changes had been made. For example, instead of ceding total jurisdiction to the state agencies upon their request, Dirksen now proposed that, if the state had not resolved the complaint in six months, the individual could take the case to the U.S. commission for another six-month period of voluntary conciliation. At the end of that second six-month period, the individual could file a civil suit in the U.S. district court to compel enforcement.[119]

The Republican activists rejected this procedure as too time consuming. They were also still opposed to Dirksen's elimination of the commission's authority to file enforcement suits in the courts on its own motion. But they found other of Dirksen's modifications more acceptable. Both sides stressed their desire to continue negotiations. The minority leader, therefore, decided he would introduce ten of his less controversial amendments on Thursday, April 16, 1964, but withhold the amendments dealing with jurisdiction and enforcement pending these further discussions.

Despite their continuing disagreements over the enforceability of Title VII (equal employment opportunity), Jacob Javits, one of the pro-civil rights Republicans, praised Dirksen's willingness to continue discussions and called him the "linchpin" in the search for cloture.[120]

Dirksen introduced his ten Title VII amendments on April 16, 1964, as promised.[121] Dirksen noted on the floor: "I have . . . had conversations with people who express the hope that the bill will be approved without a single amendment. I am afraid that people who utter that hope have no familiarity with the real legislative process. I believe the Senate is duty-bound carefully to examine all legislation."[122]

On Saturday, April 18, 1964, Humphrey and Kuchel met with Attorney General Robert Kennedy, Lawrence O'Brien, and other Justice Department and White House personnel to formulate their response to these initial proposals. The participants were in general agreement on their tactics to deal with Dirksen. They would have to see all of Dirksen's amendments, including his proposal on Title II (integration of public accommodations), before deciding whether any were acceptable. The "no amendments" policy could not be abandoned unless the bipartisan leaders could evaluate the full consequences of that change. A deal with Dirksen on his amendments, moreover, would have to include his commitment to work unreservedly to apply cloture on the entire bill.

Finally, the leaders had no problem with Dirksen leaving his mark on the bill so long as this did not jeopardize any essential aspects of the legislation and so long as he could deliver the missing votes for cloture. They also agreed to do their best to restrain the Leadership Conference lobbyists from attacking Dirksen publicly in this delicate period of maneuvering and probing. Criticism from this direction would likely harden the minority leader's position on Title VII and drive him toward the more conservative members of his party.[123]

On Tuesday, April 21, 1964, following another Republican Policy Committee luncheon, Dirksen introduced his final amendment to Title VII several hours before Talmadge unveiled his jury trial amendments.[124] The minority leader's proposal now gave state agencies three months to resolve allegations of job discrimination (six months for states with newly created agencies) before the U.S. commission could assume jurisdiction for another three months. If the case had not been settled by these voluntary efforts, the complainant could take the issue to the U.S. courts. The Justice Department could also intervene at the discretion of the court.

The bipartisan leaders were frankly disappointed. Although some improvements had been achieved, Dirksen's emphasis was still one of relying upon voluntary compliance, with the individual complainant carrying the burden of court enforcement. Following another meeting with Justice Department officials, Humphrey characterized Dirksen's amendment as "a bit troublesome." And then he added: "The more we see of the amendments, the better we like the House bill."[125]

The Senate Must Pass Judgment

Yet circumstances had combined to make some change in the declared policy of "no amendments" essential for further progress. As discussed in the preceding section, the threat of the Talmadge amendment forced Mansfield and Humphrey to take prompt counteraction to avoid a probable southern Democratic victory. Although no specific nose counts were taken at that juncture on the jury trial issue, Mansfield, Humphrey, and Kuchel agreed that the vote might be extremely close, given the issue's drawing power among some southern Democrats and most Republicans.[126] Less of an immediate threat but equally destructive of the "no amendments" policy was a growing feeling that the House bill contained certain deficiencies and weaknesses which the Senate had a responsibility to remedy. This feeling extended into the ranks of senators who otherwise were counted among the bill's supporters.

George Aiken of Vermont, a highly respected liberal Republican, spoke of these concerns in his remarks on the Senate floor on Monday, April 27, 1964: "In spite of the fact that the president has asked to have the bill approved as it came from the House, it seems to me that, if we just set aside all legislative processes and take our directive from the executive branch, we will not only be doing an injustice to our constituents but violence to our structure of our government as well. . . . President Johnson must know that continued insistence on the Senate passing the bill identically as it came from the House will likely result in killing the legislation."[127] The Senate, in other words, ought to reach some independent judgments.

When evaluated with the lack of progress in wearing down the filibuster, these sentiments caused Humphrey to begin thinking of ways the Senate could correct demonstrated weaknesses in the House version without sacrificing its essential features. He became convinced of the need to develop a procedure which permitted the Senate's independence to be expressed in ways the party leaders could control.[128] For Dirksen's part, the inability to achieve an orderly disposition of the various jury trial proposals made it appear unlikely that his package of amendments would receive sustained or thoughtful attention. Face-to-face negotiations between the bipartisan leaders and Dirksen seemed more likely to serve their respective interests than a watch-and-wait policy wholly dependent upon Russell's willingness to permit the transaction of business on the Senate floor.[129]

If Dirksen and the civil rights forces could agree on a comprehensive package of amendments which met the requirements of acceptability as defined by the president and the House of Representatives, Humphrey believed that Dirksen would readily commit himself in a final drive for cloture on the entire bill. In fact, the minority leader had told Humphrey privately that he believed passage of a strong bill was inevitable. In his opinion, not only were the southern Democrats losing their confidence of killing the bill, but support for the legislation continued to grow around the country.

In these circumstances Dirksen said he intended to see that a substantial majority of the Republican senatorial party voted affirmatively for an effective bill. He would have but one more amendment to propose, his substitute for Title II (integration of public accommodations), and it would contain only minor modifications. He also stressed his desire to have the bill completely finished in the Senate before the Republican National Convention convened in July. Dirksen's marked interest in scheduling discussions with the Democrats also suggested to the bipartisan leadership that, finally, he felt more secure with his uncommitted Republicans.[130]

Dirksen also met with House Republican leaders to discuss his Title VII amendments and reported that "some rather substantial people" found them acceptable. But reports still persisted that Representative William McCulloch (Rep., OH), in particular, did not agree with Dirksen's position. Kuchel then initiated a series of meetings with Republican civil rights supporters from the House and Senate to see what alternatives might be developed.[131]

The Dirksen Negotiations Begin

During the final week of April, the week of rising frustration over the inability to vote on the jury trial amendments, the bipartisan leaders and Dirksen agreed to open discussions on his amendments on Tuesday, May 5, 1964.[132] Held in the Capitol offices of the minority leader, the first session was attended by Mansfield, Dirksen, Humphrey, Kuchel, Attorney General Robert Kennedy, Hickenlooper, Aiken, and Magnuson. Given Dirksen's earlier assurances that he had only one more amendment to Title II (integration of public accommodations), the Democratic negotiators were startled to receive from the minority leader a heavy sheaf of mimeographed amendments divided into three categories: Class A, containing technical and clarifying amendments; Class B, amendments somewhat more substantive than those of Class A; and Class C, the major substantive amendments. In all, more than 70 separate amendments were involved.[133]

Where Humphrey had concluded earlier that Dirksen and the civil rights forces could agree relatively easily on a comprehensive package containing all amendments and decide to seek cloture, he now confessed that the exposure of Dirksen's three-category bundle of amendments altered these expectations. This unexpected realization, coupled with their near defeat on the Morton amendment and the inability to vote on the Mansfield-Dirksen substitute, brought the bipartisan leaders to their greatest discouragement of the 83-day debate.

Also discouraging was this fact. If Dirksen assumed an uncompromising posture in the negotiations and Richard Russell continued to frustrate action on the floor, the likely appearance of what Humphrey and Kuchel most feared, namely, the rise of pressures for basic changes in the bill's substance, might produce an agreement between Mansfield and Dirksen to sponsor such major amendments jointly as the only way to break the deadlock.

It also appeared that Dirksen had not, in fact, shored up sufficiently his own position among the Republicans. In the opening negotiating session on May 5, 1964, Bourke Hickenlooper (Rep., IA) announced his opposition to any enforceable Title II (integration of public accommodations) or VII (equal employment opportunity) in the bill and stalked out of the meeting. He never returned. Yet, despite all these disheartening signs, only one course of action seemed possible for the bipartisan leaders. Negotiate with Dirksen in good faith in the hope that an acceptable package of amendments could be developed.

Civil Rights Forces Disorganized

The author dictated the following observation on the evening of May 6, 1964: "There is a definite lack of urgency and lack of direction to the civil rights forces at present. But I will say that it will be somewhat of a major miracle if the pro-civil rights forces can get themselves back in order and push ahead with some degree of resolution and determination.[134]

Agreement was reached rather easily on the Class A amendments and most of those in Class B. But the issue which had separated Dirksen from the civil rights forces in the beginning still remained unsettled, i.e., the procedure for enforcing the prohibitions against discrimination in public accommodations and employment.[135] Dirksen seemed particularly concerned that the U.S. government be kept from harassing the individual businessman for complex and detailed reports or threatening him with court action in disputes which otherwise might be settled voluntarily. He also appeared to base most of his judgments on the parochial experiences of Illinois. From this perspective he continued to advocate a procedure which then placed the principal burden of court enforcement upon the individual complainant.

The Justice Department, on the other hand, saw a different aspect of the problem. Unless the authority existed to confront businessmen of a given geographical area with enforceable orders to desegregate or cease discriminatory hiring practices, there would be strong competitive advantages for individual firms to hold out as long as possible and few incentives for voluntary action. In their eyes, enforcement which relied ultimately on private individuals initiating court action against a single firm would become an essentially endless process. They argued persistently for U.S. government authority to combat massive resistance as the most effective way, not only to achieve enforcement in situations of last-ditch opposition, but also to promote voluntary compliance on a broader scale.

"Pattern or Practice"

The critical breakthrough in the negotiations occurred when Dirksen's staff finally came to understand precisely the nature of the Justice Department's concern. At that point one of Dirksen's assistants proposed that the U.S. government be given authority to initiate action only where there existed a "pattern or practice of massive resistance in any geographical area." With some minor refinements, this formula broke the impasse with Dirksen which had existed since President Kennedy's first proposals came to the Congress almost a year earlier.

The civil rights forces strengthened the federal government's leverage in this procedure by establishing later in the debate that "pattern or practice" could also refer to repeated violations by a single business establishment.[136]

Having prevailed on the vital question of U.S. government enforcement authority, the negotiators accepted Dirksen's proposals to permit an initial period of state jurisdiction over cases arising under Title II and Title VII. Under

Title II (integration of public accommodations) the state was given 30 days to act. Under Title VII (equal employment opportunity) the state was given jurisdiction for 90 days, with 180 days provided during the first year the state law was in effect.[137] There were, of course, a number of other proposals which had to be resolved, but the "pattern or practice" breakthrough made final agreement almost a certainty.[138]

By Wednesday, May 13, 1964, the principals reconvened in Dirksen's office hoping to reach final agreement on a substitute bill. Prior to the meeting the Democratic participants met in Mansfield's office to discuss their tactics on the remaining points of disagreement. These concerned Dirksen's proposals that the attorney general's authority to file suit under Titles II and VII be spelled out in a separate, new Title XII. Also that the Commission on Civil Rights be made subject to the Administrative Procedures Act. And that only the attorney general, and not the Equal Employment Opportunity Commission, be authorized to determine instances of a "pattern or practice" of discrimination.[139] The pro-civil rights leaders agreed to maintain a relatively noncompromising stance on these remaining issues since, by this time, they believed Dirksen needed them as much as they needed him.

Humphrey opened the final meeting with Dirksen by stressing that agreement on the amendments hinged ultimately on the minority leader's willingness to support cloture on the entire bill. The bipartisan leaders could not accept Dirksen's announced preference for applying cloture separately to each title. The minority leader responded that this would not be a problem if their substantive differences could be resolved.

At this point George Aiken (Rep., VT) interrupted to observe that, in his opinion, the bill in its present form was dead unless the negotiators could agree on an acceptable substitute. After a great deal of discussion, running into the afternoon, Dirksen acquiesced to most of the final demands of the bipartisan leaders. During the bargaining over Title

VII, Clark walked out of the meeting, declaring that he could not support the compromises which were being made. His abrupt departure helped illustrate a point Humphrey had been attempting to drive home. Since any changes would likely be opposed by the civil rights activists, Dirksen ought not to demand too high a price for his cooperation on cloture.

In the end, Dirksen abandoned the idea of a separate, new Title XII. The Commission on Civil Rights would not be subject to the Administrative Procedures Act, although some language would be drafted to regulate more strictly the commission's hearing procedures. And the Equal Employment Opportunity Commission was authorized to recommend to the attorney general situations which warranted intervention under the "pattern or practice" powers, although the commission could not initiate court action directly.[140]

The Deal with Senator Dirksen

By the middle of the afternoon, all outstanding differences had been resolved. Both sides acknowledged their commitment to the changes which would be offered in one package as an amendment in the nature of a substitute bill. They would also join forces in attempting to apply cloture on the full bill. Finally, neither side would ask for additional changes or alterations to the major agreements which had been hammered out.

Both sides acknowledged their probable difficulty in selling the substitute package to certain elements of their respective constituencies. Dirksen could expect some opposition from his more conservative party colleagues. Humphrey recognized the dangers of an eruption by the Leadership Conference and the more liberal Democratic senators. As the senators left Dirksen's office to announce their agreement to the waiting newsmen, Humphrey remarked that he felt like someone going down a ski jump for the first time. Once you pushed off down the slope, you could only hope that somehow you would land on your feet.[141]

The meetings over the Dirksen amendments were held from May 5 to May 13, 1964. All the sessions were deliberately scheduled in the offices of the minority leader. In a superficial sense, the meetings served as an informal substitute for a standing committee's executive session where a bill is "marked-up," i.e., voted on section by section by the committee members.

But the differences from a committee mark-up were crucial, especially in assessing the role played by the party leadership in passing the bill. The Dirksen negotiations were convened under the sponsorship and control of the elected leaders of both parties. The negotiations were designed expressly to serve the leaders' interests in finding a formula which could pass the bill. The sessions provided an informal, ad hoc forum to arrive at the kind of compromises which could not have been secured in public debate on the Senate floor, or in a standing committee. The Senate floor is an environment where control is more difficult to maintain even when a filibuster is not in progress. A standing committee is controlled by its chairman, not the Senate leadership.

Consistent with the general notion of party leaders being ill-equipped to handle complex substantive questions on the floor or in committee, the leadership found Dirksen's back room more to their liking. True give-and-take was possible, decisions were neither public nor final, and the need to sustain one's public posture on certain issues was greatly reduced. In this environment, the party leaders could explore the content of independent senatorial decisions without risking a loss of leadership control.

Moreover, the Justice Department officials, principally Nicholas Katzenbach and Burke Marshall, carried the major negotiating burden for the bipartisan leaders. Although other pro-civil rights senators and staff attended the sessions, they generally deferred to the judgment and expertise of the executive branch personnel in developing changes which met Dirksen's most urgent concerns without jeopardizing the bill's basic objectives.

The pro-civil rights senators, however, served a useful function by defining in explicit terms the activist pressures for a strong bill. For example, by taking a tough, uncompromising position on many issues, they helped push the Dirksen lawyers further toward the House bill than might otherwise have been the case. This posture also helped establish the Justice Department representatives as arbitrators to the various disputes which arose.[142]

The senators and Justice Department officials would usually attend the meetings in Dirksen's office briefly in the morning to ratify what the staff assistants had produced the previous afternoon. They also offered broad advice on the range of opinions that should be considered in drawing up the crucial sections of the bill.

This approach also permitted President Johnson's interests to be protected by Katzenbach and Marshall without his having to become publicly involved in the Senate's internal business. Indeed, the sessions served as a remarkably effective device of the senatorial party leaders for resolving differences between the executive branch and the Senate in an environment where control need not be sacrificed in the process of satisfying the essential interests of both sides.

Finally, the negotiations represented the last step in the long process of giving Dirksen his opportunity to contribute personally to the legislation, although Dirksen's resulting notoriety would also produce some difficult moments with certain of his fellow Republicans, a development that will be explored more fully in the next section.

In summary, under the conditions of a filibuster with normal committee procedures inoperative, the party leaders needed a method to secure the substantive agreements which were necessary for cloture, and cloture was the only procedure thought likely to defeat the southern Democratic opposition and make possible the enactment of an acceptable bill. The negotiations with Dirksen supplied such a method.

During this period in early May of 1964, the Leadership Conference lobbyists were almost frantic in their suspicions that the bill was being compromised irretrievably. At one point they almost released a public statement attacking Humphrey and Kuchel for meeting with Dirksen. Another time they insisted upon being admitted as full participants to the negotiations. Humphrey did arrange for them to receive verbal briefings of the general points under discussion, but they were refused access to anything in writing.

The bipartisan leaders were convinced that a frontal attack by the Leadership Conference at this juncture might destroy all hopes of concluding an acceptable package deal with Dirksen. The minority leader's apparent readiness to accept such provisions as the "pattern or practice" formula could disappear immediately under the threat of a Leadership Conference ultimatum. Humphrey and Kuchel were forced to use almost every fragment of personal credit they possessed with the Leadership Conference to avert such an explosion during the crucial moments of the negotiations.[143]

Whereas President Johnson understood the reasons for having to abandon the policy of no amendments, and whereas his interests were being tended carefully by the Justice Department, the Leadership Conference personnel could only envision a repetition of earlier civil rights fights. To them, a sellout appeared certain.

The successful evolution of what came to be called the Dirksen-Mansfield substitute bill achieved one of the bipartisan leadership's major strategic objectives: winning the support of Everett Dirksen for cloture. The tactical decision to negotiate seriously with Dirksen and abandon President Johnson's initial policy of "no amendments" proved to be the turning point in the bipartisan leadership's efforts to apply cloture on a substantively acceptable bill.

Incidentally, although the president made no effort to stop the introduction of the jury trial substitute or halt the negotiations with Dirksen, he frowned on any public discussion of the change in policy. The *New York Times* reported as late as Friday, May 1, 1964, that Humphrey allegedly had been reprimanded by President Johnson for suggesting to reporters that Senate amendments were not "precluded." Humphrey later told reporters that the president still favored the House bill.[144]

There were, of course, some risks in the decision of Humphrey and Kuchel to negotiate with Minority Leader Dirksen. If they had failed to reach agreement on Dirksen's amendments, his support for cloture would probably have been sacrificed permanently. But there were far greater risks in doing nothing. It seemed unlikely that Dirksen would ever accept H.R. 7152 as it came from the House. Aiken's comments on April 27, 1964, moreover, demonstrated further the importance of affirmative legislative action by the Senate to perfect portions of the House bill. Indeed, the decision to negotiate with Dirksen took account of the same basic factors which suggested to the bipartisan leaders at the outset the wisdom of encouraging a fair, deliberate, and reasoned debate, namely, the Senate's traditional commitment toward maintaining its sense of institutional integrity and independence. Given that fact, the risks seemed well worth taking.

It was also essential to provide Dirksen with the tactical negotiating room to develop a position on H.R. 7152 that eventually could be sustained within his own party and appeal to the broad ideological spectrum found there. If the bipartisan leaders had attacked his earlier proposals, or attempted to coerce him into agreement, his freedom to explore and experiment with various legislative approaches would have been sharply curtailed.

Nevertheless, the rising demand across the country for positive action, and President Johnson's unquestioned backing of the legislation, could not be disassociated from Dirksen's eventual decision to work for a strong bill. But these external pressures could have been counterproductive if the minority leader had not been given the chance to demonstrate his independence.

As with most legislative decisions, it was a question of balance. Dirksen had to understand the determination of the civil rights forces, particularly those inside the Senate, to enact a meaningful and effective bill. But the process of communicating this message could not be permitted to grow into a campaign of overt pressure or personal intimidation.

Notes

1. John G. Stewart, *Independence and Control: The Challenge of Senatorial Party Leadership* (Ph.D. dissertation, University of Chicago, 1968). This section is from ch. 6, pp. 206-254.

2. Theodore H. White, *The Making of the President 1964* (New York: Atheneum Publishers, 1965), pp. 182-183. See also *Revolution in Civil Rights* (Washington, D.C.: Congressional Quarterly, Inc., 1965), pp. 39, 51.

3. U.S., Congress, Senate, *Standing Rules of the United States Senate*, corrected to January 9, 1963, VIII, 10.

4. Staff memorandum to Senator Mansfield on organizational work of proponents of civil rights bill, March 9, 1964.

5. See pp. 175-178.

6. See John G. Stewart, *Independence and Control: The Challenge of Senatorial Party Leadership* (Ph.D. dissertation, University of Chicago, 1968), pp. 143-144.

7. Staff memorandum to Senator Mansfield on procedure, August 15, 1963, Washington, D.C.

8. Staff memorandum on procedure, January 22, 1964, Washington, D.C.

9. *Congressional Record*, CX, p. 2774. The relevant sec-

tion of Rule XIV reads: ". . . every bill and joint resolution of the House of Representatives which shall have received a first and second reading without being referred to a committee, shall, if objection be made to further proceeding thereon, be placed on the Calendar." U.S., Congress, Senate, *Standing Rules of the United States Senate*, corrected to January 9, 1963, XIV, sec. 4, pp. 14-15.

10. *Congressional Record*, CX, p. 3557.
11. *Congressional Record*, CX, pp. 3623-3626.
12. *Congressional Record*, CX, pp. 3557-3660.
13. *Congressional Record*, CX, p. 3584.
14. *Congressional Record*, CX, p. 3560.
15. *Congressional Record*, CX, p. 3583.
16. *Congressional Record*, CX, p. 3583.
17. *Congressional Record*, CX, p. 3583.
18. *Congressional Record*, CX, p. 3830.
19. *Congressional Record*, CX, pp. 3830-3831.
20. *Congressional Record*, CX, p. 4585.
21. In some instances, the debate never goes beyond the motion to take-up, e.g., the successful southern Democratic filibuster against the Civil Rights Act of 1966 was directed against this motion. When cloture could not be invoked, the bill returned to the calendar and died at the end of the Congress. The motion to take-up is not debatable under the rules if it is offered upon conclusion of morning business and before the hour of 2:00 p.m. See U.S., Congress, Senate, *Standing Rules of the United States Senate*, corrected to January 9, 1963, IX, 11.
22. U.S., Congress, Senate, *Standing Rules of the United States Senate*, corrected to January 9, 1963, VII, 10. See also Watkins and Riddick, *Senate Procedure: Precedents and Practice*, pp. 366-371, 372-376.
23. *Congressional Record*, CX, pp. 4573-4585. Even though the majority leader traditionally is accorded the right of prior recognition to the floor, the rules specify that reading of the Journal is the first item of morning business

in the "morning hour." The majority leader is therefore prevented from gaining recognition. *Standing Rules of the United States Senate*, corrected to January 9, 1963, VII, 9.

24. A staff memorandum to Senator Mansfield, undated, Washington, D.C., read: ". . . the leadership might consider attempting the procedure outlined herein under the heading 'Possible Morning Hour Procedure' for circumventing the amending of the Journal and allowing the Senate to take up the bill without debate during the morning hour."

25. *Congressional Record*, CX, p. 4585.

26. A staff memorandum to Senator Mansfield, March 9, 1964, Washington, D.C, read: "Thought is to adjourn each night for two or three days so that Southerners will have to go through filibuster tactic each morning on amending the Journal."

27. *Congressional Record*, CX, p. 4590.

28. ". . . a measure must actually be before the Senate in order for a senator to make a motion to refer it to a committee, and not just a motion pending to proceed to its consideration." Watkins and Riddick, *Senate Procedure: Precedents and Practice*, pp. 505-506.

29. Author's notes on bipartisan leadership meeting of March 9, 1964, Washington, D.C. The bill's supporters also continued to interrupt the filibuster in order to discuss a variety of matters extraneous to civil rights. This practice eventually produced this observation from Cotton (Rep., NH) on March 23, 1964: ". . . the *Record* ought to show that . . . apparently senators have been speaking on a variety of subjects. In all fairness, I should say that if I decide to vote for cloture, my decision will be based on the amount of time that has been exhausted by the minority of the Senate." *Congressional Record*, CX, p. 5779.

30. *Congressional Record*, CX, pp. 4645-4652.

31. *Congressional Record*, CX, p. 4828.

32. *Congressional Record*, CX, pp. 5042-5046, 5079.

33. *Congressional Record*, CX, p. 4915.

34. *New York Times*, March 17, 1964, p. 1.

35. Memorandum of bipartisan leadership meeting, March 19, 1964, Washington, D.C.

36. Memorandum of bipartisan leadership meeting, March 19, 1964, Washington, D.C. The memorandum concluded: "It was deemed crucial that these steps be considered seriously as the most constructive way to preserve the initiative in the present situation and to demonstrate the toughness which seems to be called for under the present circumstances of delay."

37. Bipartisan Civil Rights Newsletter (mimeographed), No. 2, March 11, 1964; No 7, March 17, 1964, Washington, D.C.

38. Author's notes, March 25, 1964, Washington, D.C.; *New York Times*, March 26, 1964, p. 16.

39. *Congressional Record*, CX, p. 6206.

40. *Congressional Record*, CX, pp. 6206-6207. For an analysis of Morse's tactics and Russell's hopes of winning the vote by lining up a coalition in favor of "orderly procedure," see Jerry Landauer, "Southern Senators' Fight To Divide Forces Backing Rights Bill," *Wall Street Journal*, March 24, 1964, p. 5.

41. *Congressional Record*, CX, pp. 6241-6242.

42. *Congressional Record*, CX, p. 6344.

43. *Congressional Record*, CX, pp. 6234-6241.

44. Miller, Smith, McGee, and Carlson. *Congressional Record*, CX, p. 6344.

45. Dirksen, Hickenlooper, Hayden, Mechem, Williams, Jordan of Idaho, and Walters. *Congressional Record*, CX, p. 6344.

46. Pearson. *Congressional Record*, CX, p. 6344.

47. Marjorie Hunter, "Rights Command Set Up in Senate," *New York Times*, March 22, 1964, p. 41.

48. Rowland Evans and Robert Novak, "Rights and Religion," *Washington Post*, March 20, 1964, p. A21.

49. Hubert H. Humphrey, undated memorandum on

Senate consideration of the Civil Rights Act of 1964.

50. *New York Times*, March 19, 1964, p. 21; March 21, 1964, p. 14.

51. *Congressional Record*, CX, p. 6244. See also E. W. Kenworthy, "The South's Strategy," *New York Times*, March 28, 1964, p. 25.

52. *Congressional Record*, CX, p. 7254.

53. *Congressional Record*, CX, p. 7151.

54. *Congressional Record*, CX, p. 6651.

55. Author's notes on meeting, April 6, 1964, Washington, D.C.

56. See pp. 249-252.

57. *New York Herald Tribune*, April 10, 1964, p. 2.

58. *New York Times*, April 6, 1964, pp. 1, 16.

59. *Washington Post*, April 9, 1964, p. A1.

60. *New York Times*, April 16, 1964, p. 1.

61. Author's notes on bipartisan leadership meetings, April 7, 10, 14, 16, 1964, Washington, D.C.

62. *Washington Post*, April 2, 1964, p. A3.

63. Staff memorandum to Senator Mansfield, April 9, 1964, Washington, D.C.

64. Author's notes, April 10, 1964, Washington, D.C. Memoranda of bipartisan leadership meetings of April 14 and 16, 1964, Washington, D.C. Also, on April 15, a number of Senate staff assistants met with Leadership Conference lobbyists to estimate probable votes on cloture. See author's notes, April 15, 1964, Washington, D.C.

65. *New York Times*, April 18, 1964, p. 17.

66. *Congressional Record*, CX, pp. 8221-8228.

67. Criminal contempt involves the willful disobedience of a court order for which punishment by fine or jail sentence, or both, is imposed. Civil contempt proceedings seek only compliance with the court's ruling. Punishment is suspended as soon as the defendant complies. Henry Campbell Black, *Black's Law Dictionary* (St. Paul, Minn.: West Publishing Co., 4th ed., 1951), p. 390. The southern Democrats

had been debating the question of jury trials on the Senate floor since early April.

68. *CQ Almanac—1957*, pp. 568-569.

69. *Congressional Record*, CX, pp. 9515-9516.

70. Author's notes, April 22, 1964, Washington, D.C.

71. The Supreme Court several weeks earlier had denied the appeal of former Mississippi Governor Ross Barnett and then Governor Paul B. Johnson that their convictions of criminal contempt of the Federal courts without a jury trial contravened the guarantees of the Sixth Amendment. The opinion suggested, however, that if the penalty imposed on the violator was greater than that imposed for a "petty offense," the right to jury trial might be assured (*U.S. v. Ross Barnett*, 376 U.S. 681 [1964]). In sum, the Barnett ruling supported the leaders' decision to seek a provision patterned after the 1957 jury trial compromise.

72. Author's notes of bipartisan leaders' meeting with Dirksen, April 23, 1964, Washington, D.C.

73. *Congressional Record*, CX, 8715.

74. Nevertheless, the decision to submit this amendment probably helped prepare the bipartisan leaders for the more basic decision to negotiate over the Dirksen amendments. The Leadership Conference lobbyists, however, were quite fearful that this step would open the bill up to many other debilitating amendments.

75. *New York Times*, April 24, 1964, p. 1.

76. *Congressional Record*, CX, p. 8715.

77. *New York Times*, April 28, 1964, p. 1. For an analysis of Russell's difficulties in handling the divergent views among southern Democrats as to the wisdom of voting on amendments, see E. W. Kenworthy, "Rights Foes Split on Dirksen Move," *New York Times*, April 17, 1964, p. 18.

78. *New York Times*, April 28, 1964, p. 1.

79. The reaction of Humphrey, Kuchel, and Mansfield to the threatened use of cloture contained in the author's notes, April 29, 1964, Washington, D.C.

80. *New York Times*, April 29, 1964, p. 1.

81. Author's notes, April 29, 1964, Washington, D.C.

82. *New York Times*, April 30, 1964, p. 1.

83. Although the Mansfield-Dirksen substitute could not be amended further, it was permissible to offer "perfecting" amendments to the original Talmadge amendment. These perfecting amendments would be voted on prior to the Mansfield-Dirksen substitute. See Watkins and Riddick, *Senate Procedure: Precedents and Practice*, pp. 29-30.

84. Author's notes, April 29, 1964, Washington, D.C.

85. *New York Times*, May 1, 1964, p. 1.

86. *Congressional Record*, CX, p. 9505. Even the subhead in the *Congressional Record* read, "Announcement of Possible Vote on Wednesday, May 6."

87. *Congressional Record*, CX, p. 9511. Cosponsors included Williams (Rep., DL), Miller (Rep., IA), and Jordan (Rep., ID).

88. John Sherman Cooper (Rep., KY) introduced a perfecting amendment of his own to require jury trials in criminal contempt cases arising under the bill, but he exempted the sections dealing with voting, schools, and publicly owned facilities. Cooper claimed that either the Supreme Court or Congress had outlawed discrimination in these areas. If public officials willfully defied the law of the land in these respects, they were entitled to a jury trial only at the discretion of the court. *Congressional Record*, CX, p. 9798.

89. *Congressional Record*, CX, p. 9878.

90. *Congressional Record*, CX, p. 9879. Since a vote can be reconsidered only once, the winning side offers the motion to reconsider immediately, and then moves to lay that motion on the table, in order to foreclose reconsideration at a later time by the losing side.

91. *Congressional Record*, CX, p. 9880.

92. *Congressional Record*, CX, p. 9881. Later in the session, the Cooper amendment also was defeated, 74-19 *Congressional Record*, CX, p. 9886.

93. *New York Times*, May 7, 1964, p. 1.
94. *Congressional Record*, CX, p. 9878.
95. See Stewart, *Independence and Control*, pp. 52-53.
96. *Congressional Quarterly*, CX, p. 9881.
97. *Congressional Quarterly*, CX, p. 10722. See also *New York Times*, May 17, 1964, p. 1.
98. *Congressional Record*, CX, p. 9878.
99. *Congressional Record*, CX, p. 10228.
100. Hickenlooper, Hayden, Mechem, Williams, Jordan of Idaho, Walters, Miller, and Pearson voted against the leadership. Dirksen (paired), McGee, and Smith voted for the leadership. Carlson was absent. *Congressional Record*, CX, p. 9881.
101. See (original dissertation), pp. 171-177.
102. *Congressional Record*, CX, pp. 2804-2805.
103. *Congressional Record*, CX, p. 2776.
104. *Congressional Record*, CX, pp. 3580-3581.
105. *Congressional Record*, CX, p. 6234.
106. *Congressional Record*, CX, p. 2777.
107. See p. 182.
108. Memorandum of bipartisan leadership meeting of April 15 and April 17, 1964, Washington, D.C. Memorandum of bipartisan leaders meeting with Leadership Conference representatives, April 17, 1964, Washington, D.C.
109. In drafting these and subsequent amendments, Dirksen relied primarily upon the minority counsels of the Subcommittee on Administrative Practice and Procedure, the Subcommittee on Constitutional Amendments, and the Subcommittee on Antitrust and Monopoly Legislation, all of the Judiciary Committee.
110. *Washington Post*, April 1, 1964, p. A1.
111. *New York Times*, April 5, 1964, p. E5.
112. *Washington Post*, April 8, 1964, p. A5.
113. *New York Times*, April 9, 1964, p. 18.
114. *New York Times*, April 9, 1964, p. 18. See also *Wall Street Journal*, April 8, 1964, p. 3.

115. Memorandum of bipartisan leadership meeting of April 15, 1964, Washington, D.C.

116. *New York Times,* April 13, 1964, p. 12. *Washington Post,* April 14, 1964, p. A1.

117. Author's notes of bipartisan leadership meeting with Leadership Conference representatives, April 16, 1964, Washington, D.C.

118. *Washington Post,* April 14, 1964, p. A1.

119. *Washington Post,* April 15, 1964, p. A1.

120. *Washington Post,* April 15, 1964, p. A1.

121. *Congressional Record,* CX, pp. 7834-7837.

122. *Congressional Record,* CX, p. 7937.

123. Author's notes on bipartisan leadership-executive branch meeting, April 18, 1964, Washington, D.C. See also *Washington Post,* April 19, 1964, p. A1.

124. *Congressional Record,* CX, pp. 8330-8331. *New York Times,* April 22, 1964, p. 30.

125. *Washington Post,* April 22, 1964, p. A2.

126. Memorandum of bipartisan leadership meeting, April 22, 1964, Washington, D.C.

127. *Congressional Record,* CX, p. 8850.

128. This concept of "controlled independence" of the Senate's response to the president's legislative agenda is explored more fully in Stewart, *Independence and Control,* pp. 298-308.

129. Memorandum of bipartisan leadership meeting, April 22, 1964, Washington, D.C.

130. Author's notes on Humphrey-Dirksen conversation April 21, 1964, Washington, D.C.

131. *New York Times,* April 24, 1964, p. 1.

132. Author's notes, May 6, 1964, Washington, D.C. The *New York Times* first referred to the Dirksen negotiations in their story of Friday., May 1, 1964, p. 1.

133. Author's notes, May 6, 1964, Washington, D.C. *New York Times,* May 7, 1964, p. 1.

134. Author's notes, May 6, 1964, Washington, D.C.

135. The following description and evaluation of the Dirksen position is based primarily upon the author's notes, compiled during the negotiations, and subsequent conversations with other senatorial staff assistants who participated in the sessions. This material is supplemented, as noted, by dispatches in the daily press.

136. See statement by Humphrey on June 17, 1964, *Congressional Record*, CX, p. 13745.

137. The full text of the substitute bill is printed in the *Congressional Record*, CX, pp. 11537-11546. A title-by-title analysis by Humphrey, delivered on June 4, 1964, is found in the *Congressional Record*, CX, pp. 12283-12299.

138. *New York Times*, May 1964, p. 1.

139. Author's notes, May 15, 1964, Washington, D.C.

140. Author's notes, May 15, 1964, Washington, D.C.

141. *New York Times*, May 14, 1964, p. 1.

142. Author's notes, May 13, 1964, Washington, D.C.

143. Author's notes of bipartisan leadership meeting with Leadership Conference officials, May 7, 1964, Washington, D.C.

144. *New York Times*, May 1, 1964, p. 1.

Chapter 8

The Civil Rights Act of 1964: Tactics II

John G. Stewart

The decision by Senator Everett Dirksen of Illinois to support a cloture vote on an amended version of the civil rights bill was a major victory for civil rights forces in the Senate. But Dirksen's support in and of itself did not guarantee a favorable outcome. In this next section of his doctoral dissertation, John Stewart describes the "final drive" for cloture. He then details the unanticipated problems faced by the pro-civil rights senators in the "post-cloture" environment on the Senate floor.[1]

In the months which preceded the Senate's taking up the Civil Rights Act of 1964, speculation was rife that the battle might produce a major crisis over the institution's capacity to respond effectively to the needs of the black minority as spelled out by presidents John F. Kennedy and Lyndon Johnson and as later expressed by the House of Representatives with the passage of H.R. 7152. The power of the southern Democrats, grounded firmly in the Senate's explicitly established right of extended debate, had been able to defeat or largely emasculate all earlier civil rights proposals. There was no compelling reason why their prior successes should not be repeated in 1964.

This early speculation had focused on three possible results of another failure to defeat the southern Democratic filibuster:

First, there existed the danger of a crisis of the Senate as a viable instrument of contemporary democratic government.

This crisis might damage the integrity of the legislative process or produce even more basic changes in the nature of the Senate and its role in the governmental system. A massive outpouring of public sentiment against the institution itself might result in widespread civil disobedience in the District of Columbia, the intimidation of senators, disruption of the public sessions, or even violence. Whatever the response to this kind of illegal behavior, the process of representative democracy would have been dealt a serious blow.

Second, but less likely, the Senate might respond, as it did in 1917 with the passage of Rule XXII, by reducing the power of the filibuster to the point of empowering a simple majority to act in all circumstances. This decision would strike at what many persons believed to be the Senate's unique and necessary capacity to restrain an impassioned and impatient majority through the extended deliberation of a filibuster. It would, moreover, radically alter the character of the institution and the corresponding relationships with the executive branch and the House of Representatives.

Third, there was the most probable course that the party leaders, in their inability to break the filibuster, would follow their earlier patterns of eventually acceding to the principal demands of the southern Democrats and would thereby shift to the House and to the president the burden of whether to accept the Senate's changes or abandon the entire bill. The domestic consequences of either choice were equally alarming.

Yet by mid-May the nearly 13-week battle had demonstrated quite another lesson. The Senate apparently would enact a strong and comprehensive Civil Rights Act of 1964 by having followed procedures fundamentally *in accord* with its traditional norms and practices and by having rejected any crash effort to force the legislation through by threat or intimidation. Rather than producing an institutional crisis for the Senate, the battle over the Civil Rights Act of 1964 seemed likely to be a historic affirmation and demonstration of its ability to handle even this kind of divisive and potentially explosive issue through established procedures.[2]

This favorable development produced this comment in a staff memorandum to Senator Mansfield on April 28, 1964: "The time seems fast approaching when cloture should be attempted on the civil rights bill. The many diverse elements that are part of the formula for a successful cloture vote, such as 'fairness to the southerners,' the backlog of legislation in a short election year, and boredom with the filibuster, are combining in a manner that soon should enable us to win the vote when it comes."

To overcome the formidable obstacle of the filibuster, the floor managers of the bill, Humphrey and Kuchel, had sought to channel the pressures for major concessions in the substance of the legislation, which normally arose during a filibuster, into pressures for the application of cloture on a substantively acceptable bill. With a bipartisan team of civil rights activists, they pursued this strategy during the early weeks of the debate on four reasonably separate and distinct fronts: (1) winning the support of Everett Dirksen, (2) fostering a fair, deliberate, and reasoned debate, (3) organizing the civil rights proponents in the Senate, and (4) working closely with the groups and individuals outside the Senate supporting the bill. Upon the successful conclusion of the Dirksen negotiations, the party leaders believed they stood on the threshold of possessing the necessary votes to succeed in the debate's first, and they hoped only, motion to invoke cloture.

Whether the leaders could cross this threshold, however, depended in large measure upon their ability to coordinate and synchronize the disparate elements of strategy in a final drive to secure a solid two-thirds majority behind the substantive agreement reached with Everett Dirksen. This level of support on substantive policy could then be translated into the votes needed to invoke the procedure of cloture.

Their campaign to line up the remaining uncommitted senators moved into high gear immediately upon the adjournment of the final meeting with the minority leader on May 13, 1964. The job turned out to be more difficult than the leaders had supposed.

The Drive for Cloture

As the senators and Justice Department officials left Dirksen's office, two major questions remained to be answered: (1) Would the more conservative members of the Republican Party, those senators known to hold the balance of power on cloture, join in Dirksen's sponsorship of the substitute? (2) By the same token, would the activist civil rights supporters of H.R. 7152, both inside and outside the Senate, accept the Dirksen-Mansfield revisions? If either group refused to throw its support behind the new proposals, the chances of applying cloture would be negligible.

In other words, if the conservative Republicans and the liberal northern Democrats could not come together to support this new version of the civil rights bill, with almost ten weeks of debate having elapsed since Mansfield offered the motion to consider (13 weeks since the bill arrived from the House), passage of a bill acceptable to the House and the president would become highly doubtful in the 88th Congress. And rather than having been the catalyst in the leadership's drive to defeat the filibuster, the Dirksen negotiations would stand as a tactical gamble whose failure rendered inoperable the basic strategy developed to invoke cloture and pass the bill.

Within two hours of the end of the negotiations on May 13, 1964, Humphrey called the principal officials of the Leadership Conference to his Capitol office for a briefing on the contents of the Dirksen-Mansfield substitute. Attending for the Leadership Conference were Joseph Rauh, Clarence

Mitchell, Arnold Aronson (executive director of the Leadership Conference), Andrew Biemiller (chief lobbyist for the AFL-CIO), and Thomas Harris (counsel for the AFL-CIO).[3]

Deeply anxious about the bill's fate throughout the Dirksen negotiations, the Leadership Conference personnel were noncommittal as they listened to Assistant Attorney General Burke Marshall describe the principal elements of the substitute. They wanted to study the actual language before reaching any definite conclusions. The next morning senators Joseph Clark (Dem., PA) and Philip Hart (Dem., MI), supported by Justice Department and Senate staff, resumed the discussions with the Leadership Conference people. Although the Leadership Conference officials encountered some relatively minor provisions which they opposed, their general reaction was favorable. In particular, they acquiesced to the "pattern or practice" formulation for enforcement of Titles II (integration of public accommodations) and VII (equal employment opportunity).

By the end of Thursday, May 14, 1964, Humphrey felt relatively confident that the Leadership Conference would not attack the substitute publicly, even though they could be expected to advocate privately certain minor changes. And Humphrey also believed that a little disagreement from the Leadership Conference would make Dirksen's task easier. Any bill which the civil rights representatives accepted without a murmur of dissent would be that much harder to sell to the more conservative Republican bloc.[4]

The Democratic Conference

Mansfield scheduled a Democratic party conference for Tuesday morning, May 19, 1964, to review the proposed substitute bill. All Democratic senators were invited and even a half-dozen southerners appeared. Humphrey presided for most of the conference and explained the various changes which had been worked out with Dirksen. In response, several senators asked questions about specific provisions. A few northern Democrats grumbled that Dirksen was getting too much of the credit. The southern Democrats made the predictable attacks on the bill, although they also praised the leadership for the manner in which the debate was being conducted.

Philip Hart of Michigan put the basic question to his Democratic colleagues. Can you in good conscience accept the Dirksen-Mansfield substitute? He announced his decision to do so, and this attitude seemed to sum up the general reaction of all Democratic senators previously committed to H.R. 7152.[5] Given the generally restrained response from the Leadership Conference, it appeared that support from the civil rights proponents for the Dirksen-Mansfield substitute and for the application of cloture was secure.

The Republican Conference

Dirksen, however, was experiencing more difficulty with his Republican Party colleagues. In what proved to be the first of five Republican Party conferences devoted to the substitute, the minority leader reviewed on May 19, 1964, all the amendments except those contained in Title VII dealing with equal employment opportunity. There was little time at this first session for substantive discussion or debate. After the conference, Dirksen told reporters: "I don't believe we did ourselves any harm so far as cloture is concerned."[6]

Bourke Hickenlooper of Iowa, however, had walked out of the conference, just as he had left the first negotiating session in Dirksen's office. He continued to voice severe reservations, characterizing the substitute as a "gargantuan thing" and claiming that Dirksen's amendments did not go far enough "to meet the real evils of this bill."[7] Next morning the Republican Conference reconvened and Dirksen explained the numerous changes in Title VII (equal employment opportunity). After the conference, Norris Cotton of New Hampshire went to the Senate floor and introduced an amendment limiting coverage of the act to employers with a minimum of 100 employees, as opposed to the 25-employee limit eventually reached in the substitute bill.[8]

Although the minority leader continued to talk optimistically about Republican reaction to the substitute, he had clearly run into difficulty with a number of the crucial senators, principally Hickenlooper and Cotton, who were supported by Mundt, Curtis, Hruska, Miller, and Jordan. These senators were generally opposed to any notion of an enforceable job discrimination statute. Dirksen's advocacy of Title VII and the implication that Republicans had the obligation to support their party leader on this issue was, from their perspective, especially galling. Cotton, in fact, reported privately to Humphrey that at least nine Republicans were unwilling to support Dirksen on Title VII and were prepared to oppose cloture until major changes were made in the provision.[9]

In the bipartisan leadership meeting of Wednesday, May 20, 1964, Humphrey reported on these growing problems among the Republicans. He also noted that, in his opinion, no further concessions were warranted at this time, especially since Dirksen himself had not proposed any.[10]

Three more Republican Party conferences were held as Dirksen labored to overcome these difficulties and consolidate his position within the party.[11] He agreed to seek a variety of minor adjustments to the substitute bill, but rejected all proposals for major changes, such as Cotton's amendment to Title VII. On the evening of May 25, 1964, the bipartisan group of staff assistants and the Justice Department personnel met to see what further refinements were possible.

Considering the objections raised both by the Republican senators and the Leadership Conference officials, the staff accepted many of the suggestions so long as they did not change the legislation in any fundamental way.[12]

Accommodation and Adjustment

At this point the negotiators were following two relevant principles of party leadership: (1) permitting individual senators to recognize their handiwork in the bill and their interests being served by its passage, and (2) striving to accommodate the interests of the widest cross section of the senatorial parties as a means of reducing the fragmentation which could severely hamper the leadership's ability to control the parliamentary environment. This process of marginal accommodation and adjustment was to continue until the last day before the cloture vote.

For example, Humphrey and Dirksen accepted an amendment by Karl Mundt (Rep., SD) which exempted businesses maintained on Indian reservations from coverage under Title VII (equal employment opportunity).[13]

Richard Russell's Response

The next day, Tuesday, May 26, 1964, Dirksen introduced the Mansfield-Dirksen amendment in the nature of a substitute.[14] It incorporated these most recent adjustments. The minority leader received the unstinting praise of Mansfield, Humphrey, and Kuchel for his role in drawing up the substitute provision. Richard Russell, however, asked to be excused "for not opening my remarks by adding my bouquets to the praise that covers the distinguished senator from Illinois . . . (who) is without doubt the most accomplished thespian who has ever trod this floor."

Russell then attacked the prominent role which Attorney General Robert Kennedy assumed in the negotiations, maintaining that the Senate had thereby sacrificed its independence in considering the bill. He decried how the legislation seemed directed solely at southern racial problems. "It puts Charles Sumner, Thad Stevens, and Ben Wade to shame," Russell asserted.[15] Sumner, Stevens, and Wade were so-called Radical Republicans who sought to punish the South in the post-Civil War period.

Whether Dirksen merited either the bipartisan leaders' praise or Russell's opprobrium depended in large measure upon the minority leader's ability to deliver the crucial Republican votes for cloture. The substitute had unquestionably brightened the prospects in this regard, but no one in the civil rights command seemed ready to claim without qualification that Hickenlooper and his followers were prepared to follow their floor leader without further difficulty. But with the Mansfield-Dirksen substitute introduced, only one course remained: to push ahead in lining up 67 firm commitments to end the filibuster.

Organizing Outside Support

In this drive the bipartisan leaders called upon the Leadership Conference and their constituent organizations, especially the labor and religious groups, to activate all their resources, both human and material, in support of cloture. Whereas the negotiations with Dirksen had necessarily been held behind closed doors, a situation which called for the exclusion of the Leadership Conference and caused its representatives many anxious moments and much dismay, the cloture vote would be a distinctly public event, one where the Leadership Conference could perform a major role. The party leaders wanted the undecided senators to know that their performance on cloture would be monitored closely. The Leadership Conference could deliver this message.[16]

Obtaining an Accurate Vote Count

Since mid-April, in fact, the civil rights command in the Senate had been comparing notes with the Leadership Conference on the question of cloture. Attempting to formulate a more accurate vote count than the one prepared for Mansfield at that time, a bipartisan group of staff assistants, Leadership Conference lobbyists, and Justice Department officials met on April 16, 1964, to pool their information.

They estimated, on the basis of direct conversations with senators, that by mid-May a minimum of 58 senators would vote to invoke cloture. Another six were ranked at that time as "highly probable," including Peter Dominick (Rep., CO), Howard Edmondson (Dem., OK), Roman Hruska (Rep., NE), Everett Jordan (Rep., ID), Jack Miller (Rep., IA), and Thruston Morton (Rep., KY). Six Republicans were bracketed as the "Dirksen group," including Dirksen (IL) himself, Carl Curtis (NE), Norris Cotton (NH), Karl Mundt (SD), Bourke Hickenlooper (IA), and Edwin Mechem (NM).

Taken three weeks prior to the start of the Dirksen negotiations, this first full-scale survey indicated that cloture by mid-May would be a strong possibility.[17] By April 30, 1964, an updated estimate by the bipartisan leadership and the Leadership Conference operatives projected 64 to 65 affirmative votes, assuming they had secured the support of Dirksen and his group when the vote occurred.[18]

These earlier surveys were, however, essentially hypothetical. Until the Dirksen negotiations concluded senators could only voice general attitudes. But once the substitute had been agreed upon and circulated, senators could respond specifically to its contents and express themselves accordingly. Later estimates, reflecting the continuing doubts of many Republican senators originally included in the "Dirksen group" or rated in mid-April as "highly probable," were much less optimistic. Mansfield, for example, conceded on May 16, 1964, that he lacked the votes for cloture and finding them would be "nip and tuck."[19]

An Associated Press survey released on May 24, 1964, indicated that only 56 were definitely committed to vote for cloture in early June. In this survey 17 senators, including all the Republicans sought by Dirksen and the bipartisan leaders, gave qualified or noncommittal responses.[20] And on May 25, 1964, a count by the bipartisan leaders revealed that 12 more firm votes were still needed.[21] Coming almost two weeks after the end of the Dirksen negotiations, this last count documented the minority leader's difficulties in rounding up the disgruntled conservative Republicans gathered around Hickenlooper.

Putting on the Pressure

During the period immediately following the end of the Dirksen negotiations, Leadership Conference officials in Washington initiated a final effort to secure the support of undecided senators of both parties. They coordinated their efforts with the bipartisan leaders in the Senate. An operations center was opened one block from the Capitol, manned by personnel borrowed from various constituent organizations of the Leadership Conference. From there, all available resources were focused on winning the crucial votes. If a particular group had good access to a target senator, it assumed principal responsibility for securing his commitment. Communications with each senator were often channeled through persons in his state or delegations were brought to Washington.

Since many of the midwestern Republicans were not amenable to the normal lobbying approaches used on Democrats, e.g., visits by local union leaders, the religious groups were active in spearheading the campaigns for these pledges of support. In some cases home-state bishops sent telegrams to wavering senators. Groups of ministers placed conference telephone calls. Thousands of constituents wrote letters urging their senators to support cloture.

The Commission on Religion and Race of the National Council of Churches held daily meetings and religious services in a church one block from the Capitol. Seminary students maintained a 24-hour vigil in front of the Lincoln Memorial.[22] A massive Interreligious Convocation on Civil Rights, sponsored by the National Council of Churches, the National Catholic Welfare Conference, and the Synagogue Council of America, was held in the Georgetown University field house on the evening of April 28, 1964. Over 5,000 persons attended.[23]

In the week following introduction of the Mansfield-Dirksen substitute, the cumulative impact of the coordinated efforts inside and outside the Senate began to emerge in the form of a growing consensus that the southern Democrats had had their day and that the time for cloture had arrived. With the filibuster still blocking further votes on the jury trial amendments, sentiment within the Senate continued to shift in favor of cloture as the only way of breaking the impasse. On May 27, 1964, Mansfield told reporters: "I think, by and large, the senators have just about had enough. They're tired of all this. You have to hit bedrock some time and have a showdown."[24]

Although Dirksen had not resolved completely his problems with the senators now identified by the civil rights command as the "Hickenlooper group," he continued to work unreservedly in behalf of cloture.[25] In addition, the last-minute adjustments to the substitute had been well received among most of the Republicans. These developments inside the Senate were complemented by the Leadership Conference's work in the home states and in Washington.

And the machinery of the civil rights command continued to produce a quorum whenever the need arose and a supply of senators to patrol the floor during the southern Democrats' speeches. The net formed by the Senate leadership's original four-pronged strategy was being drawn even tighter.

SETTING THE DATE FOR CLOTURE

On Monday, June 1, 1964, Mansfield and Dirksen announced their decision to file the long-awaited cloture petition the following Saturday, June 6. Under this schedule the vote on cloture would occur on Tuesday, June 9, 1964.[26] This time the floor leaders sought to limit debate on the entire bill, the tactic Humphrey and Kuchel had strongly urged on the two earlier occasions when cloture had been threatened. This time the two whips agreed that further delay on cloture would be purposeless. The issue could only be brought to a head by announcing a specific date for a showdown. Humphrey and Kuchel also felt confident of winning the vote by a two-thirds majority. Their nose count of June 1, 1964, produced an estimate of 66 affirmative votes in mid-June, including such previously doubtful senators as Everett Jordan (Rep., ID), Thruston Morton (Rep., KY), James Pearson (Rep., KA), and Frank Lausche (Dem., OH). But the six principals of the Hickenlooper group remained in the possible category.[27]

In scheduling the vote for June 9, 1964, the floor leaders had deliberately waited until after the California Republican presidential primary on June 2, which pitted Barry Goldwater, a Republican senator from Arizona, against Nelson Rockefeller, the Republican governor of New York. Goldwater had already told Dirksen of his intention to vote against cloture. Given this fact, the minority leader wanted to avoid confronting Goldwater's backers in the Senate, essentially those senators of the Hickenlooper group, with the necessity of deciding whether to follow the Arizona senator's lead on cloture until the California primary no longer stood as a factor in their decision.[28]

But Dirksen also wanted to have the civil rights issue settled before the Republican National Convention convened in San Francisco on July 13, 1964. He feared its status as a live question in the Senate at that time would only exacerbate the growing split in the Republican party between the pro- and anti-Goldwater factions.[29] On the basis of these considerations, and sensing a growing momentum for cloture, the floor leaders circled June 9, 1964, as the date for the historic vote.[30]

Unexpected Complications

In rapid succession, however, two unforeseen developments threatened the success of the bipartisan civil rights strategy in the final days of its implementation. First, Russell announced on Tuesday, June 2, 1964, the southern Democrats' willingness to halt the filibuster temporarily to permit votes on the jury trial amendments that were still pending.[31] Second, the feud between Dirksen and the Hickenlooper group, which had been brewing for months within the inner councils of the Republican party, broke into open rebellion on the Senate floor when Hickenlooper announced on Friday, June 5, 1964, that at least 17 Republicans demanded an opportunity to vote on certain amendments before casting their votes on cloture.[32]

The Counter-Filibuster

As he had done on the two earlier occasions when a cloture vote appeared imminent, Russell reactivated his tidbit tactic, i.e., decelerated the momentum for cloture by permitting a vote or two without, however, making any further commitments to finish voting on the entire bill. This time, however, the civil rights command was no longer interested in tidbits. Having announced the Senate leadership's intention to file a cloture petition on Saturday, and fearing that any intervening votes might dissipate the rising pressure for cloture, Mansfield, with a grin, explained to Russell that "beginning this afternoon there will be some speeches on the question of the pending jury trial amendment, and that beginning tomorrow a number of senators . . . have indicated their intention to speak on the Dirksen substitute."[33]

In other words, the pro-civil rights forces were about to launch a counter-filibuster to prevent any votes until Tuesday's showdown on cloture. Various senators dusted off unused speeches and consumed the time without great difficulty. Humphrey, for example, filling in for an ailing Dirksen, delivered the official explanation of the substitute.[34]

Yet Russell's move did place the bipartisan leaders in an awkward and embarrassing position. In effect, the civil rights forces were using the procedure of extended debate to tide them over until the announced time had arrived for a vote on the procedure to limit debate. In the delicate business of assigning blame for the lack of progress on the bill, some civil rights proponents feared that Russell's tactic might shift some of the burden of obstructionism from the southern Democrats to the civil rights forces. After much discussion, however, the bipartisan leaders adhered to their earlier decision to push resolutely ahead with a cloture vote on June 9 and to block all other votes in the interim.

In line with this thinking, a staff memorandum to Senator Mansfield recommended: "If the southerners at any point during the week decide to stop talking so as to allow a vote on one or more of the jury trial amendments, the leadership should prevent a vote from taking place until a count revealed that the Talmadge amendment could be safely and easily tabled."[35]

THE HICKENLOOPER REVOLT

But on Friday, June 5, 1964, these plans were suddenly scrapped. In mid-afternoon Senator Bourke Hickenlooper (Rep., IA) proposed a unanimous consent request, supported by at least 17 Republicans, that the Senate vote on three amendments before Tuesday: (1) the Morton jury trial amendment which had been narrowly defeated on May 6, (2) the Cotton amendment to limit the coverage of Title VII (equal employment opportunity) to firms with 100 or more employees, and (3) a Hickenlooper amendment to eliminate from Title IV (desegregation of public education) authorization for training institutes and federal study grants designed to assist in the process of desegregation.[36]

Goldwater's resounding victory in the California primary and Dirksen's absence from the Senate due to illness were thought to have emboldened the Hickenlooper clique. They moved to translate their general dissatisfaction with the substitute, and with their floor leader for taking the lead in producing it, into this demand for special treatment of their amendments.

Recovered from a brief illness, Everett Dirksen had come to Hubert Humphrey early in the day on Friday, June 5, 1964, with the distressing news the entire drive for cloture would be put in jeopardy by the Hickenlooper move. He referred to serious "slippage" among Mundt, Cotton, Curtis, Miller, and Hruska.[37] E. W. Kenworthy of the *New York Times* described June 5, the day of the Hickenlooper request, as "a day of huddles and scurrying to and fro, as confusing as any day since debate began March 9."[38]

Although Hickenlooper never said so explicitly in his remarks on the Senate floor, the bipartisan leaders understood clearly the terms of the unanimous consent request. Either you agree to these votes or a substantial number of Republicans will vote against cloture next Tuesday. The linkage between substance and procedure was never more evident.

The same day Cotton also expressed on the floor his dissatisfaction with the result of the Dirksen negotiations and the minority leader's refusal to accept any major changes during the five party conferences which followed. Describing how he presented his amendment to Title VII in the final conference on May 25, 1964, Cotton said: "I have never presented a proposal to a committee which received less attention than my amendment received on that occasion. . . . Senators know that we sometimes sit at a committee table and some crackpot comes in and sounds off. The chairman smiles sweetly and says, 'Thank you. We are very appreciative of your being here.' Out the man goes—and that is just the way I went out of my conference."[39]

Hickenlooper's ultimatum left Mansfield with little choice. The decision to attempt cloture had already been announced. Any postponement of this vote would be interpreted as a major admission of weakness by the civil rights command, a development which might impede the momentum that was building for cloture. But a defeat on the first cloture vote due to Republican defections would strengthen immeasurably the bargaining position of the senators who held the balance of power, essentially the same ones backing Hickenlooper in his request. More than this, however, Humphrey had been told privately by one of the rebelling senators that if the three amendments were voted on, most of the senators supporting Hickenlooper would then vote affirmatively for cloture, whether or not the amendments carried.[40]

Given the Republican renegades' subsequent support for cloture, their action was less of a determined last-ditch stand against the substance of the Mansfield-Dirksen compromise (although there was much in it with which they disagreed) than a demonstration of their independence of the agreements which Dirksen had reached with the Justice Department. There also was an implied rebuke to their floor leader for his assuming they would defer quietly on the matter. Their independent decision to disrupt the bipartisan leadership's carefully drawn schedule for cloture would communicate that dissatisfaction in language Dirksen would understand. The incident served again to illustrate the internal problems encountered by a party leader who became deeply and personally identified with a complex set of substantive issues on a highly controversial bill.

But the Hickenlooper rebels were apparently unwilling to assume responsibility for the bill's defeat at that advanced stage of the debate or even for the emasculation of its crucial titles. In fact, a small number of senators in the Hickenlooper group could have thwarted the Senate leadership's plans for cloture, and their price for cooperation could have been far higher than merely asking for an opportunity to vote on three amendments. But this leverage was never used. As one renegade senator remarked in a conversation with Humphrey: "All we really wanted was the chance to show that Dirksen wasn't the only Republican on the Senate floor."

Roman Hruska of Nebraska was one Republican senator who held this point of view. He said: "We are reluctant to surrender our right, before cloture, to speak our minds and state our positions."[41]

After he recovered from the initial shock of this unusual public display of Republican infighting, Mansfield promptly agreed to Hickenlooper's unanimous consent request for the three votes.[42] The majority leader had no difficulty in providing these Republicans with an opportunity for a show of independence and a chance to flex their senatorial party muscles. Dirksen was too deeply committed to cloture and the substitute bill to take offense. And the benefits of locking up the cloture issue by granting Hickenlooper's request far outweighed the minor inconvenience of having to postpone the cloture vote by one day.

Humphrey went even further. He pledged that any of the rebel Republican amendments adopted by the Senate would be included in the Dirksen-Mansfield substitute before cloture was voted on.[43]

Richard Russell's Dilemma

Hickenlooper's unanimous consent request, however, presented Russell with a profound dilemma. If he failed to object, he knew the crucial Republican senators probably would then be ready to vote for cloture on Tuesday. But if he blocked the request (and a single objection would be sufficient), the blame would fall upon the southern Democrats. This fact would likely compel the Republicans to vote for cloture anyway. Russell also wanted to consult with his less predictable southern Democrats so that no one would break ranks in a show of defiance similar to Thurmond's solo filibuster in 1957.

In these difficult circumstances, Russell finally asked Hickenlooper for another day in which to consider his request. Russell said: "I hope that the senator from Iowa will not compel us to make a shotgun decision on the spur of the moment here." After lengthy debate, all the senators agreed to postpone a final decision until Saturday morning, June 6, 1964. The following day Russell made no attempt to conceal his problem: "We are now caught between two rocks in a hard place. I have been in that position before, but the rocks have not been so large nor the place so hard as it is today. . . . But out of deference to the wishes of the senator from Iowa . . . I have concluded not to interpose an objection to the unanimous consent request."[44]

The Hickenlooper agreement called for the Senate to debate Morton's jury trial amendment on Monday, June 8, 1964, and to vote on this amendment early Tuesday. Debate and votes on Cotton's and Hickenlooper's amendments would occupy the remainder of Tuesday. The cloture petition would be filed on Monday, June 8, with the vote on cloture taking place on Wednesday, June 10, one day later than originally scheduled.

Prior to Russell's acceptance of Hickenlooper's unanimous consent request, Mansfield had filed the cloture petition on Saturday, June 6, 1964, to demonstrate clearly the leadership's intention to adhere to the original cloture schedule if the southern Democrats blocked the three pre-cloture votes.[45] When agreement was reached, however, Mansfield withdrew the petition and reoffered it on Monday.[46]

On Tuesday, June 9, 1964, the Morton amendment, defeated in May by the narrowest of margins, carried, 51-48. Three northern Democrats reversed their earlier positions on the Morton amendment: Stuart Symington (MO), Edward Long (MO), and Henry (Scoop) Jackson (WA).[47] But given the accelerating momentum for cloture, the bipartisan leaders were not particularly distressed by the defeat. A month earlier when cloture was still very much in doubt, and both sides were sparring cautiously to gain the initiative in the debate, approval of the jury trial amendment would have constituted a grave reversal for the civil rights forces. The Justice Department, while favoring a bill without these procedures for prosecuting cases of criminal contempt, concluded that adoption of the Morton amendment did not hinder unduly the legislation's enforcement machinery.[48]

The Cotton amendment to Title VII (equal employment opportunity) and the Hickenlooper amendment to Title IV (desegregation of public education) were both easily defeated.[49] Sam Ervin (Dem., NC) also managed to obtain a vote on his proposal to strike Title VII from the bill. It lost, 64-33, by almost the 2-1 margin needed for cloture.[50] Buoyed by these three substantial victories, and no longer seriously alarmed by the impact of the Morton jury trial amendment on the legislation itself or on the parliamentary situation,[51] the bipartisan leaders looked confidently ahead toward Wednesday's historic vote on cloture.

ROUNDING UP THE VOTES

Mansfield was satisfied to have Humphrey manage final details of the leadership's cloture drive. The majority whip had kept the White House fully advised of the progress toward cloture, but he never felt it necessary to call for President Johnson's personal intervention with any senator. Whether the president did so on his own initiative was not known. It was, however, rumored that, due to the president's urging, Senator Carl Hayden (Dem., AZ) either agreed to absent himself or vote affirmatively if it meant the difference between defeat or victory. Hayden remained in the cloakroom until a two-thirds majority had voted for cloture and then came onto the Senate floor to vote against it.[52]

But the Leadership Conference, especially the labor organizations, spared no effort in the last days. Leadership Conference members concentrated principally on the few remaining undecided Democratic senators, e.g., Howard Cannon (NV), Howard Edmondson (OK), and Ralph Yarborough (TX). The union officials complemented similar efforts being made within the Senate by the Democratic leadership.[53] After their day of glory on Tuesday, the Republican supporters of Hickenlooper's minor coup came quietly without additional persuasion from Dirksen or outside sources.

On Tuesday evening, June 9, 1994, Humphrey made final calculations in his Capitol office and, before leaving for home, he told President Johnson that cloture would be invoked the next day. Early in the evening, Humphrey had counted only 65 sure votes. Then the news tickers carried the story of Hickenlooper's announcement of his intention to vote affirmatively. The total stood at 66. At this point the absence of one senator would have been sufficient to guarantee a two-thirds majority of those present and voting. Senator Clair Engle (Dem., CA) was critically ill with brain cancer and not expected by most people to appear the next morning.[54]

But Humphrey continued to work on the Democratic holdouts. He placed phone calls to Edmondson, Yarborough, and Cannon and followed up with them again Wednesday morning. In a dictated memorandum Humphrey noted: "I had worked very hard even the night before to nail down the votes of Edmondson, Yarborough, and Cannon. It was doubtful about Cannon, but we were terribly pleased when he came through. I informed the president on Tuesday night at 7:30 that we had the votes. He said he hoped so, but he said it would be difficult. I told him I was sure of it."

One hour before the vote Humphrey passed a note to Philip Hart (Dem., MI) predicting 69 to 70 affirmative votes. His three Democrats had all responded favorably. Even this prediction proved to be one vote shy.[55]

Cloture Day

On the 75th day of debate, the Senate prepared itself for the historic roll call on cloture. As the appointed hour of 11:00 a.m. approached, an air of drama and expectancy suffused the Senate chamber to a degree seldom experienced by even the most senior members. The public galleries had been filled for hours. Outside on the Capitol lawn, a TV reporter stood ready to relay to the nation a vote-by-vote capitulation of the roll call.[56] Roger Mudd, the CBS-TV newsman, received a verbal report of each vote by telephone from the press gallery. He then recorded it immediately on the cloture scoreboard set up on the lawn. Many of the senatorial staff assistants, barred from the Senate floor during the vote, were unable to squeeze into the public galleries and retreated to a senator's Capitol office and followed the vote through Mudd's TV report.

A number of senators delivered statements prior to the vote, but Mansfield, consistent to the end, permitted Dirksen to close the debate. The minority leader responded to the moment with one of his better oratorical efforts, remembered principally for his use of Victor Hugo's aphorism: "Stronger than all the armies is an idea whose time has come."

Dirksen also intoned: "The time has come for equality of opportunity in sharing in government, in education and in employment. It will not be stayed or denied. It is here."[57] He closed with a plea for Republicans to uphold the campaign pledges of their party. "Were these promises on civil rights but idle words for vote-getting purposes," Dirksen asked, "or were they a covenant meant to be kept? If all of this was mere pretense, let us confess the sin of hypocrisy now and vow not to delude the people again."[58]

In almost total silence, the clerk called the roll. All 100 senators responded. Even Clair Engle (Dem., CA), critically stricken with brain cancer, was wheeled in in a wheel chair. Barely able to speak, he indicated an affirmative vote by pointing to his eye. Lee Metcalf (Dem., MT), the acting president pro tempore, announced the result: "71 yeas; 29 nays. Two-thirds of the senators present having voted in the affirmative, the motion is agreed to."[59] There were four votes to spare.

Of the 12 senators identified in mid-February as "crucial" by the Democratic Policy Committee staff study, 9 voted to apply cloture (Dirksen, Carlson, Hickenlooper, Jordan of Idaho, Miller, Pearson, Smith, McGee, and Williams of Delaware) and 3 were opposed (Hayden, Mechem, and Walters). This 9-3 division, in itself, would not have been sufficient to secure the necessary two-thirds majority. The victory ultimately resulted from a combination of the 9 "crucial" senators and 7 originally classified as "reasonably sure against," including Cannon, Monroney, Edmondson, Yarborough, Hruska, and Curtis.

Reasons for Success

For the first time since Rule XXII was adopted in 1917, cloture had been invoked on a civil rights bill.[60] It was a striking vindication of the strategy which the Democratic party leaders began devising a year earlier, as well as the tactical decisions which had been made in the course of the debate itself. In retrospect, two decisions appeared crucial: (1) abandonment of the "no amendments" policy and (2) holding back on any serious bargaining with Dirksen until he became convinced of the necessity for cloture.

Once Russell's tactics had demonstrated to the minority leader the futility of attempting to change the bill on the floor by piecemeal amendments, and once the civil rights proponents had established the credibility of their intention to hold out until cloture was invoked, the bipartisan leaders could deal with Dirksen in an atmosphere where controlled negotiation was possible. They could demand the federal enforcement of Titles II (integration of public accommodations) and VII (equal employment opportunity) while yielding to Dirksen on other pre-enforcement procedures. They also acknowledged that Dirksen's lesser amendments generally helped clarify a number of smaller ambiguities and inconsistencies found in the House-passed bill.

The exercise, in short, provided a method controllable by the party leaders for the Senate to demonstrate its independence from the executive branch and the House of Representatives and for the minority party, led by Dirksen, to participate in shaping the final legislative product. Given the major obstacles created by the bitter southern Democratic filibuster, the assertion of bipartisan independence was an essential step in the process of compiling the two-thirds majority for cloture.

The brief Republican rebellion organized by Hickenlooper testified primarily to the numerous restraints under which any elected party leader must operate. Despite Dirksen's elaborate and painstaking efforts to maintain a unified front among his Republicans, many of the senators supporting Hickenlooper simply felt that Dirksen was getting too much of the credit while he was actually selling out to Lyndon Johnson and the Justice Department on the vital point of enforcement. The Hickenlooper unanimous consent agreement, while it put the capstone on the drive for cloture, demonstrated the party leadership's inability to silence dissident senators or simply to command their loyalty. But the narrow scope of the Hickenlooper agreement suggested further that, if party leaders could not command support, they could control the legislative result by carefully structuring the choices open to the senators. The payment demanded by the Hickenlooper group was surprisingly low.

In a dictated memorandum Humphrey observed: "I do believe that this . . . Hickenlooper unanimous consent package brought us the extra votes that we needed for cloture. I can recall Senator Russell complaining that we hadn't cooperated with him when he wanted to vote, and I said to him somewhat in jest, but also in truth, 'Well, Dick, you haven't any votes to give us in cloture and these fellows do.' That was the sum and substance of it."[61]

Major factors in the leadership's ability to maintain this control in the final stages of the cloture drive were the effective organization of the civil rights forces in the Senate and the external pressures brought to bear on uncommitted senators by the Leadership Conference groups. One senator finally admitted in exasperated tones: "Every time I'd try to argue, . . . they'd get down on their knees and start to pray. How can you win an argument against God?"[62]

The exclusion of the Leadership Conference lobbyists during the Dirksen negotiations, and their heavy participation in the final cloture drive, suggested that party leaders could use this type of mass organizational pressure most effectively at those points in the legislative process which were visible to the public, such as floor debate, where the behavior of senators could be monitored and where they could be held accountable for their actions. The kind of intimate, person-to-person relationship between a lobbyist and a senator, a far different kind of outside pressure, would be more likely to achieve results on the committee level and in the cloakroom. To this degree the elected party leaders seemed to share with the president an interest in maintaining the ability to generate mass organizational pressure at critical moments of floor debate.

Finally, Richard Russell's lack of tactical flexibility in the several weeks prior to cloture, his inability to drop tidbits more frequently, helped the civil rights forces build up the image of total southern obstructionism. If voting had continued in early May on the jury trial amendments, for example, the outcome of the Dirksen negotiations might have been far different. The minority leader might have been less willing to concede the critical point of federal enforcement in the private bargaining sessions and more likely to have taken the issue to the Senate floor for final disposition. But the southern Democrats also had their dissidents and rebels, and Russell consequently had to sacrifice tactical flexibility as the price for maintaining internal unity of the southern forces.

In summary, almost three months of patient, unremitting pressure in an environment which permitted the Senate to affirm its institutional independence achieved what few persons thought possible: cloture on a civil rights bill with all essential substantive provisions intact.

The Final Days

The strategy of the bipartisan leaders had been devised to produce a two-thirds majority on the motion to invoke cloture. After 75 days of debate, it had succeeded brilliantly. But few preparations had been made for controlling the debate in the period after the application of cloture until final passage of H.R. 7152, the period where the immediate majority would again be operative.

There had been a small amount of preparation. For example, on June 10, 1964, the day of the cloture vote, the Bipartisan Civil Rights Newsletter carried this admonition in capital letters: "If this morning's cloture vote is successful and cloture is imposed, the leadership expects that there will be voting on amendments soon thereafter. As the Senate convened on Monday [June 8, 1964], a total of 411 amendments had been offered; a substantial number have been introduced since then. *For this reason senators are urged to avoid engagements that will take them away from the Capitol when the Senate is in session.*"[63] There had not, however, been the systematic preparation with the senators individually or in groups that had taken place in the earlier segments of the debate.

On the surface it appeared that the civil rights forces were then unstoppable, that cloture had destroyed the southern Democrats' will to resist further. Yet a closer look suggested that the battle was by no means ended. Approximately 560 amendments qualified for consideration under the terms of Rule XXII, and each senator had one hour of speaking time in which to call up these amendments.[64] The adoption of many of these amendments would, moreover, drastically alter the substance of the legislation. But, so great had been the leadership's concentration on cloture, they had ignored totally the job of organizing their forces to protect the bill's substance in the post-cloture period.

Since only amendments "presented and read" prior to cloture qualified for consideration, a successful southern Democratic amendment probably could not be countered subsequently by another amendment offered by the civil rights command because it could not be introduced except by unanimous consent. Under these conditions, the bipartisan leaders could ill afford any miscalculations in the numerous roll call votes which lay ahead.

THE ERVIN DOUBLE JEOPARDY AMENDMENT

Immediately upon the announcement that cloture had been imposed, the bipartisan Senate leadership's lack of planning became evident. As commotion and chaos replaced the silence and tenseness which had gripped the Senate during the roll call on cloture, Senator Sam Ervin of North Carolina called up his amendment which prohibited a person who was acquitted or convicted of a specific crime under the bill from also being charged with criminal contempt and vice versa. This "double jeopardy" amendment carried, 49-48. In the commotion on the floor after the cloture vote, the chair first announced erroneously that Ervin's amendment had been defeated, 48-47.[65]

Only when the correct vote had been announced did the bipartisan leaders realize that Ervin's amendment appeared to open a serious loophole in the enforcement machinery by permitting a state to acquit a person for a crime related to the legislation and thereby prevent any subsequent U.S. prosecution for criminal contempt. But the leaders also discovered that in the confusion on the floor Ervin had not offered his amendment to the Dirksen-Mansfield substitute. Instead he had amended the House text, which would be eliminated entirely upon adoption of the substitute. In short, Ervin's double jeopardy amendment, despite its adoption, would survive only until passage of the Mansfield-Dirksen substitute just prior to third reading of the bill.

This comedy of mistakes surrounding the Ervin amendment confronted the bipartisan leaders with the urgent necessity of deciding their policy of response to the numerous southern Democratic amendments that would be called up. After defeating Russell's amendment to postpone the effective date of Title II (integration of public accommodations) for two years, Mansfield hurriedly recessed the Senate until 3:00 p.m. in order to "give us a chance to regroup, rethink and recollect."[66]

Post-Cloture Strategy Making

Meeting later that afternoon and again at 9:00 a.m. on Thursday, June 11, 1964, the civil rights proponents disagreed sharply among themselves on the specific problem of their response to Ervin's demand that he be permitted to reoffer his amendment in proper form to the Dirksen-Mansfield substitute and, more generally, on their strategy of response to all southern Democratic amendments. Should the leaders oppose every southern amendment as a matter of explicit policy or should they retain some flexibility and, where possible, attempt to develop an acceptable version of the amendment?[67]

Mansfield, supported by Humphrey, reacted to the situation in a thoroughly consistent and predictable fashion. Maintain the pre-cloture posture of fairness and consideration of all senators, including the southern Democrats, even though the party leaders now possessed, at least potentially, the power to execute a much less generous policy. Instead of voting down every southern Democratic amendment regardless of its substance, the majority leader and whip advocated taking positive steps that would ease the burden of the southerners' crushing defeat on cloture and would help reunify the party.

In the opinion of the Democratic party leaders, that at least meant being receptive to those amendments which might ameliorate a particularly acute personal or constituency problem and which did not make any basic change in the legislation. At one point Mansfield even suggested giving the southern Democrats additional time to offer amendments under cloture. Humphrey stressed that a policy of voting down all amendments might possibly backfire unexpectedly at some point. "You can only push senators around for so long," he said. "Suddenly you'll have a revolt on your hands." He seemed particularly concerned that amendments to Title VI (cutoff of U.S. funds) might carry if strict policies of rejecting all amendments were announced by the leadership.

Humphrey recalled the bitter feelings which certain liberal senators still harbored about the leadership's decision to table numerous of their amendments during the 1962 debate over establishing the Communications Satellite Corporation. He stressed that tabling motions should not be used in 1964 to dispose of the southern Democratic amendments to H.R. 7152 for fear of reviving these antagonisms among otherwise friendly senators.[68]

On the other side of the argument were several northern Democrats who assigned less importance to the party leadership's concern over reestablishing cordial relations with the southern Democrats. Philip Hart (Dem., MI) and Joseph Clark (Dem., PA), in particular, argued that a policy of deliberate conciliation toward the southerners would dissipate the momentum of the cloture triumph and prolong unnecessarily final passage of the bill. They also asserted the impossibility of reacting intelligently to dozens of skillfully drafted southern amendments. "How can you accept some and not others?" asked Hart. "Once you begin such a process, every senator who doesn't have his favorite amendment accepted is going to be sore at the leadership."

As if to prove Hart's argument correct, within an hour of this 9:00 a.m. meeting, Norris Cotton (Rep., NH) made the following statement on the Senate floor in response to a unanimous consent request to permit Russell Long (Dem., LA) to offer an amendment to Title VI: "If we are going to start granting unanimous consent with relation to amendments that are not printed and at the desk, I merely wish to say that I shall offer mine, and if objection were made to my amendment, I suggest that there would be discrimination."[69]

Back at the leadership meeting, John Pastore (Dem., RI), focusing on the specific issue of the Ervin amendment, responded that he, for one, was not ready to vote against the concept of protecting a citizen from double jeopardy. He predicted that other superficially attractive amendments would be offered during the debate. Unless the bipartisan civil rights leadership was willing to consider developing relatively innocuous alternatives to these amendments, some might be adopted, as illustrated by Ervin's victory.[70]

The leaders also discussed the problem of ending the debate as expeditiously as possible. Under cloture every senator had only one hour of speaking time. However, in just 30 seconds a senator could call up an amendment and demand a roll call vote, but he was not then charged with the time actually required to call the roll, approximately 15-20 minutes, nor the time for a quorum call after the vote on the amendment.

In short, an expenditure of 30 seconds of a senator's hour could consume half an hour of clock time. At that rate the process of disposing of the southern Democratic amendments, even under cloture, might require several weeks if the southerners decided to oppose the bipartisan leadership to the bitter end.

Mansfield suggested, therefore, that a more sympathetic treatment of the southerners' amendments at the outset might, in turn, encourage them to conclude the debate more quickly. Also, a policy of absolute opposition to all southern Democratic amendments might reinforce their determination to resist. For these reasons the majority leader favored negotiating a compromise with Ervin. Mansfield would agree to support Ervin's reoffering of his double jeopardy amendment to the substitute bill but in a form that would not impair the bill's enforcement machinery. Then Mansfield suggested offering similar treatment to other southern Democrats if their amendments were not totally unacceptable.

Hart and Clark, on the other hand, continued to advocate getting tough with the southern Democrats and anyone else who called up amendments.[71]

When the Senate convened at 10:00 a.m. on Thursday, June 11, 1964, a general strategy toward southern Democratic amendments had not been agreed upon, although Mansfield had won support for an accommodation on the Ervin amendment. This absence of a broader policy, however, had immediate consequences. Within minutes, Humphrey agreed voluntarily with Russell Long (Dem., LA) to develop acceptable language for a Long amendment to Title VI that allegedly would insure against its application to enforce nondiscrimination in the U.S. government insured home mortgage market—a policy which Pastore, floor captain of Title VI, claimed had already been included in the bill. Pastore also charged that Long's amendment would have invalidated President Kennedy's executive order which barred discrimination in housing insured by the Veterans Administration and the Federal Housing Administration.

After extended controversy on the floor, and over Pastore's strong objections, Humphrey stood by his commitment to Long.[72] Later in the day the Justice Department produced a version of the amendment which satisfied Long but read that Title VI did not affect the U.S. government's existing antidiscrimination policy on home mortgages one way or the other. It was added to the bill.

Following this exchange, the redrafted and now harmless Ervin amendment won overwhelming approval, 80-16. Only a hard core of 16 pro-civil rights senators voted against the compromise.[73]

Although Humphrey and Mansfield, usually after consulting with Dirksen,[74] occasionally accepted or had modified a handful of other amendments, a procedure began to emerge naturally on the Senate floor that differed in few respects from the process of across-the-board rejection advocated by Clark, Hart, and other pro-civil rights senators. Unless a senator on his own initiative sought the assistance of the party leaders in devising acceptable language, his amendment was dispatched swiftly and surely. Only a handful of votes were close. In most cases the southern Democrats proposed changes so basic that no compromise was possible and, in fact, few were sought.

The southerners appeared more interested in compiling a record of total hostility to the legislation rather than resolving specific substantive problems through the good offices of the party leadership. And so, without debate or soul searching, the bipartisan forces disposed of the amendments one after the other. Aiken enunciated his formula for deciding how to vote in these circumstances: "It is perfectly obvious that the sponsor of an amendment cannot explain it in less than 5 minutes. . . . When the sponsor of an amendment asks for less than 5 minutes, it is obvious that he does not care whether I understand his amendment or not. So I vote 'nay.' It is a very simple formula, which is available to any senator."[75]

One can speculate whether the standing offer of the party leaders to work out particular substantive problems in amendments offered by the southern Democrats and others averted any general revolt against the party leaders in this period of numerous roll call votes and quorum calls. However, given the complexities of adjusting the few problems which were brought to the leadership's attention, primarily by Russell Long of Louisiana, it appeared fortunate that no more southern Democrats availed themselves of the opportunity. The problem of deep substantive involvement by party leaders was well illustrated by their few attempts to be kind to their southern colleagues. But there were no serious rebellions against the leadership in this exhausting period after cloture. Instead, pressure intensified among the senators for the southern Democrats to end their repetitious offering of amendments which were doomed to defeat.

A Lack of Southern Strategy

In proposing their many amendments, the southern Democrats followed no discernable pattern or prearranged plan. Russell and his charges seemed no better prepared for the period under cloture than the bipartisan leaders. A southern senator would obtain the floor and offer a series of amendments, often in random order, drifting from one title of the bill to another.

Humphrey remarked privately that a carefully prepared strategy by the southern Democrats for proposing their amendments might have produced some unexpected reverses for the civil rights forces, but this never happened.[76] Nor did more of the southern senators exploit the willingness of Mansfield and Humphrey to help devise alternative language that could be included in the bill. Russell Long (Dem., LA) was, in fact, the only southern senator to take the initiative in bargaining with the bipartisan Senate leadership. Three of his amendments were ultimately adopted, although each one needed substantial rewriting by the Justice Department staff.

Instead of bargaining with Mansfield and Humphrey, the southerners seemed satisfied to propose dozens of amendments that were certain to lose. By Monday, June 15, 1964, Russell informed Mansfield and Humphrey of his desire to conclude the debate as quickly as possible and said that he had no further amendments to propose personally. The southern Democratic leader acknowledged the futility of prolonging the struggle further.[77] Russell told the *New York Times* that "he himself had no more amendments and he thought his colleagues would not call up any of substance."[78]

But three of Russell's southern colleagues—Strom Thurmond (Dem., SC), Sam Ervin (Dem., NC), and Russell Long (Dem., LA)—had other plans. Continuing to exhibit the independence which had hampered Richard Russell before cloture, they made clear their intention to sustain the fight for at least a few more days. As long as they rationed their debating time carefully, the three senators were well supplied with amendments. At the time cloture was invoked Ervin had introduced 128 amendments, Long 93, and Thurmond 94. It also was permissible for these three senators to call up any other amendment that had been introduced, even if another senator was its author.

This southern intransigence was made clear following a southern Democratic caucus on Tuesday, June 16, 1964. Richard Russell announced that the debate would continue with southern Democrats calling up as many amendments as possible.[79]

In these circumstances Mansfield, who had deliberately sought to avoid late-night sessions, decided to bear down. On Tuesday, June 16, 1964, the Senate worked from 10:00 a.m. until midnight and voted on 33 amendments, an all-time record for roll call votes in one calendar day.[80] By early evening on Tuesday, as fatigue and discouragement spread through the ranks of both parties, senators began to chafe openly at the southern tactics. Patrick McNamara (Dem., MI) complained that the debate had become a "form of filibuster, with senseless and useless quorum calls in order to kill time. . . . I hope (the leaders) will keep us here all night, and that we run a 'tough show' from here on."[81]

A Motion to Adjourn

About an hour later Senator James Eastland (Dem., MS) took the most unusual step of moving to adjourn, a procedural motion reserved strictly for the majority leader or his designee. It was a challenge which neither Dirksen nor Mansfield could have ignored and still have presumed to preside over activities on the Senate floor. During the roll call on Eastland's motion, two Republicans, Peter Dominick of Colorado and Edwin Mechem of New Mexico, voted in the affirmative. They thus were opposing both Mansfield and Dirksen, who were busy lining up every non-southern Democratic vote to crush this minor rebellion against the prerogatives of the floor leadership.

Outraged at this unexpected slap at the party leaders, Dirksen dispatched a covey of pages to locate the errant Republican senators before the vote ended. Dominick was the first to return and quickly changed his vote to "nay." After some delay, Dirksen and Mechem entered the chamber and walked down the center aisle. The minority leader looked Mechem squarely in the eye and commanded, "Now vote!" Whereupon Mechem quietly responded: "Nay." By the margin of 73-18 the Senate rejected the motion to adjourn and upheld the party leaders' prerogatives on such a strictly procedural question as the hour of the Senate's adjournment.[82]

Tuesday's exhausting session had the desired effect. The southern Democrats decided to call up their final amendments on Wednesday, June 17, 1964, even though several southerners could have held out for a few more days. A bit of humor even returned to grace the proceedings. Richard Russell proposed, after scribbling the amendment at his desk, that the bill be retitled "The Dirksen-Humphrey-Kennedy Civil Rights Act of 1964." When Mansfield refused Russell's request for unanimous consent, the senator from Georgia remarked: "Does not the senator from Montana recognize that all of us soon will pass from this mortal scene. . . . But if we emblazon their names on the front page of the bill, their names will remain there for all time to come, until the American people rise in their wrath and defeat it."[83]

In the early evening, Strom Thurmond (Dem., SC) finally made his long-awaited announcement: "This is the last amendment I shall offer."[84] When it had lost, like so many of its predecessors, the southern Democratic struggle to block the Civil Rights Act of 1964 in the Senate was over. In all, 10 amendments were accepted, including the principal Dirksen-Mansfield substitute, while 99 amendments were defeated.[85]

Final Passage

Quickly the Senate passed the Mansfield-Dirksen amendment in the nature of a substitute, as amended, by the margin of 76-18.[86] The bill received its third reading, closing it to further amendment, and the Senate adjourned. All that remained were the closing speeches and the final vote.

Thursday, June 18, 1964, was devoted entirely to speeches. Both proponents and opponents wanted their respective positions clearly on the record. Interest centered on Senator Barry Goldwater's (Rep., AZ) expected statement about his position on the final vote. Even though the man, now seemingly assured of the 1964 Republican presidential nomination, had voted against cloture, the press continued to carry reports about his alleged desire to support the bill on final passage.[87] But stressing instead his belief that the legislation bestowed unconstitutional authority on the U.S. government in Titles II and VII, Goldwater announced his intention to vote against H.R. 7152.[88]

On Friday, June 19, 1964, one unexpected vote took place on a motion by Albert Gore, Sr. (Dem., TN) to recommit H.R. 7152 to the Judiciary Committee for the purpose of adding an amendment to Title VI (cutoff of U.S. funds) that would have prevented termination of U.S. financial assistance to any school district unless a U.S. court desegregation order had been violated. Following Gore's motion, Humphrey made the point of order that it was out of order on two counts: (1) it had not been "presented and read" prior to the cloture vote, and (2) H.R. 7152 had already received its third reading.

To his surprise, however, Humphrey learned that Gore had received unanimous consent on the prior afternoon to offer his amendment. Therefore, the motion was in order and Humphrey withdrew his point of order. Gore claimed that he had "waited until the Democratic leadership was on the floor of the Senate" before offering his unanimous consent request. He seemed quite offended that Humphrey had termed the request "unusual."[89] In fact, the leadership did not know of Gore's intention to propose the unanimous consent request. If they had been so aware, they would have objected to it.

When the Senate voted 74-25 against Gore's motion to recommit, there were those who suggested that the magnitude of the defeat stemmed at least partially from general disapproval of Gore's procedure in scheduling the vote without the explicit sanction of the party leadership.[90]

In their final remarks on Friday, June 19, 1964, the principal architects of the victory stressed their pride in the Senate's ability to legislate successfully on this complicated and emotionally charged issue. Humphrey, drawing from Benjamin Franklin's closing remarks at the Constitutional Convention in 1787, declared that he would "consent to this measure because I expect no better and because I am not sure it is not the best."[91]

Mansfield suggested that the moment of the final vote was "perhaps of even greater significance than the outcome of the vote itself, for it underscores, once again, the basic premise of our government. . . . That a people of great diversity can resolve even its most profound differences, under the Constitution, through the processes of responsible, restrained and reciprocal understanding."[92]

And, as on the cloture vote, Mansfield deferred again to Dirksen in delivering the closing speech. "What has happened in 'the year that was' is a tribute to the patience and understanding of the country, of the Senate, and generally the people of this Republic," declared the minority leader. "There is involved here the citizenship of people under the Constitution who, by the 14th Amendment, are . . . citizens of the United States of America. That is what we deal with here. We are confronted with the challenge, and we must reckon with it."[93]

Indeed, the day of reckoning had arrived. Moments after Dirksen concluded his address, H.R. 7152 passed by the vote of 73-27.[94] On the 83rd day of debate, the Civil Rights

Act of 1964 went back to the House of Representatives for its consideration of the Senate amendments.

Immediately after the Senate passed the civil rights bill, Majority Leader Mike Mansfield, true to character, disclaimed any credit for the victory. He even refused to pose for photographs with Dirksen, Humphrey, Kuchel, and other senators who had been instrumental in the triumph.[95]

Diminished Elation

Two events diminished the sense of elation which many of the bipartisan leaders otherwise would have felt upon the bill's passage. First, on June 17, 1964, Humphrey learned of the serious illness of his eldest son, Robert, who had a cancerous lymph node removed from his neck. Fortunately he recovered fully in the coming weeks. Second, following the final vote, senators Birch Bayh (Dem., IN) and Edward Kennedy (Dem., MA) left Washington in a private plane to attend a party rally in Massachusetts, only to crash. As it turned out, Kennedy's back was badly injured, but early reports of the accident claimed that Kennedy had been killed.

House Action

The bipartisan civil rights leadership in the House already had decided to accept the Senate amendments without requesting a conference to resolve the differences between the acts as passed by the respective houses. Both the bipartisan leaders in the Senate and Justice Department officials, principally Deputy Attorney General Nicholas Katzenbach, had kept in close touch with the bipartisan leaders in the House. Due to his statements during the House debate, Representative William McCulloch (Rep., OH) received special attention in order to make sure that the Senate amendments would be acceptable. Once the full scope of the Mansfield-Dirksen substitute bill had been determined, all of the House leaders indicated their willingness to accept the changes.

It was crucial that this happen. If the House had insisted on a conference, the report of the conferees would have to be approved by each house. This would have given the southern Democrats in the Senate another opportunity to conduct a filibuster.[96]

As soon as the Committee on Rules voted out a resolution authorizing the House to accept H.R. 7152, as amended by the Senate, the House could approve the resolution of acceptance and dispatch the act to President Johnson for his signature. In order to prevent Howard W. Smith (Dem., VA), chairman of the Committee on Rules and an implacable foe of the legislation, from stalling action further by not convening the committee, the Democrats initiated the procedure to authorize a meeting without the chairman.[97] In response to this pressure, Smith scheduled a Rules Committee meeting for June 30, 1964, and the bipartisan majority for the bill promptly approved the resolution, 10-5.[98] On July 2 the House voted, 289-126, to accept the bill as amended by the Senate.[99]

A few hours later, after addressing the nation in a televised ceremony from the East Room of the White House, and in the company of the massive coalition of senators, representatives, and private citizens who fought for the bill, President Johnson signed H.R. 7152 into law.[100]

Notes

1. John G. Stewart, *Independence and Control: The Challenge of Senatorial Party Leadership* (Ph.D. dissertation, University of Chicago, 1968). This section is from ch. 7, pp. 255-288.

2. See E. W. Kenworthy, "Civil Rights Bill—Why It Is Taking So Long," *New York Times*, May 17, 1964, p. E12. See also *New York Times*, May 18, 1964, p. 1.

3. Author's notes, May 13, 1964, Washington, D.C.

4. Author's notes on bipartisan leadership meetings of May 14 and May 1, 1964, Washington, D.C.

5. Author's notes of Democratic party conference, May 19, 1964, Washington, D.C. *New York Times*, May 20, 1964, p. 1.

6. *New York Times*, May 20, 1964, p. 34.

7. *New York Times*, May 20, 1964, p. 34.

8. *New York Times*, May 20, 1964, p. 1.

9. Author's notes, May 19, 1964, Washington, D.C.

10. Memorandum of bipartisan leadership meeting, May 20, 1964, Washington, D.C.

11. One conference was held on Friday, May 22, and two on Monday, May 24, 1964. *New York Times*, May 26, 1964, p. 27.

12. Author's notes of final negotiating session with Dirksen's staff, May 25, 1964, Washington, D.C.

13. See U.S., Congress, *H.R. 7152*, 88th Congress, 2nd Session (1964), Title VII, Sec. 703 (i).

14. *Congressional Record*, CX, pp. 11537-11538. Although the Dirksen-Mansfield substitute in effect stood as a complete bill in its own right, it was introduced as an amendment in the nature of a substitute to H.R. 7152. In this capacity, it would be the last amendment to H.R. 7152 voted on before "third reading," the point in the parliamentary process when amendments could no longer be considered, and after all other amendments to the Dirksen-Mansfield substitute had been voted up or down.

15. *Congressional Record*, CX, p. 11554.

16. Robert E. Baker, "Rights Leaders Urged To Mobilize Opinion," *Washington Post*, May 20, 1964, p. A1.

17. Author's notes and memorandum of cloture survey, April 16, 1964, Washington, D.C. A staff memorandum to Senator Mansfield dated April 28, 1964, also noted: "This

could indicate that with proper preparation cloture can be obtained. The question arises as to what procedural tactics should be employed in this effort. These include, briefly, timing, length of sessions, and amendments."

18. Memorandum of bipartisan leadership—Leadership Conference meeting, April 30, 1964, Washington, D.C.

19. *Baltimore Sun*, May 17, 1964, p. 1.

20. *Washington Evening Star*, May 24, 1964, p. 1.

21. Staff memorandum on cloture prepared for bipartisan leadership, May 25, 1964, Washington, D.C. See also Rowland Evans and Robert Novak, "The Big Manhunt," *Washington Post*, May 20, 1964, p. A17.

22. For various activities of lobbying groups, see Bipartisan Civil Rights Newsletter (mimeographed), No. 42, April 29, 1964; No. 55, May 15, 1964. See also the periodic "Memos" (mimeographed) published by the Leadership Conference on Civil Rights announcing the various groups and delegations coming to Washington to lobby for the bill.

23. *New York Times*, April 29, 1964, p. 1.

24 *New York Times*, May 28, 1964, p. 14.

25. The "Hickenlooper group" of Republicans generally included Hruska (NE), Curtis (NE), Cotton (NH), Hickenlooper (IA), and to a lesser degree Miller (IA) and Mundt (SD). See also Jerry Landauer, "Civil Rights Forces To Try To End Filibuster in Senate in June," *Wall Street Journal*, May 25, 1964, p. 1. See also Richard Wilson, "Hickenlooper and the Rights Bill," *Washington Evening Star*, May 25, 1964, p. 9.

26. *Congressional Record*, CX, pp. 11856-11857.

27. Staff memorandum on cloture prepared for bipartisan leadership, June 1, 1964, Washington, D.C.

28. Robert C. Albright, "California Primary Delays Cloture," *Washington Post*, May 21, 1964, p. 45. See also *Washington Post*, May 22, 1964, p. 1.

29. *Washington Post*, June 1, 1964, p. A1.

30. *Congressional Record*, CX, p. 11856.

31. *Congressional Record*, CX, p. 12013.

32. *Congressional Record*, CX, p. 12408.

33. *Congressional Record*, CX, p. 12013.

34. *Congressional Record*, CX pp. 12281-12299. *New York Times*, June 4, 1964, p. 18.

35. Staff memorandum to Senator Mansfield, June 2, 1964, Washington, D.C.

36. *Congressional Record*, CX, p. 12408. Hickenlooper's amendment would have eliminated Sections 404, 403, 406 of H.R. 7152.

37. Author's notes, June 11, 1964, Washington, D.C.

38. *New York Times*, June 6, 1964, p. 1.

39. *Congressional Record*, CX, pp. 12308-12389.

40. Author's notes, June 11, 1964, Washington, D.C.

41. Hruska (NE) also characterized Senator Cotton's description of Dirksen's conduct in the Republican party conference "as most restrained, and may tend to be somewhat charitable." *Congressional Record*, CX, p. 12391. See also *New York Times*, June 6, 1964, pp. 1, 10, and June 8, 1964, p. 1.

42. *Congressional Record*, CX, p. 12409.

43. *Congressional Record*, CX, p. 12417. Unless these adjustments were made, the successful amendment would eventually be vitiated upon adoption of the Mansfield-Dirksen amendment in the nature of a substitute. When the Morton amendment carried, the leadership introduced just prior to cloture on June 10 an entirely new substitute containing the Morton provision. See *Congressional Record*, CX, p. 12857.

44. *Congressional Record*, CX, p. 12427.

45. *Congressional Record*, CX, p. 12425.

46. *Congressional Record*, CX, p. 12489.

47. *Congressional Record*, CX, p. 12611.

48. Author's notes, June 11, 1964, Washington, D.C.

49. The Cotton amendment lost, 63-34. See *Congressional Record*, CX, p. 12653. Hickenlooper's amendment lost, 56-40. See *Congressional Record*, CX, p. 12600.

50. *Congressional Record*, CX, p. 12645.

51. As noted earlier, the jury trial issue had appealed to some northern liberals concerned with civil liberties and to labor unions traditionally opposed to judges enforcing their own injunctions. These factors, totally unrelated to the question of applying cloture on a civil rights bill, also made it possible for the bipartisan leaders largely to discount the effect of their defeat. *New York Times*, June 10, 1964, p. 1.

52. *New York Times*, June 11, 1964, p. 21.

53. *New York Times*, June 11, 1964, p. 21. Author's notes, June 11, 1964, Washington, D.C.

54. Author's notes, June 11, 1964, Washington, D.C.

55. Author's notes, June 11, 1964, Washington, D.C.

56. *New York Times*, June 11, 1964, p. 21. *Washington Post*, June 11, 1964, p. A1.

57. *Congressional Record*, CX, p. 12866.

58. *Congressional Record*, CX, p. 12867.

59. *Congressional Record*, CX, p. 12875.

60. Eleven earlier attempts had failed. On only four of the prior efforts were the civil rights proponents able to produce even a simple majority. See *Congress and the Nation* (Washington, D.C.: Congressional Quarterly, Inc., 1965), p. 1637. See also Anthony Lewis, "The Strategy of Cloture," *New York Times*, June 11, 1964, p. 21. See also Rowland Evans and Robert Novak, "Cloture Post Mortem," *Washington Post*, June 18, 1964, p. A23.

61. Humphrey memorandum.

62. Related to the author by Senator Humphrey. See author's notes, June 21, 1964, Washington, D.C.

63. Bipartisan Civil Rights Newsletter, No. 74, June 10, 1964.

64. Only amendments "presented and read" prior to the cloture vote could be called up except by unanimous consent. All amendments and motions, moreover, had to be germane. *Standing Rules*, XXII, 24.

65. *Congressional Record*, CX, p. 12876.

66. *Congressional Record*, CX, p. 12878.

67. Author's notes, June 11 and June 15, 1964, Washington, D.C.

68. Author's notes, June 11 and June 15, 1964, Washington, D.C.

69. *Congressional Record*, CX, p. 12969.

70. Author's notes, June 15, 1964, Washington, D.C.

71. Author's notes, June 15, 1964, Washington, D.C.

72. *Congressional Record*, CX, pp. 12968-12969, 12996.

73. *Congressional Record*, CX, p. 12970. The Justice Department had prepared an amendment which simply reaffirmed a person's existing rights against double jeopardy in the federal courts and eliminated the possibility of spurious acquittals or convictions in state courts.

74. For example, a package of minor amendments was presented by Miller (Rep., IA). *Congressional Record*, CX, pp. 12993-12994. Another amendment was presented by Long (Dem., LA) which stated that a person could not be convicted of criminal contempt unless there was an "intentional" violation. *Congressional Record*, CX, p. 13729.

75. *Congressional Record*, CX, p. 13410.

76. Author's notes, June 15, 1964, Washington, D.C.

77. Author's notes, June 15, 1964, Washington, D.C.

78. *New York Times*, June 16, 1964, p. 1.

79. *New York Times*, June 17, 1964, p. 1.

80. *Washington Post*, June 17, 1964, p. A2.

81. *Congressional Record*, CX, p. 13416.

82. *Congressional Record*, CX, p. 13438. *Washington Post*, June 17, 1964, p. A2.

83. *Congressional Record*, CX, p. 13707.

84. *Congressional Record*, CX, p. 13743.

85. *Revolution in Civil Rights* (Washington, D.C.: Congressional Quarterly, Inc., 1965), p. 66.

86. *Congressional Record*, CX, p. 13746.

87. *New York Times*, June 10, 1964, p. 1.

88. *Congressional Record*, CX, pp. 13825-13826.

89. *Congressional Record*, CX, p. 13934.

90. *Congressional Record*, CX, p. 13943. The reaction of other senators is noted in the author's notes of June 20, 1964, Washington, D.C.
91. *Congressional Record*, CX, p. 13945.
92. *Congressional Record*, CX, p. 14010.
93. *Congressional Record*, CX, p. 14012.
94. *Congressional Record*, CX, p. 14013.
95. Author's notes, June 20, 1964, Washington, D.C.
96. Author's notes, June 15, 1964, Washington, D.C.
97. *Washington Post*, June 23, 1964, p. A6.
98. *New York Times*, June 25, 1964, p. 1, and July 1, 1964, p. 1.
99. *Congressional Record*, CX, p. 14982.
100. *New York Times*, July 3, 1964, p. 1.

Chapter 9

Independence and Control

John G. Stewart

At the conclusion of his doctoral dissertation, John Stewart sought to relate the successful passage of the Civil Rights Act of 1964 to the tradition of "independence" among members of the United States Senate. He notes that Senate leaders must somehow find a way to exercise "control" over a group of individuals who, by the very nature of their elected office, are entitled to operate in a highly "independent" manner. Stewart concludes that it was only by respecting the traditional "independence" of their Senate colleagues that the pro-civil rights Senate leadership was able to overcome the filibuster and produce such significant, far-reaching legislation.[1]

The Senate passed the Civil Rights Act of 1964 on Friday, June 19, 1964. After the roll call on final passage, the victorious team of bipartisan leaders gathered in Majority Leader Mansfield's office for a round of hand shaking, press statements, and photographs. In spite of the fact that he was the top party leader in the Senate, Mike Mansfield's dislike of personal publicity caused him, even in this great victory for the party leadership, to avoid being included in any of the press photographs.[2]

One hour later a crowd of several thousand persons still ringed the approaches to the Senate wing of the Capitol, waiting to congratulate and applaud the senators who had led the successful battle. Responding to natural instincts, a number of the leaders left the majority leader's office and walked down the Senate steps to acknowledge the cheers of their joyous supporters.

And fully three hours later, when the bill's floor manager, Hubert Humphrey, left the Senate for a downtown restaurant, he was astounded to find several hundred persons still encamped outside. Their enthusiasm appeared boundless. In his 15 years in the Senate, the majority whip could recall no similar outpouring of public sentiment over a bill's passage.[3]

These details are recounted only to suggest the drama which surrounded the Senate's consideration of the civil rights bill and the importance which many persons attached to the outcome. Its passage was to many critics of senatorial norms and traditions an unexpected demonstration of the institution's ability to act without a prior change in the filibuster rule or related practices. The Senate had not merely survived its most notable institutional challenge of the post-World War II era, but its supposed outworn and unworkable procedures never looked better when the southern Democrats were beaten at their own game.

The final product of the 83-day debate was considerably expanded and strengthened over the version submitted to Congress a year earlier by President John F. Kennedy. The principal addition was Title VII, establishing a national nondiscrimination program in employment under the direction of the Equal Employment Opportunity Commission. Franklin D. Roosevelt, Jr., the son of the former president, was named the first chairman of the commission.

No essential element of the act received from the House of Representatives had been abandoned or weakened in the Senate. The Senate's past treatment of civil rights legislation and the initial unfavorable reaction of many uncommitted senators to the public accommodations and equal employment titles made the outcome especially satisfying for the bill's proponents. Years of disappointment and defeat for civil rights supporters were redeemed, if not forgotten, in this moment of victory.

Pressures for Victory

Many factors contributed to this striking reversal of form. One might, for example, assemble evidence to support Everett Dirksen's conclusion that the passage of the Civil Rights Act of 1964 was essentially the result of "an idea whose time had come." In this view the senatorial party leaders had only to preside over a debate whose outcome was fundamentally guaranteed by the interplay of several considerable forces.

The Leadership Conference on Civil Rights and the many religious groups working for the bill's passage placed great significance on the mass expressions of support which came from a multitude of private citizens previously silent on the civil rights issue. With a strong emphasis on the alleged morality of the bill's objectives, this sentiment proved to be especially effective among uncommitted midwestern Republicans. President John F. Kennedy's assassination also seemed to mute overt criticism of the bill's more controversial parts by some persons, especially during its debate in the House of Representatives.

The civil rights groups managed to submerge their internal differences in a common fight for the bill, and national civil rights leaders headed off any widespread civil disobedience or other attempts to intimidate the members of Congress during the long months of the bill's debate. The urban riots in Philadelphia, Pa., Rochester, N.Y., and New York, N.Y., were not to occur until later in the summer of 1964. In summary, public support had been aroused to a degree never before achieved in earlier civil rights battles.[4]

President Lyndon Johnson's unswerving determination to pass the bill provided the party leaders in Congress, and especially those in the Senate, with a mandate to wage the battle in terms of total victory. Richard Russell, the leader of the southern Democrats, had seen the possible consequences of this posture even before the debate commenced. In early March of 1964 he observed:

> I think President Johnson feels that if he loses any substantial part of it, that will cast all of his statements in support of it in doubt as to their sincerity. That really makes it a much more difficult position as to any possible compromise that there would have been had President Kennedy not met his tragic fate.[5]

But the position of the president, in itself, did not guarantee success. Presidents have often been defeated by Congress on measures they backed without qualification. It did, however, reduce greatly the leadership's latitude for pursuing a course of concession and compromise, the traditional response to the stresses of a filibuster.

And this position of the president's also provided the leaders with a bona fide excuse for demanding of their colleagues an extra measure of effort when the pressures of the filibuster began to take their toll in April and May. With much the same effect, the bipartisan coalition which eventually backed the legislation in the House of Representatives, together with the public statements by leading House members about their refusal to acquiesce to any major concessions by the Senate, limited the propensity for compromise during the bill's journey through the Senate.

Finally, the southern Democrats' reliance upon a strategy of almost total obstructionism, forsaking numerous opportunities early in the debate for amending the bill's controversial sections, helped drive the uncommitted senators into the civil rights coalition for the vote on cloture. Had the southern Democrats been more imaginative, had they allowed more votes on amendments designed to appeal to the "crucial" senators, the civil rights forces would have been hard pressed to sustain their case that cloture was the only feasible alternative to deadlock.

For example, the bipartisan leaders generally believed that an amendment by Norris Cotton (Rep., NH) to limit the coverage of Title VII (equal employment opportunity) to firms with 100 or more employees would have carried easily in the opening weeks of the debate. When the Senate finally voted on it, the day before cloture, it lost, 63-34.[6]

But, as discussed earlier, Richard Russell's tactical flexibility was hampered by internal divisions within the southern bloc. And so, with the exception of votes on the motion to consider and the Morton and Cooper jury trial amendments, the opponents' words flowed on while the frustrations of everyone else mounted.

These were the factors which differentiated 1964 most distinctly from the earlier civil rights struggles in 1957, 1960, and 1962. And perhaps these forces were sufficient in their own right, regardless of the behavior of the senatorial party leaders. One can, of course, never really know.

But the process of managing any major bill is complex and demanding. Little can be taken for granted. And opportunities to commit grievous strategic and tactical errors are plentiful, especially when a well-organized coterie of opponents is anxiously watching for the slightest misstep which might relieve its hard-pressed circumstances. Although the various pressures which developed in the 1964 debate were missing in earlier civil rights battles, the senatorial leaders channeled these forces in a manner which suggested that the successful outcome was not preordained. Indeed, without the leadership's contribution, the bill might have foundered.

"Controlled Independence" in 1964

What had the party leaders contributed to the successful effort to pass the Civil Rights Act of 1964 which otherwise could not be accounted for? In brief, they had applied the pro-civil rights pressures in ways which made them affirmative factors in controlling the Senate's decision on cloture and related issues. A major element in the leaders' ultimate success, moreover, was their conscious decision to use these pressures in a manner which retained the Senate's opportunity for reaching independent decisions on the substance of the legislation.

As revealed in the frequent past skirmishes in the Senate over Rule XXII (the filibuster rule), the tradition of senatorial independence has included the notion that simple majorities may be called upon to prove themselves persistent and undoubted.[7] This proof had to be assembled by the party leaders before the majority could act in 1964. Neither Mansfield nor Humphrey believed this could be done simply by unleashing the considerable forces supporting immediate action on the House-passed bill.

The uncommitted senators, whose votes would determine the outcome of cloture, held deep reservations about certain titles. They were, moreover, unreceptive to the direct appeals of the bill's more fervent advocates. Instead, the party leaders believed they had to establish a legislative environment where the doubts of the uncommitted senators could be expressed and acted on, within the limits of acceptability laid down by the president and the House of Representatives.

In short, the leadership's open acceptance of the legitimacy of independent senatorial action, and their willingness to provide opportunities in the debate for the expression of these independent views, helped establish a credible parliamentary situation where the opposition of the uncommitted senators could eventually be overcome and where control by the party leaders over the crucial decisions could be established.

On the basis of the 1964 experience, adequate control by the party leaders over closely fought issues depends upon establishing a legislative environment where appropriate deference can be paid to the senatorial norms of independence and autonomy, obligations of party notwithstanding. With considerable variation in technique arising from shifts in the political environment, differing strategies of leadership, and the nature of the particular issue, this quest for "controlled independence" sums up the challenge of senatorial party leadership.

In 1964 the party leaders initiated a number of positive steps to achieve an independent evaluation of the bill's more controversial sections but in a manner which ultimately strengthened their control over crucial substantive decisions.

During the period of the bill's gestation, for example, a period extending roughly from late March until early May of 1964, the party leaders rebuffed a number of tactical suggestions by the Leadership Conference on Civil Rights which, in their opinion, would have threatened too directly the Senate's efforts to conduct a searching evaluation of the bill, e.g., conducting round-the-clock sessions, arresting senators who failed to answer quorum calls, and enforcing the two-speech rule. In these weeks Mansfield and Humphrey, in particular, wanted to establish beyond question that the southern Democratic opponents had received every opportunity to make their case to the public and to their senatorial colleagues.

The party leaders also kept Dirksen well insulated from massive outside pressure, and they emphasized repeatedly the importance of lobbyists avoiding anything which smacked of threat or intimidation. Many other uncommitted senators were also protected from overzealous solicitation by outside groups in these formative weeks. The southern Democrats were not attacked personally, and their motives in opposing the bill were not questioned. Indeed, the party leaders went out of their way to maintain an atmosphere of good relations and mutual respect.

In these circumstances the party leaders believed their major objective of passing an acceptable bill would be advanced by providing undecided senators an opportunity to evaluate the legislation free from the pressures of outside persons often unable to understand a senator's lack of enthusiasm for a certain provision. The party leaders believed further that, once the uncommitted senators had examined the bill independently, they would become more susceptible to the external and internal pressures needed for victory on cloture and other major issues.

The party leaders' decision to abandon President Johnson's policy of defeating all Senate amendments to H.R. 7152 revealed both their concern for achieving some display of senatorial independence and their skill in controlling the effect of such action. In their sponsorship of the Mansfield-Dirksen jury trial amendment, the leaders believed they had outflanked the southern Democrats on parliamentary procedure. They were confident that the joint sponsorship of the substitute amendment by both floor leaders would insure a clear majority.

Things seemed to be under control. Although the Senate would demonstrate its independence by adding the jury trial provision to the bill, no serious damage would be done to the bill's enforcement mechanism. However, Richard Russell's parliamentary skill in developing the Morton perfecting amendment, and the Democratic party leadership's reduced capacity for mobilizing its forces on the roll call vote, almost handed the victory to the southern Democrats. These needless miscalculations nearly sacrificed the leadership's control of the debate in one of its critical moments.

The negotiations with Dirksen came to a more satisfactory conclusion. Stimulated in large measure by a growing feeling that verbatim approval of the House text could be defended no longer, i.e., that the uncommitted senators were determined to amend certain critical sections, the negotiations were conducted on an informal, off-the-record basis which guaranteed flexibility and control to both sides. It provided a forum where the exercise of senatorial independence would not destroy the essential parts of the bill.

Trial balloons could be released and retrieved. Unresolved issues could be dropped temporarily and raised again later. The entire agreement could be stitched together in a way which met the vital interests of both sides before any isolated part was made public.

Ostensibly a discussion between Dirksen and the bipartisan leaders, the principal bargaining in fact took place between Justice Department officials and Dirksen's staff. And in terms of the political forces which had to be brought into agreement in order to produce a bill, the negotiations were, in effect, conducted between the president, as represented by the Justice Department personnel, and the uncommitted senators, as represented by Dirksen.

The party leaders then brought forth the compromise package of amendments as a substitute bill. This technique permitted the bipartisan leaders to develop a bill which both the uncommitted senators and the civil rights forces could ultimately accept, without incurring the grave risks of hammering out such a delicate compromise in public on the Senator floor. The Dirksen negotiations, in short, represented a striking example of "controlled independence" in operation.

What factors helped the party leaders establish control of the civil rights debate in the midst of the Senate's display of its institutional independence? In the early weeks of the debate, the civil rights forces within the Senate had to establish without question their capacity to outlast the southern Democratic filibuster no matter how long it went on. Past filibusters had demonstrated that many of the bill's 55 original proponents would assign higher priority to their immediate personal interests rather than linger in the Senate corridors waiting for quorum calls. An invitation to address the home-state Rotary convention or the state labor council would be accepted. The quorum calls would be forgotten.

The party leaders, however, arranged a daily schedule assigning each proponent specific days for quorum duty and clearing other days for more personal activities. This routine attendance mechanism, established by the party leadership, was a device seemingly far removed from the great issues over which the debate was waged. But this attendance mechanism proved to be a vital factor of control. It generated the internal pressures to withstand the filibuster. These pressures, in turn, helped produce the negotiations which resolved the major policy issues.

Another opportunity for establishing control grew out of the majority leader's recognized initiative in matters of procedure. Mansfield followed a zig-zag course which alternated between regular and extraordinary procedural tactics, a course explained most satisfactorily by his concern for creating conditions of "controlled independence." The complicated process of bypassing the Senate Judiciary Committee permitted the party leaders to keep the House-passed bill out of Chairman James Eastland's hands and under their jurisdiction on the Senate calendar. At the same time, Mansfield's decision to follow normal procedures on the motion to consider H.R. 7152 helped head off criticism among the uncommitted senators that the bill was being rammed through the Senate.

The outside groups backing the legislation contributed significant leverage which enhanced the party leader's control. Although the Senate leadership had deliberately restrained the outside groups from applying direct pressure in the formative stages of the debate, these restraints were removed once the substantive issues had been resolved through the negotiations with Senator Dirksen. The substitute bill, representing the Senate's independent contribution to the final act, could then provide a focal point to the outside lobbying efforts.

In these circumstances the party leaders urged the most vigorous application of external pressure in the final drive for cloture. The Leadership Conference on Civil rights and the religious groups swung into action. Union leaders, bishops, housewives, and stated clerks responded. The results were impressive.

One of those impressed was Richard Russell, the southern Democratic leader. In his final speech prior to the cloture vote, Russell said on the Senate floor: "I have observed with profound sorrow the role that many religious leaders have played in urging passage of the bill, because I cannot make their activities jibe with my concept of the proper place of religious leaders in our national life. During the course of the debate, we have seen cardinals, bishops, elders, stated clerks, common preachers, priests, and rabbis come to Washington to press for passage of the bill. . . . Day after day, men of the cloth have been standing on the Mall and urging a favorable vote on the bill. They have encouraged and prompted thousands of good citizens to sign petitions supporting the bill."[8]

Finally, the operational meaning of "controlled independence" was demonstrated again in the bipartisan leaders' response to the revolt of Hickenlooper and his followers in the last days before cloture. A measure of independence was exercised. Hickenlooper received unanimous consent to vote on three amendments prior to cloture, and the Senate leadership had to reschedule the cloture vote by one day. But by this time the network of controlling pressures supporting the drive for cloture had curtailed the price which the uncommitted rebels could demand, even though their votes still stood as the difference between defeat or victory on the critical motion to limit debate. In the wake of Hickenlooper's brief flurry, the drive for cloture went over the top.

In summary, for the Civil Rights Act of 1964 to pass the Senate, more was needed than pressure by the president, by the House of Representatives, and by outside groups. Even the sterility of the southern Democratic strategy did not guarantee victory. The missing element, and the element which the Senate party leaders provided, was the application of these considerable forces in a manner which permitted some expression of the Senate's sense of "independence" without, in the process, sacrificing the leadership's ultimate "control."

Indeed, these demonstrations of senatorial independence created an environment where the pressures for the bill's passage had maximum impact in the final drive for cloture. Once the Dirksen compromise had been worked out, the uncommitted senators had no credible basis for continuing their opposition to cloture or to the bill itself. . . .

There is surely one lesson from the battle to pass the Civil Rights Act of 1964. Where individuals are willing to work, organize, debate, and when they can refrain from castigating their opponents for moral weakness or an abnormally large consignment of original sin, positive results are possible.

NOTES

1. John G. Stewart, *Independence and Control: The Challenge of Senatorial Party Leadership* (Ph.D. dissertation, University of Chicago, 1968). This section is from ch. 8, pp. 289-298, 311.
2. Author's notes, June 21, 1964, Washington, D.C.
3. Author's notes, June 21, 1964, Washington, D.C.
4. See "Strategy Leading to Enactment of Rights Bill Analyzed," *Revolution in Civil Rights* (Washington, D.C.: Congressional Quarterly, Inc., 1965), p. 52.
5. *New York Times*, March 2, 1964, p. 12.
6. Author's notes, June 11, 1964, Washington, D.C.
7. Stewart, *Independence and Control*, pp. 129-135.
8. *Congressional Record*, CX, p. 12856.

Chapter 10

The Impact and Aftermath of the Civil Rights Act of 1964

Robert D. Loevy

The primary impact of the Civil Rights Act of 1964 was the almost immediate elimination of racial discrimination in places of public accommodation throughout the United States. Five months after Lyndon Johnson signed the 1963-64 civil rights bill into law, the Supreme Court ruled that the commerce clause of the U.S. Constitution gave the Congress all the legal power it needed to integrate hotels, motels, restaurants, snack bars, swimming pools, and other public places. In the decision, *Heart of Atlanta Motel v. United States*, the high court defined the concept of commerce broadly, applying the new civil rights law to restaurants that received their food and supplies from out of state, even when their customers all came from within the state.[1]

In addition to opening up public accommodations to African Americans and other minorities, the Civil Rights Act of 1964 instituted the hotly debated "cutoff" of U.S. Government funds to governmental programs that practiced discrimination. As the backers of this provision hoped, the need and desire for U.S. Government dollars inspired state and local governments throughout the nation, but particularly in the South, to integrate all their facilities and services. Congress subsequently used the cutoff extensively as a means of getting state governments to comply with congressional law, particularly when Congress passed legislation guaranteeing equal access to public facilities for women and the physically handicapped.

It could be argued that the most important provision of the Civil Rights Act of 1964 was the one instituting equal employment opportunity. There was an immediate and highly visible increase in the number of women and monority group members who gained employment in the nation's factories and offices. The work force in the United States, particularly the highly skilled and professionalized work force, went from being predominantly white male to having substantially increased proportions of women and minorities.

Political Impact

In July 1964 the Republican Party held its National Convention in San Francisco, California. Although the majority of Republicans in the U.S. Senate had supported the Civil Rights Act of 1964, the Republican Party nominated for president Senator Barry Goldwater of Arizona, who had voted against both cloture and final passage. Goldwater, who defined himself as an ardent conservative, said the newly enacted civil rights law represented too great an extension of U.S. Government power over states' rights.

Incumbent Democratic President Lyndon Johnson easily defeated Senator Goldwater in the 1964 presidential election. Because of his opposition to the Civil Rights Act of 1964, Republican Goldwater was able to carry the "Deep South" states of Louisiana, Mississippi, Alabama, Georgia, and South Carolina. He also carried his home state of Arizona. That was all, however. In one of the great landslides in presidential election history, President Johnson won every other state in the Northeast, the Midwest, the West, and the Upper South. In addition, President Johnson had long "coattails" and carried large numbers of Democrats into both the Senate and the House of Representatives with him.

Black voters in particular rewarded President Johnson for his highly visible and very skillful support of the Civil

Rights Act of 1964. In many predominantly black precincts in large cities in the North, Johnson received more than 95 percent of the vote in the 1964 presidential election. This was almost 20 percent better than John F. Kennedy had polled with black voters in the 1960 presidential election. This strong shift of black voters to the Democratic Party endured to the mid-1990s, and even then showed no signs of ending.

It can be argued that the Republican Party's 1964 presidential nominee, Barry Goldwater, undid much of the good work that Everett Dirksen had performed in the Senate for the Republican Party in the spring of 1964. Dirksen, after all, had rounded up the critical Republican votes needed to cloture the civil rights bill. Under other conditions, these actions on Dirksen's part might have moved significant numbers of black voters to vote for the GOP candidate for president. However, Goldwater was so outspokenly against the civil rights bill, and so much more visible than Dirksen, that black voters in 1964 abandoned the Republicans and began giving near-unanimous electoral support to the Democrats.

The Protest at Selma

In early 1965 Lyndon Johnson was well aware that his landslide presidential victory and the large Democratic majorities in both houses of Congress offered an unusual opportunity for governmental action. In a speech in December 1964 he said: "Great social change tends to come rapidly in periods of intense activity before the impulse slows. I believe we are in the midst of such a period of change."[2]

In the field of civil rights, one of the remaining arenas for action and change was voting rights. The Civil Rights Act of 1960 had dealt with voting problems for blacks in the South, but the judicial solutions proposed had not been effective in overcoming state literacy tests that were administered in such a way that blacks could not pass them and gain the ballot. President Johnson pledged in his State of the Union address in January 1965 that he would call on Congress to eliminate "all barriers to the right to vote." He repeated this promise of voting rights legislation to Martin Luther King, Jr., when the now-renowned civil rights leader visited Johnson at the White House in early February 1965.[3]

On January 18, 1965, King had begun a series of voting rights demonstrations in Selma, Alabama. Dallas County, where Selma was located, had more black citizens than white citizens, but 9,700 whites were registered to vote compared to only 325 blacks. When King staged a march on the county courthouse in Selma, he and 2,000 other blacks were jailed for "parading without a permit." Later, when King attempted to lead a march from Selma to the state capital in Montgomery, he and his fellow marchers were confronted by Alabama state troopers as they walked across the Alabama River highway bridge leading out of Selma.

Once again the television sets and front-page newspaper photographs of America showed white state troopers attacking civil rights demonstrators. The state police, many of them mounted on horseback, fired tear gas at the marchers and then beat them back with clubs. The demonstrators, almost all of them black, were chased, bleeding and limping, all the way to their headquarters church in Selma. Millions of Americans were outraged, and civil rights advocates from throughout the North and the West, both black and white, began to pour into Selma to support Martin Luther King and his voting rights campaign.

Lyndon Johnson seized the opportunity presented by Selma to introduce his proposed voting rights bill to both Congress and the country. Addressing the Senate and the House of Representatives meeting together at a special evening session, Johnson said situations such as the one in Selma could not be allowed to continue. He ended his speech with the title of the civil rights marchers' hymn, "We Shall Overcome."

The Voting Rights Act of 1965

The Johnson Administration's voting rights bill was greatly influenced by what had happened with the Civil Rights Act of 1964. The Justice Department began immediate negotiations with Everett Dirksen of Illinois, the Republican leader in the Senate, and a "consensus" on the provisions of the bill was reached early in the bill's consideration by Congress. As a result, the Senate debate on the voting rights bill ended early with a successful cloture vote on May 25, 1965. The southerners had barely gotten their filibuster going when the cloture vote stopped them. It was the second time in two years—but only the second time in the nation's history—that the Senate had voted to forcefully end debate on a civil rights bill.

But the speed of this legislative action was significant. It had taken more than a year to get the Civil Rights Act of 1964 through Congress. It took only five months to enact the Voting Rights Act of 1965. The quick cloture vote of 1965 had been "made much easier by the precedent of the victorious cloture vote of 1964."[4]

The new law took direct aim at black nonvoting in the South. It targeted those areas where fewer than 50 percent of adults eligible to vote were actually voting, which in effect meant the bill would enfranchise blacks in Alabama, Georgia, Louisiana, Mississippi, North Carolina, South Carolina, and Virginia. In those states that failed to meet this 50 percent "triggering" test, U.S. Government "examiners" appointed by the executive branch would come into the state and take over the registration process from local officials. It could be argued this sending in of "Federal registrars" represented the ultimate triumph of national policy toward minorities over state and local policies.

The effects of the voting rights law were immediate and extensive. By 1967 black voter registration in six southern states had increased from 30 percent to more than 50 percent of those eligible.[5] There was a substantial increase in the number of blacks elected to political office in the South. In 1976, when Democrat Jimmy Carter was elected president of the United States in a very close election, newly enfranchised southern blacks were given a large share of the credit for his victory.[6]

Andrew Young, a former aide to Martin Luther King, Jr., was working in the Carter for President campaign. When Young heard that even the deep South state of Mississippi had voted for Carter, thanks to a heavy Democratic vote from Mississippi blacks, Young remarked: "When I heard that Mississippi had gone our way, I knew that the hands that picked cotton finally picked the president."[7]

The Splintering of the Civil Rights Movement

In many ways the protest at Selma and the rapid enactment of the Voting Rights Act of 1965 represented the peak of the civil rights movement. Martin Luther King, Jr., enjoyed widespread support throughout the North and the West when he confronted the Alabama state troopers at the bridge in Selma. The vast majority of Americans, black and white, clearly supported the haste with which Congress moved to grant that most basic of all democratic rights—the vote—to minority Americans.

But just days after the Voting Rights Act was signed into law, blacks living in the Watts section of Los Angeles rioted, burning and looting their own and neighboring sections of that city. There were subsequent riots in other major cities, and these riots "were in no sense demonstrations for [minority] rights."[8] They thus tended to greatly weaken white support for the minority cause.

In 1966, when Martin Luther King, Jr., led a drive for equal employment and equal housing opportunity in Chicago, much of the white community there opposed him rather than supported him. King eventually withdrew from Chicago without achieving the major goals of his Chicago Freedom Movement. On Capitol Hill, a housing rights bill failed to gain the requisite two-thirds vote for cloture when Senate Republican leader Everett Dirksen declined to support it.

Within the civil rights movement itself, there was disagreement over the proper way to further the minority cause in the United States. New leadership at the Congress of Racial Equality (CORE) and the Student Nonviolent Coordinating Committee (SNCC) began to question the effectiveness of Martin Luther King's nonviolent protests and openly advocated more confrontational techniques. Other voices and organizations, such as the Black Muslims, talked of "black nationalism," "black separatism," and "black power." The unity and singleness of purpose that had characterized the civil rights movement in the early 1960s had begun to dissipate and fall apart by the late 1960s.[9]

The Memphis Sanitation Workers Strike

In March of 1968 Martin Luther King, Jr., went to Memphis, Tennessee, to support a labor strike by municipal sanitation workers, all of whom were black. The strike was for union recognition, higher wages, fringe benefits, and safer working conditions. The strike was a bitter one, and white Memphis city officials had stood firm against the black strikers' economic demands.

During a King-led protest march in downtown Memphis on March 28, 1968, some of the demonstrators cast aside King's nonviolent principles and began breaking plate-glass windows and looting stores. The Memphis police force responded with hostility toward all the marchers. It was the first time King and his fellow organizers had ever lost control of a protest march and had it result in black, rather than white, violence. As the situation became more tense and uncontrollable, King's colleagues forced him to leave the march against his will in order to guarantee his personal safety.

The night of April 3, 1968, King addressed a black rally in Memphis supporting the sanitation strike. He concluded with a reference to his own mortality, suggesting that he might not live long enough to see the promised land of racial justice for which he and so many others had been working for so long. "I may not get there with you," he concluded his talk, "but we as a people will get to the promised land."[10]

The following evening Martin Luther King, Jr., was killed by a bullet from a high-powered rifle as he stood on the balcony of his motel in Memphis. As the news spread throughout the nation, riots broke out in the African-American sections of more than 130 cities, including Washington, D.C. During the weeklong course of the riots, forty-six people were killed, all but five of whom were black. Some 2,600 fires were started that caused property damage of more than $100 million. State governors had to call out the national guard to quell the violence. In a number of larger cities, President Lyndon Johnson was forced to order in regular Army troops. Over 20,000 rioters were arrested. It was "the most concentrated week of racial violence Americans had ever known."[11]

The Housing Rights Act of 1968

Throughout the spring of 1968, as Martin Luther King, Jr., was helping the Memphis sanitation workers, a major civil rights bill was once again making its way through Congress. The bill was originally designed to extend U.S. Government protection to civil rights workers, but it was amended also to prohibit discrimination in the sale and rental of housing.

The Birmingham protests had launched the Civil Rights Act of 1964, the Selma protests had inspired the Voting Rights Act of 1965, but this new housing rights bill resulted mainly from the efforts of Clarence Mitchell, Jr., the Washington director of the NAACP. The bill picked up real speed when Senate Republican leader Everett Dirksen, harkening back to his earlier days as a principal designer and supporter of civil rights bills, put his considerable influence behind the legislation. Prior to Dirksen's announcement of support, three cloture votes on the southern filibuster of the bill had failed to get the required two-thirds majority. On March 4, 1968, with Dirksen now on board, cloture was voted by an extremely slim 65 to 32 margin. There was not one vote to spare.

The bill then moved to the House of Representatives, where it was believed the bill would be subjected to weakening amendments. Unlike in 1964, when the House was more liberal than the Senate on civil rights issues, the House had grown increasingly conservative as the result of urban riots and black-power oratory. After the House weakened the bill, it was thought, a Senate-House conference committee would write a compromise version, which would then be repassed by both houses.

The wave of national remorse over the assassination of Martin Luther King, Jr., intervened dramatically in this legislative scenario. On April 9, 1968, the day of Martin Luther King's funeral, the House Rules Committee voted to send the housing rights bill directly to the House floor and permit only one hour of debate and no amendments. King's assassination had generated irresistible pressure to pass the strong Senate bill and pass it quickly. The bill passed the House on April 10, 1968, by a vote of 229 to 195. President Johnson signed the Civil Rights Act of 1968, often referred to as the Housing Rights Act of 1968, into law the next day.

The housing rights bill was the last of the three great civil rights acts of the 1960s to be enacted by the U.S. Congress and signed into law by the president. Years later observers would look back and see the housing rights act as the final legislative achievement of the civil rights movement. "It was a landmark . . . , though less a sign of resurgent reform than the coda [in music, the closing section] to a passing era of legislative gains."[12]

School Busing

In 1970 a U.S. judge in North Carolina ordered that black students be bused to white schools and that white students be bused to black schools. This crosstown "school busing," it was hoped, would end the de facto segregation of public schools caused by white students living in predominantly white neighborhoods and black students living in predominantly black neighborhoods. One year later this use of busing to achieve school integration was upheld unanimously by the U.S. Supreme Court in the landmark case *Swann v. Charlotte-Mecklenburg*.

Other U.S. judges turned to busing as a way to end de facto school segregation, in the North as well as in the South. Although the North was thought to be much more favorable to civil rights than the South, there were a number of heated protests from white parents who opposed their children being bused long distances across the city to attend black schools. Some parents also opposed black students being bused into white schools. Among the most violent and well-publicized of these protests was the white opposition to school busing in the cradle of the American Revolution—Boston, Massachusetts.

In June of 1974 U.S. Judge Arthur Garrity ruled that the Boston School Committee was intentionally keeping the city's schools segregated and was forcing blacks to attend the oldest, most crowded, and most poorly staffed schools. He ordered that 17,000 Boston school children be bused in a manner that would reduce the unacceptably high racial concentrations in the schools. White families responded by organizing resistance, both legal and illegal, to the concept of mandatory school busing.

The first trouble point was South Boston High, a previously all-white school in a mainly working class, Irish Catholic neighborhood. Whites expressed their disapproval of busing on opening day in 1974 by urging their children to boycott classes. The boycott was 90 percent effective. When black students walked out of the school to get on the buses and ride back to their homes in Roxbury, a black ghetto, they were pelted with stones. Once on the buses, the students were hit by shattered glass as hostile crowds of whites threw heavier stones through the bus windows.

The newspaper photographs and television reports from South Boston looked a great deal like the ones from Birmingham and Selma a decade earlier. Once again crowds of hostile whites were attacking blacks fighting for their civil rights. There was one important difference in Boston and other northern cities attempting school busing, however. The local and state police were trying to protect the children being bused rather than staying neutral or joining the attack, as had happened in so many southern civil rights protests.

In mid-October 1974 a white student was stabbed during a racial confrontation at Boston's Hyde Park High School. Some 450 national guardsmen had to be sent in to restore order. Two months later, after a white student at South Boston High was stabbed by a black student, a white mob surrounded the school and kept 135 black students trapped inside the building for four hours. Shortly thereafter, a 500-person police guard was required to keep order at South Boston High, which had only 400 students.

White parents organized an anti-busing lobby group named ROAR (Restore Our Alienated Rights). In early October 1974 over 5,000 Bostonians marched through the streets of South Boston to publicly demonstrate their opposition to "forced busing." Significant numbers of state legislators, city councilpersons, and members of the Boston

School Committee, the group specifically charged by the U.S. Court to implement busing, walked prominently in the parade.

The racial turmoil in Boston over school busing eventually began to drive white families out of the city and into the de facto segregated Boston suburban schools. By 1976 it was estimated that more than 20,000 white students had transferred to parochial schools, private schools, or had moved out of town with their families. As a result, by the late 1970s black students constituted a clear majority of Boston's school population. People began to talk about "resegregation," the concentration of blacks in central cities and the fleeing of large numbers of whites to the surrounding suburbs.[13]

In 1987, thirteen years after Judge Garrity first ordered school busing in Boston, that city's school system was released from supervision by the U.S. Courts. Two years later Boston school officials tried a new strategy to achieve racial integration. The city was divided into three zones for elementary and middle schools. Parents were allowed to send their child to any school they pleased in their particular zone, but school officials monitored and sometimes overruled parent choices in order to facilitate racial balance. School officials reported that, in the first year of the new program's operation, 80 percent of elementary school children were able to go to the school their parents chose for them.

MILLIKEN V. BRADLEY

Many observers believed that, for school busing to be effective as an instrument of school integration, black students should be bused out of the central cities into schools in the outlying suburbs. Only in this way, it was argued, could busing be instituted without having the effect of driving the remaining white families out of the city. The Supreme Court did not agree with this proposed solution, however, ruling 5 to 4 in *Milliken v. Bradley* that the suburbs had not caused the de facto segregation in the central cities and thus were not required to help provide a solution to the problem.

The *Milliken* decision represented a turning point for the Supreme Court where racial matters were concerned. Richard M. Nixon, a Republican, had been elected president of the United States in 1968, succeeding Democrat Lyndon B. Johnson. Nixon did not share Johnson's enthusiasm for rapid advancement in the civil rights arena, and his Supreme Court appointments had reflected this less-involved attitude. All four Nixon appointees voted with the majority in the *Milliken v. Bradley* decision. The central cities were to cope alone with the problem of de facto segregation of public schools. The suburbs had been granted judicial permission to remain "lily white."

After the *Milliken* decision, school administrators in central cities searched for imaginative new ways to provide some measure of racial integration in their school systems. One idea was creating "magnet schools" with specialized curricula, such as advanced science or music classes, that students from the suburbs would want to attend. Improved school buildings often were combined with enriched academic programs to make magnet schools extra attractive to suburban students and their parents.[14]

A Change in the Cloture Rule

The Democratic Party scored significant gains in the congressional elections of 1974. The large numbers of new Democrats elected to the Senate and the House of Representatives were in a reformist mood, and one of the things they wanted to reform was Congress itself.

In 1975 in the Senate, the number of votes required to cloture a filibuster was reduced from two-thirds to three-fifths, from 67 votes to 60 votes if all senators were present and voting. It was believed that this lowered number of votes required for cloture would make it more difficult to sustain a filibuster in future debates, and the end result would be the Senate would have an "easier time" enacting civil rights bills.

This new cloture rule did not reduce the use of the filibuster in the U.S. Senate, however. In fact, if anything, it appeared to make the filibuster a more acceptable legislative weapon, even for non-southerners. Groups of senators began to filibuster non-civil rights bills, thus requiring the Senate leadership to produce a three-fifths vote or give up on the particular bill in question. Senators found filibusters to be a particularly effective way to kill bills they opposed late in the legislative session when there was little time remaining and the leadership was anxious to enact more important bills prior to adjournment.

The Bakke Case

The Civil Rights Act of 1964 called for the elimination of racial discrimination in employment. A variety of government agencies and institutions receiving U.S. Government funds, such as colleges and universities, began to take *affirmative action* to hire more women and minorities. They sought to compensate for the consequences of past discrimination by rapidly increasing the employment and promotion of groups that had been traditionally underrepresented in the work force.

Affirmative action was applied to college and university admission policies as well. Educational institutions made an extra effort to see that more women and minorities were accepted into their undergraduate, graduate, and professional programs. Since admission to institutions of higher education is often highly competitive, affirmative action meant that women and minority candidates were accepted who might otherwise have not been accepted. They took the places of other candidates, mainly white males, who were rejected and, in some cases, limited to attending less prestigious colleges and universities. Opponents of affirmative action soon were calling this process *reverse discrimination.*

The Supreme Court was called upon to address the constitutionality of affirmative action. Alan Bakke was a young white male who had an excellent academic record at both the University of Minnesota and Stanford University. He also was a Vietnam War veteran. Twice, in 1973 and 1974, he applied for admission to the medical school at the University of California at Davis. Both times he was rejected, but students with weaker academic records and lower aptitude/achievement test scores were accepted.

Under the affirmative action program for the medical school at the University of California, Davis, 100 students were admitted each academic year. Of these 100 admissions, 16 were set aside for African Americans, Chicanos, Asian Americans, and Native Americans. Whites were not considered for any of these sixteen spots. When U.C. Davis rejected Bakke's application the second time, Bakke filed suit in the U.S. Courts, arguing he had been rejected solely because of his race.

Title VI, the equal employment opportunity section, of the Civil Rights Act of 1964 was the impetus for the affirmative action program at U.C. Davis. Ironically, Bakke sued for admission on the grounds that his rights under Title VI of the Civil Rights Act of 1964 had been violated.

In 1978 the Supreme Court ruled that the U.C. Davis affirmative action plan was unconstitutional. It found that Bakke had been excluded because of race and for no other reason. The decision, *University of California Regents v. Bakke,* became one of the most well-known and ardently debated Supreme Court decisions of the decade. The immediate effect of the decision was that Alan Bakke was admitted to the medical school at U.C. Davis and went on to get his M.D. degree and pursue a medical career.

But the Supreme Court did not eliminate the concept of affirmative action altogether. The Court ruled that colleges and universities, and by inference employers, may take race and ethnicity into consideration as one of a number of factors when offering admission or employment. The key point was that prospective students or employees could not be denied entrance or employment *only* on account of race. This subtle distinction gave educational institutions and employers the flexibility they needed to keep the core elements of their affirmative action programs in place.

Affirmative action, and the frequently heard charge of reverse discrimination, remained a major part of U.S. politics in the 1990s. The Congress, the state legislatures, and both the state and U.S. courts continued to struggle to eliminate racial bias in employment and college/university admissions without unfairly favoring one group in society over another.

Perfecting Civil Rights Laws

The three great civil rights laws of the 1960s—the Civil Rights Act of 1964, the Voting Rights Act of 1965, and the Housing Rights Act of 1968—were never substantially amended in the three decades following their enactment. In the mid-1990s they continued to define the major legal protections for minorities in American society.

Subsequent laws were passed, however, that expanded and further defined the scope of these three great civil rights acts. A number of these laws sought to bring additional groups under the protection of the nation's civil rights laws.

The Age Discrimination in Employment Act (1967) outlawed discrimination against workers or job applicants on account of age. The law applied to workers ages forty through sixty-five. In 1986 the law was amended to prohibit mandatory retirement in all but the most age-sensitive jobs, such as airline pilots.

The Education Amendment of 1972 sought to guarantee women equal treatment in all facets of the educational process. The law provided that "no person . . . shall, on the basis of sex, be excluded from participation in . . . any educational program or activity receiving Federal financial assistance." This law was instrumental in increasing efforts for women's sports programs to be given equal importance and equal funding at American colleges and universities.

The Rehabilitation Act (1973) reauthorized programs to rehabilitate the handicapped and simultaneously required affirmative action programs to hire and promote "qualified handicapped individuals" in U.S. Government financed programs and activities. The Americans with Disabilities Act (1991) prohibited discrimination based on disability and required that work places, public facilities, and public accommodations be made accessible to the handicapped.

The Civil Rights Restoration Act of 1988 was designed to overturn the Supreme Court decision in *Grove City College v. Bell*. The high court had ruled that violating the anti-sex discrimination provisions of the Education Amendment of 1972 would only cut off U.S. Government aid to the particular program in which the gender discrimination was taking place. It would not cut off all U.S. Government aid to the entire institution. Congress reversed the court decision by passing a new law that cut off all federal aid, even when only one program at an institution was found to be discriminatory.

The Fair Housing Act Amendments (1988) sought to tighten up enforcement of the Housing Rights Act of 1968. Instead of the victims of housing discrimination having to pursue their claims in court (an expensive process), under the new law their complaints would be investigated by the

Department of Housing and Urban Development and decided by administrative law judges.

In the early 1990s the Congress became concerned over a series of Supreme Court decisions that appeared to be weakening the equal employment opportunity provisions of the nation's civil rights laws. After a long series of negotiations between Congress, which had Democratic majorities in both houses, and President George Bush, a Republican, the Civil Rights Act of 1991 was passed and signed into law. Employers were required to more clearly justify instances of discrimination against women and minorities, such as not permitting women to do heavy lifting, or not permitting pregnant women to work with electronic equipment or chemicals that were considered harmful to the unborn baby. The new law also prohibited discrimination in handing out job promotions and established a commission to study why there were such a relatively small number of women and minorities serving in management and executive positions.[15]

The Minority Bill of Rights

Taken together, the Civil Rights Act of 1964, the Voting Rights Act of 1965, and the Housing Rights Act of 1968 constitute what might be called the Minority Bill of Rights. Although the three laws are legislation and not part of the U.S. Constitution, they spell out in considerable detail the rights and protections that are granted to minorities in the United States. In the thirty years from the 1960s to the 1990s, these laws withstood all major efforts to weaken them or alter them in a significant way. If Martin Luther King's "A Letter from the Birmingham Jail" is the "Declaration of Independence of the civil rights movement," then the three great civil rights acts of the 1960s surely are the "Bill of Rights of the civil rights movement."

NOTES

1. Schwartz, *Statutory History of the United States: Civil Rights*, Part II, pp. 1453-1455. See also *Heart of Atlanta Motel v. United States*, 379 U.S. 241 (1964).

2. *Public Papers of the Presidents, 1963-64*, pp. 1653-56.

3. *New York Times*, February 9, 1965.

4. Loevy, *To End All Segregation*, p. 326.

5. *Washington Post*, July 7, 1967.

6. Garrow, *Protest at Selma*, pp. xii-xiii. In addition to Garrow's thorough account of the events at Selma and their effect on the Voting Rights Act of 1965, see Charles E. Fager, *Selma, 1965: The March That Changed the South* (Boston, Mass.: Beacon Press, 1985; reprint of 1974 ed.). For brief accounts of the Voting Rights Act of 1965 going through Congress, see Sundquist, *Politics and Policy*, pp. 271-275, and *Revolution in Civil Rights*, pp. 84-90. For commentary and selections from the congressional debate, see Schwartz, *Statutory History of the United States: Civil Rights*, Part II, pp. 1469-1625.

7. Stephen F. Lawson, *In Pursuit of Power: Southern Blacks and Electoral Politics, 1965-1982* (New York: Columbia University Press, 1985), p. 256.

8. *Revolution in Civil Rights*, p. 93.

9. See "Negro Revolution: The Next Steps," in *Revolution in Civil Rights*, pp. 91-94. See also Weisbrot, *Freedom Bound*, pp. 154-261, and Cashman, *African-Americans and the Quest for Civil Rights: 1900-1990*, pp. 193-210.

10. For the major writings and speeches of Martin Luther King, Jr., see James Melvin Washington, ed., *A Testament of Hope: The Essential Writings of Martin Luther King, Jr.* (San Francisco: Harper and Row, 1986). This particular quote p. 286.

11. Weisbrot, *Freedom Bound*, pp. 267-271. For a book-length treatment, see Joan Turner Beifuss, *At the River*

I Stand: Memphis, the 1968 Strike, and Martin Luther King (Brooklyn, N.Y.: Carlson Publishing, 1985).

12. Weisbrot, *Freedom Bound*, p. 272.

13. The Boston school-busing controversy is covered in Weisbrot, *Freedom Bound*, pp. 289-291. See also J. Harvey Wilkinson, *From Brown to Bakke: The Supreme Court and School Integration, 1954-1978* (New York: Oxford University Press, 1979).

14. Cashman, *African-Americans and the Quest for Civil Rights, 1900-1990*, pp. 273-274.

15. This list of civil rights laws is adapted from James McGregor Burns et al., *Government by the People* (Englewood Cliffs, N.J.: Prentice Hall, 1995), 16th ed., pp. 124-125. See also *Social Policy*, May 13, 1989, p. 1122.

Chapter 11

A Chronology of the Civil Rights Act of 1964

Robert D. Loevy

February 28, 1963. President John F. Kennedy sends a "Special Message on Civil Rights" to Congress along with proposed improvements in voting rights laws and an extension of the Civil Rights Commission. Civil rights supporters praise Kennedy for his stirring words but criticize his legislative proposals as "weak."

April-May, 1963. The Reverend Martin Luther King, Jr., leads an extended series of civil rights protests against racial segregation in Birmingham, Alabama. King is arrested and writes his famous "A Letter from the Birmingham Jail." Blacks riot for four hours following the bombing of King's motel room (King was out of town that night) in Birmingham.

June 11, 1963. Alabama Governor George Wallace "stands aside" at the University of Alabama and two black students register for classes. That evening, President Kennedy addresses the nation on television and pledges to send a strengthened civil rights bill to Congress. The president says: "The fires of frustration and discord are burning in every city, North and South, where legal remedies are not at hand. . . . Next week I shall ask the Congress . . . to make a commitment . . . to the proposition that race has no place in American life or law."

June 19, 1963. Strengthened Kennedy civil rights bill submitted to Congress. The new bill guarantees blacks access to public accommodations (hotels, motels, restaurants, snack bars, etc.), permits the U.S. Government to file suits to desegregate public schools, and cuts off U.S. Government funds to state and local programs that discriminate.

In the Senate, a "backup" bill is introduced that only integrates public accommodations. This bill is routed to the Senate Commerce Committee, chaired by Warren Magnuson (Dem., WA), a strong civil rights supporter. If the Kennedy administration bill is defeated or substantially altered in the House of Representatives, Senator Magnuson will introduce his backup public accommodations bill for action in the Senate. As it turns out, this backup Senate bill is not needed.

May 8-August 2, 1963. House of Representatives Judiciary Subcommittee No. 5 holds hearings on the Kennedy civil rights bill. Emanuel Celler, a Democrat from New York, chairs both the Judiciary Committee and Subcommittee 5. Celler is strongly pro-civil rights. The subcommittee goes "out of control," reporting out a much stronger civil rights bill than the Kennedy administration wants. The president and his advisers are convinced such a strong bill cannot get the Republican votes needed to overcome a southern filibuster in the Senate and thus will not be enacted into law.

July 24, 1964. Representative Adam Clayton Powell (Dem., NY), a black from New York City, proposes that an equal employment opportunity bill be brought immediately to the House of Representatives for a vote. Powell proposes using the "Calendar Wednesday" procedure, under which a committee chairman (Powell) can bring a bill to the floor on a particular Wednesday without the bill first going to the House Rules Committee. The House Rules Committee is a renowned center of southern opposition to civil rights bills.

Civil rights supporters in the House reject Representative Powell's suggestion, fearful that the Calendar Wednesday ploy will not work and thus will end up hurting the Kennedy administration civil rights bill. Powell drops the "Calendar Wednesday" idea for equal employment opportunity.

August 28, 1963. Over 200,000 persons participate in the peaceful "March on Washington for Jobs and Freedom." The Reverend Martin Luther King, Jr., gives his famous "I Have a Dream" speech. President Kennedy does not attend the march, but afterwards he meets at the White House with King and other prominent civil rights leaders.

September 15, 1963. Four young African-American girls attending Sunday School are killed when a bomb is thrown into the 16th Street Baptist Church in Birmingham, Alabama. The church had been a central headquarters for civil rights meetings during the Birmingham demonstrations the previous spring.

October 15-16, 1963. The president's brother, Attorney General Robert F. Kennedy, appears before the House Judiciary Committee and asks for a more moderate bill than the one approved by Subcommittee 5.

October 29, 1963. A new version of the bill, partly hammered out at a midnight meeting at the White House called by President Kennedy, is adopted by the House Judiciary Committee. This bill has the support of both Republican and Democratic civil rights supporters and has been specifically tailored to have a good chance of getting a two-thirds cloture vote in the Senate. William McCulloch of Ohio, the ranking Republican on the House Judiciary Committee, strongly supports the Kennedy administration desire for this more moderate bill.

There has been considerable support to include a Fair Employment Practices Commission (FEPC) in the civil rights bill. An FEPC is included in this House Judiciary Committee bill, but it is now labeled the Equal Employment Opportunity Commission (EEOC). The job of the EEOC is to work to eliminate employment discrimination against minorities.

November 20, 1963. The civil rights bill is reported out by the House Judiciary Committee and sent to the House Rules Committee to be scheduled for debate on the House floor. Civil rights supporters are fearful of Representative Howard W. Smith, a Democrat from Virginia, who is chairman of the Rules Committee and a well-known opponent of civil rights legislation.

November 22, 1963. President Kennedy is assassinated in Dallas, Texas, and the vice president, Lyndon B. Johnson, becomes president. In his first address to Congress following the assassination, President Johnson states his strong support for civil rights and says: "No memorial oration or eulogy could more eloquently honor President Kennedy's memory than the earliest possible passage of the civil rights bill for which he fought so long."

December 9, 1963. Skeptical that Rules Committee Chairman Smith will ever release the civil rights bill for debate on the House floor, civil rights supporters in the House file a discharge petition. If enough House members sign the petition, the civil rights bill will be forced out of the Rules Committee despite the committee chairman's opposition.

January 30, 1964. Chairman Smith allows the House Rules Committee to vote out the civil rights bill. Although the discharge petition still lacks the requisite number of signers, the *threat* of the discharge petition is given some of the credit for getting Smith to release the bill. John F. Kennedy also is given credit. Prior to being assassinated in Dallas, President Kennedy lined up Republican support for the bill on the

Rules Committee at his now-famous "midnight meeting" at the White House in October 1963.

January 31, 1964. House of Representatives begins debate on the civil rights bill. Civil rights groups pack the House galleries with civil rights supporters to make certain that pro-civil rights representatives vote against any and all weakening amendments.

February 10, 1964. House passes civil rights bill by a vote of 290-130. The House bill closely resembles the bill negotiated by the Kennedy administration in October 1963. A surprise amendment adopted on the House floor guarantees women as well as minorities the protections of the equal employment opportunity section of the bill.

February 26, 1964. The House-passed civil rights bill is placed directly on the Senate calendar without first going to the Senate Judiciary Committee. James O. Eastland, a Democrat from Mississippi, is chairman of the Judiciary Committee and would have used his powers as chairman to "bottle up" the bill. Eastland "killed" over 100 civil rights bills in the late 1950s and early 1960s by not allowing them to be reported out of the Judiciary Committee.

At this point an argument breaks out among civil rights supporters over whether to enact the Johnson administration's wheat and cotton subsidy bill prior to taking up the civil rights bill. One group argues that, since the southern senators want the cotton subsidy in the bill, the southerners can be pressured to end the expected civil rights filibuster by putting wheat and cotton on the Senate agenda after the civil rights bill. Senator Humphrey, however, being from the wheat growing state of Minnesota, wants the wheat and cotton bill passed as quickly as possible. Humphrey prevails, and the wheat and cotton bill is debated and enacted prior to the Senate taking up the civil rights bill.

February 27, 1964. Senate Democratic Leader Mike Mansfield surprises the civil rights forces by asking unanimous consent that the civil rights bill be sent to the Senate Judiciary Committee with instructions to report the bill back *unamended* in seven days. Senator Wayne Morse of Oregon supports this procedure as a way to hold committee hearings on the civil rights bill but not have the bill watered down or killed by Chairman Eastland. Democratic whip Humphrey thinks this procedure is a waste of time and supports bypassing the Judiciary Committee. The argument is ended by Senator Richard Russell of Georgia, the southern leader, who objects to Mansfield's unanimous consent motion, thereby defeating it.

March 9, 1964. The Senate attempts to begin formal debate on the House-passed civil rights bill. The southern opponents launch a filibuster of the effort to bypass the Senate Judiciary Committee, arguing that such action violates the rules of the Senate and weakens the committee system of reviewing legislation. This "mini-buster," as it comes to be known, takes up sixteen days of debate. The southerners stop the mini-buster voluntarily, not wanting to face a cloture vote so early in the debate.

March 30, 1964. Formal Senate debate on the civil rights bill itself begins. The southerners launch the expected filibuster, and the Senate settles down to the boring process of listening to the southerners attempt to "talk the bill to death." Hubert Humphrey of Minnesota, the Democratic floor leader for the civil rights bill, needs to get a two-thirds vote (67 of 100 votes) to cloture the bill, stop the debate, and have the Senate vote the bill up or down. The Republican floor leader for the bill is Thomas H. Kuchel of California.

April 23, 1964. Senator Richard Russell, the southern leader, says he will allow a roll call vote on a jury trial amendment favored by Senate moderates. The civil rights bill restricts the use of juries in civil rights cases because of the problem of the "free white jury that will never convict." Democratic leader Mike Mansfield and Republican leader Everett Dirksen hammer out a jury trial amendment that provides for waiving jury trials in civil rights cases only when fines are low and jail terms are less than thirty days. When Senator Russell changes his mind and will not allow a vote on the jury trial amendment, Senator Dirksen threatens to have a cloture vote to force action on the amendment. This upsets Senator Humphrey, who does not yet have enough votes (two-thirds of the Senate) for cloture. Fortunately for the civil rights forces, Senator Dirksen backs away from having an early cloture vote on the jury trial amendment.

May 5, 1964. Senator Humphrey begins negotiations with Everett Dirksen of Illinois, the Republican leader in the Senate. Dirksen has the support of eight to ten Republican senators, and Humphrey cannot achieve cloture without those Reblican votes. Dirksen presents Humphrey with a large package of amendments which Dirksen wants added to the bill. Civil rights supporters are fearful that Dirksen's many amendments will substantially weaken the bill, particularly the public accommodations and the equal employment opportunity sections.

May 13, 1964. After lengthy negotiations and many changes in Dirksen's original proposals, Humphrey and Dirksen reach agreement on Dirksen's amendments. Dirksen then publicly announces his support for this latest version of the civil rights bill. The major effect of Dirksen's amendments is to require that the U.S. Government enforce integration only after state and local remedies have been exhausted. Civil rights supporters agree with Humphrey that Dirksen's amendments do *not* weaken the bill substantially. President Johnson, who has been pressing for a strong civil rights bill from the White House, announces his support for the Dirksen-amended bill.

June 5, 1964. Senator Bourke B. Hickenlooper, a Republican from Iowa, objects to Everett Dirksen's tight control over the civil rights bill and demands that he and his small group of Republican allies in the Senate be allowed to present three amendments to the bill. Without the support of Hickenlooper and his small band of GOP senators, Humphrey and Dirksen do not have the necessary two-thirds vote for cloture. Hickenlooper therefore is allowed to present the three amendments for debate and a vote. Two of the amendments are defeated but the third, which gives southern officials greater access to trial by jury, is adopted. Allowing Hickenlooper to vote on these three amendments turns out to be a very wise move, because Hickenlooper and his Republican supporters subsequently vote for cloture.

June 10, 1964. The Senate votes 71-29 for cloture, four votes more than the sixty-seven needed. For the first time in American history, a southern filibuster of a civil rights bill has been stopped with a cloture vote. Civil rights supporters are cheered by the fact that the bill integrates virtually all public accommodations, cuts off U.S. Government funds to programs that discriminate, and guarantees equal employment opportunity.

June 11, 1964. Once cloture is invoked, the civil rights forces find themselves in a very difficult situation. Amendments introduced by the southerners prior to the cloture vote can be brought up and voted upon in the post-cloture period. No new amendments can be introduced after cloture, however. This means that, if any of the southern amendments pass and are later discovered to be harmful to civil rights, the civil rights forces cannot introduce new amendments to undo the work of the southern amendments. The civil rights forces quickly adopt a policy of voting down all southern amendments, even those that, at first glance, appear to strengthen the bill.

In the post-cloture period, each senator is allowed one hour of debate time. The civil rights forces have no choice but to wait while those southern senators who wish to do so use their final hour of debate to criticize the bill.

June 19, 1964. Final adoption of the civil rights bill in the Senate. The bill is returned to the House of Representatives for approval of the Senate amendments. If the House will agree to the Senate amendments without adding more amendments of its own, the bill will not have to return to the Senate for further consideration—and a second filibuster and cloture vote.

June 30, 1964. A bipartisan coalition of civil rights supporters wrests control of the House Rules Committee from Chairman Smith, who had planned to "filibuster" the bill and delay its presentation to the House a full ten days. The bipartisan coalition sends the civil rights bill, exactly as amended in the Senate, directly to the House floor.

July 2, 1964. The House of Representatives approves the civil rights bill, with no amendments, by a vote of 289 to 126. At 6:45 p.m., Eastern Daylight Time, in one of the largest bill-signing ceremonies ever held at the White House, President Lyndon B. Johnson signs the civil rights bill, now the Civil Rights Act of 1964, into law.

About the Editor

Robert D. Loevy was born in St. Louis, Missouri, on February 26, 1935. At the age of five he moved with his family to Baltimore, Maryland, where he spent his early youth.

Loevy received his A.B. degree from Williams College in 1957 and his Ph.D. from Johns Hopkins University in 1963. While at Johns Hopkins he conducted research and wrote position papers for the House of Representatives Republican Policy Committee.

During the 1963–1964 academic year, Loevy served as an American Political Science Association Congressional Fellow in the office of United States Senator Thomas H. Kuchel of California, the Republican floor manager in the Senate for the civil rights bill that later became the Civil Rights Act of 1964. After his fellowship ended, Loevy spent a second year working for Senator Kuchel as the legislation that became the Voting Rights Act of 1965 moved through the Senate.

In 1968 Loevy joined the faculty at Colorado College in Colorado Springs, Colorado, where he currently serves as professor of political science. His major research interests are minority rights and electoral politics in the United States.

Loevy is the author of *To End All Segregation: The Politics of the Passage of the Civil Rights Act of 1964*. He also is the author of *The Flawed Path to the Presidency 1992: Unfairness and Inequality in the Presidential Selection Process* and *The Flawed Path to the Governorship 1994: The Nationalization of a Colorado Statewide Election*. He is the coauthor of *Colorado Politics and Government: Governing the Centennial State* and *American Government: We Are One*.

Bibliography

Books

Ambrose, Stephen E. *Eisenhower: Volume Two: The President.* New York: Simon and Schuster, 1984.

Anderson, J. W. *Eisenhower, Brownell, and the Congress.* Published for the Inter-University Case Program by University of Alabama Press, 1964.

Beifuss, Joan Turner. *At the River I Stand: Memphis, the 1968 Strike, and Martin Luther King.* Brooklyn, N.Y.: Carlson Publishing, 1985.

Berman, Daniel M. *A Bill Becomes a Law.* 2d ed. New York: Macmillan, 1966.

Bolling, Richard. *House Out of Order.* New York: E. P. Dutton, 1966.

Branch, Taylor. *Parting the Waters: America in the King Years, 1954-1963.* New York: Simon and Schuster, 1988.

Brauer, Carl M. *John F. Kennedy and the Second Reconstruction.* New York: Columbia University Press, 1977.

Burns, James MacGregor. *The Deadlock of Democracy: Four-Party Politics in America.* Englewood Cliffs, N.J.: Prentice Hall, 1963.

Carson, Clayborne. *In Struggle: SNCC and the Black Awakening of the 1960s.* Cambridge, Mass.: Harvard University Press, 1981.

Cashman, Sean Dennis. *African-Americans and the Quest for Civil Rights, 1900-1990.* New York: New York University Press, 1991.

Chafe, William H. *Civilities and Civil Rights: Greensboro, North Carolina, and the Black Struggle for Freedom.* New York: Oxford University Press, 1980.

Clark, Joseph S. *Congress: The Sapless Branch*. New York: Harper and Row, 1964.

———. *The Senate Establishment*. New York: Hill and Wang, 1963.

Congress and the Nation. Washington, D.C.: Congressional Quarterly, 1965.

Congressional Quarterly Almanac. Washington, D.C.: Congressional Quarterly, 1957, 1960-64.

Dorman, Michael. *We Shall Overcome*. New York: Delacorte, 1964.

Eisenhower, Dwight D. *The White House Years: Waging Peace: 1956-1961*. Garden City, N.Y.: Doubleday, 1965.

Evans, Rowland, and Robert Novak. *Lyndon B. Johnson: The Exercise of Power*. New York: New American Library, 1966.

Fager, Charles E. *Selma, 1965: The March That Changed the South*. Boston: Beacon, 1985.

Farmer, James. *Lay Bare the Heart: An Autobiography of the Civil Rights Movement*. New York: Arbor House, 1985.

Forman, James. *The Making of Black Revolutionaries*. Washington, D.C.: Open Hand, 1985.

Garrow, David J. *Bearing the Cross: Martin Luther King, Jr., and the Southern Christian Leadership Conference*. New York: William Morrow, 1986.

———, ed. *Birmingham, Alabama, 1956-1963: The Black Struggle for Civil Rights*. Brooklyn, N.Y.: Carlson, 1989.

———. *Protest at Selma: Martin Luther King, Jr., and the Voting Rights Act of 1965*. New Haven, Conn.: Yale University Press, 1978.

———, ed. *The Montgomery Bus Boycott and the Women Who Started It: The Memoir of Jo Ann Gibson Robinson*. Knoxville: University of Tennessee Press, 1987.

Kane, Peter Evans. *The Senate Debate on the 1964 Civil Rights Act*. Ph.D. dissertation, Purdue University, Lafayette, Ind., 1967.

King, Martin Luther, Jr. *Stride Toward Freedom: The Mont-*

gomery Story. New York: Harper and Row, 1958.

Lawson, Stephen F. *In Pursuit of Power: Southern Blacks and Electoral Politics, 1965-1982*. New York: Columbia University Press, 1985.

Levy, Peter B. *Let Freedom Ring: A Documentary History of the Modern Civil Rights Movement*. New York: Praeger, 1992.

Lewis, David L. *King: A Biography*. Urbana: University of Illinois Press, 1978.

Loevy, Robert D. *To End All Segregation: The Politics of the Passage of the Civil Rights Act of 1964*. Lanham, Md.: University Press of America, 1990.

Lubell, Samuel. *White and Black: Test of a Nation*. 2d ed. New York: Harper and Row, 1966.

Meier, August, and Elliott Rudwick. *CORE: A Study in the Civil Rights Movement, 1942-1968*. New York: Oxford University Press, 1973.

Mills, Norbert. *The Speaking of Hubert Humphrey in Favor of the 1964 Civil Rights Act*. Ph.D. dissertation, Bowling Green State University, Bowling Green, Ohio, 1974.

Morris, Aldon D. *The Origins of the Civil Rights Movement: Black Communities Organizing for Change*. New York: Free Press, 1984.

Navasky, Victor S. *Kennedy Justice*. New York: Atheneum, 1971.

Oates, Stephen B. *Let the Trumpet Sound: The Life of Martin Luther King, Jr.* New York: Harper and Row, 1982.

Parks, Rosa, with Jim Haskins. *Rosa Parks: My Story*. New York: Dial Books, 1992.

Peck, James. *Freedom Ride*. New York: Simon and Schuster, 1962.

Potenziani, David Daniel. *Look to the Past: Richard B. Russell and the Defense of Southern White Supremacy*. Ph.D. dissertation, University of Georgia, Athens, Ga., 1981.

Revolution in Civil Rights. Washington, D.C.: Congressional Quarterly, 1965.

Riddick, Floyd M. *The U.S. Congress: Organization and Procedure*. Manassas, Va.: National Capital Publishers, 1949.

Schlesinger, Arthur M., Jr. *A Thousand Days: John F. Kennedy in the White House*. Boston: Houghton Mifflin, 1965.

Schwartz, Bernard. *Statutory History of the United States: Civil Rights*. New York: Chelsea House, 1970.

Sellers, Cleveland, with Robert Terrell. *The River of No Return: The Autobiography of a Black Militant and the Life and Death of SNCC*. New York: William Morrow, 1973.

Sorensen, Theodore C. *Kennedy*. New York: Harper and Row, 1965.

Stewart, John G. *Independence and Control: The Challenge of Senatorial Party Leadership*. Ph.D. Dissertation, University of Chicago, Chicago, Ill., 1968.

Sundquist, James L. *Politics and Policy: The Eisenhower, Kennedy, and Johnson Years*. Washington, D.C.: Brookings, 1968.

Washington, James Melvin, ed. *A Testament of Hope: The Essential Writings of Martin Luther King, Jr.* San Francisco: Harper and Row, 1986.

Watkins, Charles L., and Floyd M. Riddick. *Senate Procedure: Precedents and Practice*. Washington, D.C.: U.S. Government Printing Office, 1958.

Weisbrot, Robert. *Freedom Bound: A History of America's Civil Rights Movement*. New York: Norton, 1990.

Whelan, Charles and Barbara. *The Longest Debate: A Legislative History of the 1964 Civil Rights Act*. Cabin John, Md.: Seven Locks Press, 1985.

White, Theodore H. *The Making of the President, 1964*. New York: Atheneum, 1965.

Wilkins, Roy, with Tom Mathews. *Standing Fast: The Autobiography of Roy Wilkins*. New York: Viking, 1982.

Wilkinson, J. Harvey. *From Brown to Bakke: The Supreme Court and School Integration, 1954-1978*. New York:

Oxford University Press, 1979.
Wofford, Harris. *Of Kennedys and Kings: Making Sense of the Sixties*. New York: Farrar, Straus, and Giroux, 1980.
Wolff, Miles. *Lunch at the Five and Ten: The Greensboro Sit-ins: A Contemporary History*. New York: Stein and Day, 1970.
Zinn, Howard. *SNCC: The New Abolitionists*. 2d ed. Boston: Beacon, 1965.

Articles and Periodicals

Albright, Robert C. "A Rights Bill 'If It Takes All Summer,'" *Washington Post*, March 8, 1964.
———. "California Primary Delays Cloture," *Washington Post*, May 21, 1964.
Baker, Robert E. "Rights Leaders Urged to Mobilize Opinion," *Washington Post*, May 20, 1964.
Evans, Roland, and Robert Novak. "Rights and Religion," *Washington Post*, March 20, 1964.
———. "The Big Manhunt," *Washington Post*, May 20, 1964.
———. "Cloture Post Mortem," *Washington Post*, June 18, 1964.
Galloway, George B. "Limitation of Debate in the U.S. Senate," *Public Affairs Bulletin No. 64*. Washington: Library of Congress, Legislative Reference Service, 1956.
Hunter, Marjorie. "Rights Command Set Up in Senate," *New York Times*, March 22, 1964.
"I Am What I Am: Mansfield Answers Critics," *U.S. News and World Report*, December 9, 1963.
Kenworthy, E. W. "Civil Rights: Bill Moves on to Tougher Senate Battleground," *New York Times*, February 9, 1964.
———. "The Coming Filibuster," *New York Times*, February 23, 1964.
———. "The South's Strategy," *New York Times*, March 28, 1964.

———. "Rights Foes Split on Dirksen Move," *New York Times*, April 17, 1964.

———. "Civil Rights Bill—Why It Is Taking So Long," *New York Times*, May 17, 1964.

Landauer, Jerry. "Southern Senators' Fight To Divide Forces Backing Rights Bill," *Wall Street Journal*, March 24, 1964.

———. "Civil Rights Forces To Try To End Filibuster in Senate in June," *Wall Street Journal*, March 25, 1964.

Lewis, Anthony. "The Strategy of Cloture," *New York Times*, June 11, 1964.

"Once More to the Filibuster Over Civil Rights," *National Observer*, March 9, 1964.

Public Documents

Brown v. Bd. of Education, 347 U.S. 483 (1954).

Brown v. Bd. of Education, 349 U.S. 294 (1955).

U.S. Congress. *House Bill 7152*. Committee Print, October 2, 1963.

U.S. House of Representatives. *Majority Report, Civil Rights Act of 1963*. Report No. 914. 88th Cong., 1st Sess., 1963.

U.S. House of Representatives. Subcommittee No. 5 of the Committee on the Judiciary. *Hearings on Miscellaneous Civil Rights Proposals*. 88th Cong., 1st Sess., 1963.

U.S. v. Ross Barnett, 376 U.S. 681 (1964).

U.S. Senate. *Majority Report, Equal Employment Opportunity, S. 1937*. Report No. 867. 88th Cong., 2d Sess., 1964.

U.S. Senate. *Majority Report, S. 1732*. Report No. 872. 88th Cong., 2d Sess., 1964.

U.S. Senate. *Standing Rules of the United States Senate*. Corrected to January 9, 1963.

Index

A

Administrative Procedures Act, 118, 258–259
affirmative action, 346–348
AFL-CIO, 53, 83, 98, 157, 192, 230, 279
Age Discrimination in Employment Act, 348–349
Aiken, George, 112, 116, 118, 119, 253, 255, 258, 307
Alabama, University of, 18, 40, 155, 353
Albert, Carl, 61, 80
Allott, Gordon, 84
Amendments, U.S. Constitution; 13th, 3; 14th, 3, 6–7, 57, 312; 15th, 3, 10
Americans for Democratic Action (ADA), 49, 51, 55, 69
Anderson, Clinton, 79
armed forces integrated, 15
arrest absent senators, 69, 110, 192, 194, 327
Aronson, Arnold, 55, 157, 279
Associated Press, 285

B

Baker, Bobby, 123
Bakke, Alan, 347–348
Bakke case, see *University of California Regents v. Bakke*
Baltimore, MD, 21
Barnett, Ross, 39
bar the school house door, 40
Bayh, Birch, 147, 313
Biemiller, Andrew, 53, 56, 83, 157, 279
Bill of Rights of the civil rights move ment, 350
Birmingham, AL, 24, 26, 38, 42, 51–52, 78, 154, 161, 187, 340, 353, 355
Black Codes, 3–4
Black Muslims, 339
black nationalism, 339
black power, 339
black separatism, 339
black voters, 334–335
Bolling, Richard, 61
Boston, MA, 342–344
Boston School Committee, 342–344
Brotherhood of Sleeping Car Porters, 14, 22, 161
Brown, Clarence, 61
Brownell, Herbert, 16, 26–28
Brown v. Board of Education, 16, 17–18, 31, 41, 114
bus boycott, 22–24, 41
Bush, George, 350
bypass Senate Judiciary Committee, see motion to consider

C

Calendar Wednesday, 57–58, 354–355
California primary, 99, 103, 127–128, 135, 287–288, 290
California, University of, Davis, 347–348
Cambridge, Maryland, 160
Cannon, Howard W., 74, 91, 102, 129, 295, 296, 297
Caplan, Marvin, 55
Carlson, Frank, 297
Carter, Jimmy, 338
Case, Clifford, 74, 100, 123, 188, 190, 220, 249, 250
CBS News, 196, 200
Celler, Emanuel, 33, 34, 56, 58–59, 64, 80, 122, 156–159, 354
Central High School (Little Rock, AR), 31–32
Chicago Freedom Movement, 338–339

Index

Chicago, IL, 19, 160, 338
Church, Frank, 184
Civil Rights Act of 1870, 4
Civil Rights Act of 1871, 4
Civil Rights Act of 1875, 4, 6
Civil Rights Act of 1957, 26–31, 177–178, 213
Civil Rights Act of 1960, 33–37, 335
Civil Rights Act of 1964, vii–viii, 19, 24, 28–38, 40–42, 333–335, 337, 340, 348, 350, 361
Civil Rights Act of 1968, 340–342, 348, 350
Civil Rights Act of 1991, 350
Civil Rights Cases of 1883, 6–8
Civil Rights Commission, 26, 31, 33, 51, 118–119, 155, 183, 258–259, 353
Civil Rights Division, 26, 27, 31, 39, 41
civil rights movement, 41–42, 338–339, 350
Civil Rights Restoration Act of 1988, 349
Civil Rights Section, 13, 17, 26, 41
Civil War Amendments, 3
Civil War (U.S.), 2–4, 14, 42, 283
Clark, Joseph, 79, 81–82, 100, 106, 116–117, 119–120, 121–122, 132, 140, 180, 183, 186, 220, 259, 279, 304, 305
cloture drive, 278–296
cloture means compromise, 193
cloture rule changed, 345–346
cloture vote, 10, 30, 36–37, 66–67, 74, 91, 125–127, 150–154, 296–297, 360
cloture vote (jury trial amendment), 104–112
commerce clause, 57, 333
Commerce Committee (Senate), 172–173, 354
Commission on Civil Rights, see Civil Rights Commission
Commission on Religion and Race, 194, 227, 286
Committee of the Whole, 63
Committee on Civil Rights, 15
Communications Satellite debate, 150, 196
Community Relations Service, 155, 158, 183
Congressional Hotel, 63, 64
Congressional Quarterly, 123
Congressional Record, 84, 130, 141, 146, 217, 220
Congress of Racial Equality (CORE), 19–22, 37, 199, 230, 339
Connor, T. Eugene (Bull), 52, 53
Constitutional Convention (U.S.), 2, 312
controlled independence, 325–332
Conway, Jack, 157
Cooper amendment, 111–112, 114, 325
Cooper, John Sherman, 85, 111–112, 190, 220
Coordinating Committee for Funda mental American Freedoms, 68–69, 199, 227
Corman, James, 64
corporal's guard, 185
Cotton amendment, 72–74, 128–129, 281, 290–291, 293–294, 325
Cotton Curtain, 41
Cotton, Norris, 72, 84, 90, 128, 135, 136, 190, 281, 284, 290–291, 304, 325
counter-filibuster, 127–128, 134, 288–289
Curtis, Carl, 90, 129, 281, 284, 290, 297
cut off U.S. Government funds, see funds cutoff

D

Dallas County, AL, 336
Daly, Chuck, 63
Declaration of Independence, 2
Democratic Conference (Senate), 121–122, 279–280
Democratic National Convention (1948), 77
Democratic Policy Committee, 66, 190, 202–203
Democratic Study Group, 159–160
Dexter Avenue Baptist Church (Montgomery,AL), 23
Dirksen, Everett M.: amendments, 35, 66, 69, 226, 230; California primary, 99, 287–288; closing speech, 312; cloture drive, 278–297; comic behavior, 144; compromised by Gold-

water, 335; early cloture proposal, 236–239; evaluated, 97, 298–300, 328–329; feared big government, 99; feared by Leadership Conference, 193–195; Hickenlooper revolt, 72–73, 90, 290–294, 360; housing rights, 339, 341; idea whose time has come speech, 297, 323; illness, 127–128, 134–137, 289, 290; insulated from pressure, 327; jury trial amend ments, 98–112, 234–236, 359; Morton amendment, 239–245; motion to adjourn, 309–310; motion to consider debate, 221–222; needed for cloture, 97, 101, 277; negotiated amendments, 245–264; negotiated with Humphrey, 69–72, 94–96, 112–113, 116–120, 123–125, 126, 359; negotiated with John Kennedy, 79, 170–171; negotiated with Mansfield, 169–174, 201; negotiated with Robert Kennedy, 170–171; opposed two-speech limit, 232; photo session, 313; picketed by CORE, 199; praised by Humphrey, 86–88; Republican Conference, 249; Republican Policy Committee, 248–249, 250; supported state-local involvement, 87–88; voting rights, 337
Dirksen-Mansfield substitute amendment, see Mansfield-Dirksen substitute amendment
discharge petition, 34, 61, 356
District of Columbia, 25, 276
Dodd, Thomas, 183
Dominick, Peter, 144, 284, 309–310
double jeopardy, 130, 137–138, 302, 303, 305
Douglas, Paul, 74, 177, 183, 186, 213, 220
Drummond, Roscoe, 95

E

Eastland, James O., 28, 35–36, 65, 144, 173, 178, 213, 216, 309, 330, 357, 358
Edmondson, Howard, 91, 129, 295, 296, 297
Education Amendment of 1972, 349
Eisenhower, Dwight D.: *Brown v. Board of Education*, 15–19; civil rights program, 25; executive powers, 25; Civil Rights Act of 1960, 33–37, 195; Civil Rights Act of 1957, 26–31, 195; Little Rock, 31–33, 38; sit-ins, 37–38
Ellender, Allen J., 220
Engle, Clair, 73, 74, 75, 295–296, 297
equal employment opportunity (Title VII), 14, 49, 51, 52–54, 56–58, 64, 66, 70, 72, 79, 80, 82, 87, 90, 94, 98, 117, 127–129, 155–158, 180, 183, 190, 192, 200, 219, 226, 249–252, 254, 256–259, 279, 281, 282, 290–291, 293–294, 298, 311, 322, 325, 334, 354–355, 355–356, 357, 359, 360
Equal Employment Opportunity Commission, 258–259, 322, 356
Ervin double jeopardy amendment, 130–131, 132, 137–140, 302, 303, 305
Ervin, Sam, 80, 107, 121, 129, 130, 137–140, 143, 145, 219, 239, 294, 302, 303, 305, 308
Evers, Medgar, 155
executive powers, 13-15, 25

F

Face the Nation, 200
Fair Employment Practices Committee (FEPC), see equal employment opportunity
Fair Housing Act Amendments, 349–350
Faubus, Orval, 31–32
Fauntroy, Walter, 56
Federal blackjack, 30
Federal Housing Administration, 306
Ferris, Charles, 66, 83
filibuster, 10, 29, 30, 36–37, 55, 65–75, 150–154, 275–277, 358–360
Florida, 8–9
Foley, William, 59
Franklin, Benjamin, 312

Index

freedom ride, 20–22
free white jury that will never convict, 8–9
Fulbright, William, 241
funds cutoff (Title VI), 52, 79, 80, 87, 130, 131, 140–141, 146, 183, 200, 219, 304, 306, 311, 333, 354, 360

G

gallery watchers, 62–63
Gandhi, Mahatma, 19
Garrity, Arthur, 342, 344
Georgetown University, 83, 286
Goldwater, Barry M., 99, 127–128, 135, 247, 287–288, 290, 311, 334–335
Gore, Albert, Sr., 131, 139, 141, 146, 311–312
great man hook, 95
Greenfeld, Jerry, 83
Greensboro, NC, 37
Grove City College v. Bell, 349
Gunther, Violet, 55

H

Haley, James A., 65
Halleck, Charles A., 60, 80, 158
Hamilton, Jim, 56
Harlan, John Marshall, 9
Harris poll, 69
Harris, Thomas, 279
Hart, Philip, 82, 91, 106, 116, 121-122, 180, 183, 186, 220, 279, 280, 296, 304, 305
Hayden, Carl, 74, 295, 297
Hayes, Rutherford B., 4
Heart of Atlanta Motel v. United States, 333
Herald Tribune Syndicate, 95
Hickenlooper amendment, 72–74, 128–129, 290, 293–294
Hickenlooper, Bourke B., 72-73, 90, 112, 113, 122, 125, 128, 134–137, 255, 256, 280–281, 283–288, 290–295, 297, 298–299, 331, 360
Hickenlooper revolt, 72–74, 90–91, 134–137, 290–294, 298–299, 331, 360
Hill, Lister, 143, 219
hold their feet to the fire, 152
Holland, Spessard, 68
Hood, James, 40
Hoover, Herbert, 12
Housing and Urban Development Department, 350
Housing Rights Act of 1968, see Civil Rights Act of 1968
Hruska, Roman L., 67, 84, 90, 128, 136, 190, 281, 284, 290, 291, 297
Hubert H. Humphrey Papers, ix, 93
Hugo, Victor, 297
Humphrey, Hubert H.: AFL-CIO, 53; biography, 77–78; celebrated victory, 322; civil wrongs statement, 231; closing speech, 312; cloture drive, 122, 278–297; debated with Russell, 102; early cloture proposal, 231–232, 236–239; evaluated, 325–332; failed quorum call, 229–230; Hickenlooper revolt, 90–91, 290–294; involved Mansfield, 88; jury trial amendments, 98–112, 134, 234–236; maintained Republican support, 185–191; Morse motion, 358; Morton amendment, 239–245; motion to consider debate, 212–224; named floor manager, 81, 172, 178–180, 358; needed patience, 86; negotiated with Dirksen, 69–72, 94–96, 112, 116–117, 182, 245–264, 277, 359; negotiated with Leadership Conference, 120, 122–123, 185, 191–195; opened the debate, 83, 228–229; opposed Gore motion, 311–310; photo session, 313; post-cloture period, 130–132, 139–142, 145–147, 303–306, 308; praised Dirksen, 86–88; quorum of frustration speech, 242; responsible for passing bill, 162–163; round-the-clock sessions, 232; strategy for passing bill, 65–68, 167, 178–198, 202–203, 226–227, 277–278; Talmadge amendment, 233–234; two–speech limit, 232;

urged strong bill, 78–79; wheat and cotton bill, 81, 357; worked with President Johnson, 195–198; wrote memorandum, vii
Humphrey-Dirksen substitute amend ment, see Mansfield-Dirksen substitute amendment
Humphrey, Robert, 145, 146–147, 313
Hyde Park High School, 343

I

Indian amendment, 120, 282
Interreligious Convocation on Civil Rights, 83, 106, 286

J

Jackson, Henry R. (Scoop), 73–74, 129, 294
Jackson, Mississippi, 160
Jamestown, VA, 1
Javits, Jacob, 79, 84, 100, 106, 116, 188, 190, 215–216, 220, 233, 247, 249, 250, 251
Jefferson, Thomas, 2
Jim Crow line, 20
Johnson, Lyndon B.: before the impulse slows speech, 335; books of law speech, 60–61, 159; Cannon cloture vote, 129; Civil Rights Commission, 31; cloture on jury trial amendments, 108–109; defeated Goldwater, 334–335; Dirksen and program, 126; exactly in its present form statement, 197; filibuster strategy (1957 and 1960), 161; housing rights, 341; jury trial amendments (1957), 233; King assassination, 340; last hundred sessions combined speech, 196; no amendments policy, 167, 189, 203, 213, 230, 235, 251–253, 262, 298, 328; opening-day baseball game, 68; relied on Katzenbach, 17; signed bill, 75, 314, 333, 361; rated more effective than Kennedy, 95–96; recommended Dirksen negotiations, 171; supported bill, 54, 66, 89, 195–198, 263–264, 295, 323–324, 356, 359–360; Supreme Court appointments, 345; telephoned Joseph Rauh, 64–65; told that Humphrey had the votes, 91; voting rights, 38, 335–338; western Democrats, 124
Jordan, B. Everett, 128, 136, 281, 284, 287, 297
Judiciary Committee (Senate), 28–29, 34–36, 65, 198, 213, 246, 330, 357, 358
Judiciary Committee (House), 33, 55, 56–60, 80, 124, 156–159, 354, 355–356
jury trial amendments, 72–74, 88, 90–91, 97–112, 127–129, 130–134, 137–140, 232–245, 290, 293–294, 300, 325, 328, 358–359, 360

K

Kastenmeier, Robert W., 56, 64, 157
Katzenbach, Nicholas, 17, 66, 80, 100, 101, 105, 106, 110, 112, 122, 183, 197, 238, 260–261, 313
Keating, Kenneth, 74, 79, 84, 188, 190, 216, 220, 249
Kennedy, Edward M. (Ted), 147, 184, 229, 313
Kennedy, John F.: Alabama, University of, 18, 40; assassinated, 60, 159, 323, 356; Birmingham demonstrations, 26; black voters, 335; Civil Rights Division, 31; defeated Humphrey, 77; evaluated by Russell, 95–96; fires of frustration speech, 353; jury trial amendments (1957), 233; King meeting, 355; Mississippi, University of, 18, 38–39; public housing integrated, 25, 131, 306; relied on Robert Kennedy, 16–17; strengthened bill to Congress, 42, 53, 79–80, 154–156, 173, 187, 322, 353; Sunday school bombing, 161; weak bill to Congress, 50–52, 78–

79, 195–196, 353; White House midnight meeting, 33, 59–60, 80, 158–159, 355, 357
Kennedy, Robert F., 16–17, 59, 78–79, 80, 105, 106, 110, 112, 116, 118–119, 158, 177, 197, 238, 251, 255, 283, 355
Kenworthy, E. W., 290
King, Martin Luther, Jr.: assassinated, 340, 341; Birmingham demonstrations, 51–52, 154, 353; Chicago Freedom Movement, 338–339; dismayed by obstacles, 55; housing rights, 340–341; I have a dream speech, 355; Letter from the Birmingham Jail, 350, 353; March on Washington (1963), 54, 355; Memphis sanitation workers strike, 339–340; Montgomery bus boycott, 23–24; promised land speech, 340; provoked segregationist response, 42; Selma march, 336
Knowland, William, 177, 213
Kuchel, Thomas H.: attended early meetings, 79; civil wrongs statement, 231; cloture drive, 287; considered amending bill, 188; Dirksen amendments, 72; early cloture proposal, 231, 236–239; jury trial amendments, 234–236; Leadership Conference, 193–195; met with Johnson, 100; Morton amendment, 239–245; motion to consider debate, 212, 215, 220–223; named floor manager, 65, 84, 183, 358; negotiated with Dirksen, 112, 247, 250, 251, 255, 277; not informed by Dirksen, 108; opened the debate, 83, 228–229; photo session, 313; praised Dirksen, 282; strategy for passing bill, 65–67, 167, 172, 189–191, 203, 226–227, 277–278; Talmadge amendment, 233–234, 253

L

Lausche, Frank, 121, 287
Leadership Conference on Civil Rights: after failed quorum call, 229–230; agreed to Dirksen amendments, 70–71, 122–123, 278–279, 280, 282; cloture drive, 283–286; communications system for House voting, 159–160; described, 49; early meeting, 51; evaluated, 299, 323, 327, 330; excluded by Humphrey, 97, 101; met with Humphrey, 82–83, 85, 110, 120, 185; opposed negotiations with Dirksen, 70, 231, 248, 250, 252, 259, 262; post-cloture period, 139; published pamphlet, 68–69; role in passing bill, 54–64, 66, 73, 156–157, 227, 243, 295; strategy for passing bill, 191–195; supported bypassing Judiciary Committee (Senate), 213
leprosy bill, 78
Letter from the Birmingham Jail, 350, 353
Lincoln, Abraham, 2–3, 12
Lincoln Memorial, 58, 286
Lindsay, John, 64
literacy tests, 5, 11–12, 335–336
Little Rock, AR, 31–33, 38
live pair, 241
Loevy, Robert D., 363
Long amendment, 130–131, 132, 141
Long, Edward, 129, 183, 294
Long, Russell, 130–131, 141, 143, 144, 219, 304, 306, 307, 308

M

MacGregor, Clark, 64
magnet schools, 345
Magnuson, Warren, 82, 112, 116, 129, 172–173, 180, 183, 255, 354
Malone, Vivian, 40
Manatos, Mike, 105, 116
Mansfield-Dirksen substitute amendment, 71–72, 121–122, 137–138, 278–296, 302, 310, 311, 314
Mansfield-Dirksen substitute jury trial amendment, 97–112, 115, 234–236, 242, 244, 255, 278–296, 328, 359

Index

Mansfield, Mike: argued with Clark, 132, 140; Bobby Baker inquiry, 123; bypassed Judiciary Committee (Senate), 65; celebrates victory, 321; closing speech, 312; cloture drive, 72, 278–297; crossroads speech, 168; distributed Dirksen amendments, 122; early cloture proposal, 105, 236–239; early meetings, 78–79; evaluated, 325–332; failed quorum call, 229–230; involved by Humphrey, 88; jury trial amendments (1957), 233; jury trial amendments (1964), 98, 115, 234–236, 359; longer sessions, 143, 145; moment for the Senate speech, 218; moral perfection speech, 176; Morse motion, 224–225, 358; Morton amendment, 114, 239–245; Moss incident, 114; motion to adjourn, 309–310; motion to consider, 212–224; named Humphrey floor manager, 77; negotiated with Dirksen, 108, 112, 169–174, 245–264; negotiated with Johnson, 197; negotiated with Leadership Conference, 193–195; parliamentary pyrotechnics speech, 175; photo session, 313; post-cloture period, 131, 132, 140, 143, 145, 302–306, 308–309; praised Humphrey, 122; strategy for passing bill, 162–163, 167–178, 201–203, 225–226; Talmadge amendment, 233–234; treatment of southern Democrats, 176–178
March on Washington (1941), 14
March on Washington (1963), 54, 58, 161, 355
Marshall, Burke, 31, 80, 100, 110, 112, 116, 118, 120, 140, 183, 197, 260–261, 279
marshals (U.S.), 17–18, 39, 40
Mathias, Charles McC., 64
McClellan, John, 219, 241
McCormick, John W., 58, 61, 80
McCulloch, William, 58–60, 64, 80, 100, 122, 158, 160, 245, 254, 313–314, 355
McGee, Gale W., 297
McIntyre, Thomas, 184
McNamara, Patrick, 184
Mechem, Edwin, 144, 284, 297, 309–310
Meet the Press, 95, 189
Memphis sanitation workers strike, 339–340
Memphis, TN, 339–340
Meredith, James, 39
Metcalf, Lee, 215, 297
Miller, Jack, 126, 128, 136, 281, 284, 290, 297
Milliken v. Bradley, 344–345
mini-buster, 358
Minneapolis, MN, 77
Minnesota Historical Society, ix, 93
Minnesota, University of, 77
Minority Bill of Rights, 350
Mississippi State Sovereignty Commission, 227
Mississippi, University of, 18, 39
Missouri ex rel. Gaines v. Canada, 11
Missouri, University of, 11
Mitchell, Clarence, Jr., 8–9, 49, 51, 56, 66, 69, 70, 82, 95, 97, 101, 110, 120, 157, 191–195, 197, 231, 278–279, 341
Moore, Arch, 59
Moore, Harry T., 8–9
Moore, Pauline, 82
Monroney, A. S. (Mike), 297
Montgomery, AL, 22–24, 41, 336
morning hour, 217–218
Morrow, Frederic, 25
Morse, Wayne, 67, 111, 183, 215, 219, 224–225, 226, 246, 358
Morton amendment, 72–74, 111, 114, 128–129, 134, 239–244, 255, 290, 293–294, 325, 328
Morton, Thruston B., 72, 111, 187, 239–240, 284, 287
Moss, Frank, 114, 241
motion to consider, 28–29, 65, 67, 212–224, 325, 330
Mudd, Roger, 296
Mundt, Karl E., 67, 90, 120, 128, 135, 136, 281, 282, 284, 290
Muskie, Edmund, 74, 184
mustard plaster on a cancer, 104

Index

N

National Association for the Advancement of Colored People (NAACP), 8–9, 11, 14, 21, 39, 49, 51, 54, 95, 155, 191, 341
National Catholic Welfare Conference, 194, 286
National Council of Churches, 56, 67, 194, 227, 286
Nelson, Gaylord, 184
New Deal, 12–13
newsletter, 66, 82, 185, 220, 301
New York, 11, 54, 55, 160, 323
New York Post, 60
New York Times, 196, 239, 290
New York World's Fair, 230
Nixon, E. D., 22
Nixon, Richard M., 345
no amendments policy, 30, 189, 251–253, 262, 298, 328
no compromises, see no amendments policy
nonviolence, 19–22, 42, 339

O

O'Brien, Lawrence, 105, 110, 116, 197–198, 238, 251
Ole Miss, see Mississippi, University of

P

Palisades Amusement Park, 21
Parks, Rosa, 22–23
Part III, 26–27, 29–30, 33, 36–37, 51, 54, 56, 59, 157–158, 192, 195
Pastore, John, 140, 183, 220, 233, 304–305, 306
pattern or practice, 35, 71, 257, 279
Paul Young's restaurant, 147
Pearson, James, 287, 297
Philadelphia, PA, 188, 323
physically handicapped, 333
Plessy v. Ferguson, 9
political party problem, 5–6
poll taxes, 5
Pope, 67
post-cloture period, 130–133, 137–145, 300–313, 360–361
Powell, Adam Clayton, 57–58, 79, 354–355
Powell amendment, 79
public accommodations (Title II), 5, 6, 19-22, 37-38, 51–60, 64, 70–71, 82, 87, 94, 130, 139, 141, 155, 171, 172, 180, 183, 190, 192, 196, 200, 219, 226, 246, 254, 256, 257–258, 279, 298, 302, 311, 333, 354, 359, 360
public housing, 25–26, 131, 140–141

Q

quorum calls, 85, 151, 229–230, 287, 329
quorum duty list, 82, 184, 194, 329–330

R

Randolph, A. Philip, 14, 161
Rauh, Joseph L., Jr., vii, ix, 49–50, 56, 62, 69, 82, 120, 122–123, 157, 193–195, 197, 231, 278–279
Reconstruction, 3–4, 14, 29
referral with orders to report, 224–225, 226
Rehabilitation Act, 349
religious support, 89
Republican Conference (Senate), 122, 249, 280–281
Republican National Convention (1964), 95, 103, 254, 288, 334
Republican Policy Committee (Senate), 248–249, 250, 252
resegregation, 344
Restore Our Alienated Rights (ROAR), 343
Reuther, Walter, 54, 55, 70
Revenue Act of 1964, see tax cut bill
reverse discrimination, 347–348
Ribicoff, Abraham, 220
Robertson, Willis, 220
Rochester, NY, 323
Rockefeller, Nelson, 127, 135, 287
Rodino, Peter W., 56, 64, 157
Rogers, Byron G., 56, 59, 64, 157

Rogers, William P., 16, 18, 34–35
Roosevelt Coalition, 13
Roosevelt, Franklin D., 12–13, 14, 15, 40–41, 49
Roosevelt, Franklin D., Jr., 322
Roosevelt Hotel (New York, NY), 54
round-the-clock sessions, 36–37, 85, 151–152, 192–193, 231, 232, 327
Rules Committee (House), 34, 55, 57, 60–62, 75, 159, 162, 314, 341, 354, 356–357, 361
Roxbury, MA, 343
Russell, Richard: bill aimed at South statement, 71; cardinals, bishops, elders, stated clerks speech, 331; Civil Rights Act of 1957, 29–30; complained to Humphrey, 91; counter-filibuster, 127, 133–134; credited Johnson with victory, 95–96, 323–324; evaluated, 131, 138, 298–300; Federal blackjack, 30; filibuster strategy, 151, 198–201; handwriting on wall, 124; Hickenlooper revolt, 128, 136, 293–294; jury trial amendments, 88, 109–111, 230, 232–233, 236, 238–239, 254, 255, 358–359; limited by southern colleagues, 109–110, 143, 325; lost a skirmish speech, 227; met with Robert Kennedy, 177; Morse motion, 358; Morton amendment, 115, 239–245, 328; motion to consider, 215–218, 223–224; mustard plaster on a cancer speech, 104, 236; opposed bypassing Judiciary Committee (Senate), 65; opposed cloture, 282–283; post-cloture period, 308–310; public accommodations amendment, 138–139, 302; rules mistake, 102; Talmadge amendment, 107; tidbit tactic, 288–289

S

Saltonstall, Leverett, 116–117, 119
San Francisco, CA, 288, 334
Sargeant-at-Arms (Senate), 69
Saturday debacle, 68
school busing, 342–345
Scott, Hugh, 79, 84, 187, 188, 190
Selma, AL, 24, 38, 335–336, 340–341
separate but equal, 9
sit-ins, 20–22, 37–38
slavery, 1
slavery in the territories, 2
Smathers amendment, 242–243
Smathers, George, 232, 242
Smith, Howard, 34, 60–62, 64, 75, 159, 314, 356, 361
Smith, Margaret Chase, 297
Sorensen, Ted, 80
South Boston High School, 343
Southern Christian Leadership Conference (SCLC), 56
southern strategy, 85–86, 102, 103, 107, 109–111, 115, 130–133, 138–139, 142–143, 151, 158, 198–201, 217–218, 275–279, 293–294, 298–300, 302–310, 324–325
Sparkman, John, 219
Springfield, IL, 10
stall-in, 230
Stennis, John, 143, 219–220
Stevens, Thad, 283
Stewart, John G., vii, ix, 83, 89, 93–94, 106, 149–150
St. Louis, MO, 21
Student Nonviolent Coordinating Committee (SNCC), 38, 339
Subcommittee No. 5, 33, 56–59, 80, 156–159, 191–192, 354, 355
Sumner, Charles, 283
Supreme Court (U.S.), 6–7, 9, 16–17, 23–24, 41, 333, 342, 344–345, 346–347, 349, 350
Swann v. Charlotte-Mecklenburg, 342
Symington, Stuart, 129
Synagogue Council of America, 286

T

Talmadge amendment, 97–112, 115, 130, 137, 232–234, 243–244, 252,

Index

253, 289
Talmadge, Herman, 97–98, 232, 252
tax cut bill, 188, 214
Teasdale, Ken, 66, 83, 102, 105,106, 135
television, 24, 41
Thompson, Frank, 63
three-fifths compromise, 2
Thurmond, Strom, 109–110, 143, 145, 200–201, 238–239, 293, 308, 310
tidbit tactic, 288–289
Tilden-Hayes election, 4
title captains, 81–82, 183–184
Title XII, 116
To Secure These Rights, 15
Tower, John, 200
triggering test, 337
Truman, Harry S., 15, 25
two speech limit, 69, 193, 194, 232, 327

U

United Auto Workers, 70
University of California Regents v. Bakke, 346–348

V

Valeo, Francis, 105, 116
Veterans Administration, 306
Vinson, Fred, 16
Volstead Act, 121
Voting Rights Act of 1965, 24, 35–38, 337–338, 340–341, 348, 350
vultures in the galleries, 65

W

Wade, Ben, 283
Waldorf Hotel (New York, NY), 55
Wallace, George, 40, 155, 199, 230, 353
Walters, Herbert S., 297
Warren, Earl, 16
Watkins, Charley, 102
Watts riot, 338
Weltner, Charles L., 75
wheat and cotton bill, 81, 188, 214, 357
white-only primary elections, 5
Wilkins, Roy, 54
Williams, John J., 74, 297
Wisconsin primary, 230
Wolfinger, Ray, 83
Women's Political Council, 23
women's rights, 333–334, 349, 357

Y

Yarborough, Ralph, 91, 129, 295, 296, 297
Young, Andrew, 338